MIKE FORCE

Lt. Col. L.H. "Bucky" Burruss, USA (Ret.)

D0711343

AN AUTHORS GUILD BACKINPRINT.COM EDITION

Mike Force

AN AUTHORS GUILD BACKINPRINT.COM EDITION

Published by iUniverse.com, Inc.

For information address:
iUniverse.com, Inc.
5220 S 16th, Ste. 200
Lincoln, NE 68512
www.iuniverse.com

Originally published by Pocketbooks

ISBN: 0-595-16524-9

Printed in the United States of America

For Frank and Otis
and all the others

THE STRIKERS ARE THE ONLY
ONES WHO DIE IN THE JUNGLE
AND NOBODY CARES.

  —Translation of a sign found
   tacked to a tree deep in the
   Vietnam jungle.

DEMILITARIZED ZONE

SOUTH VIETNAM

LANG VEI

ASHAU
THUONG DUC
DANANG
AN HOA
KHAM DUC

LAOS

I CORPS

DAK PEK
DAK SEANG
BEN HET
DAK TO

PLEIKU

II CORPS

DUC LAP
TRUNG DUNG
NHA TRANG

CAMBODIA

CAM RANH BAY

KATUM
THIEN NGON
BUNARD

III CORPS

NUI KHET
CHI LANG
NUI COTO

SAIGON
☆

SOUTH CHINA SEA

VUNG TAU

CAN THO

IV CORPS

CA MAU PENINSULA

Organization of the 5th Special Forces Group in Vietnam

During the time of its employment in Vietnam, the 5th Special Forces Group was task-organized to meet the needs of the diverse missions it was assigned. There was a Group Headquarters in Nha Trang which provided command and control, intelligence, and administrative and logistical support for all of the subordinate detachments of the Group. The Group Headquarters was sometimes referred to as the SFOB—Special Forces Operations Base.

Each of the four Corps Tactical Zones into which South Vietnam was divided—I Corps through IV Corps—contained a Special Forces C Detachment, designated C-1 through C-4.

Subordinate to each C Detachment were a number of B Detachments, which in turn controlled several of the basic detachments in the Special Forces structure, the Special Forces Operational Detachment A, more commonly known as the A Team.

The A Team normally comprised two officers and ten noncommissioned officers, although this number, too, varied with the needs of the detachments' missions. The scores of border camps which Special Forces manned, each with several companies of Civilian Irregular Defense Group troops recruited largely from the ethnic minorities of Vietnam, were where most of the closely knit A Teams were located. Each camp had a Vietnamese Special Forces detachment, as well.

The numerical designations of the various detachments corresponded to that of the detachment to which it was subordinate; for example, A-421 fell under B-42, which in turn was subordinate to C-4, the detachment which controlled all the Special Forces elements in IV Corps.

The detachments which fell directly under Group Headquarters, and those designated as special projects, had numerical designations beginning with "5." These detachments included the following:

A-502—The reinforced A Team whose mission was to provide security in the region around Group Headquarters.

A-503—the Nha Trang Mike Force, which is the primary focus of this book. A-503 was later expanded to a B Team, designated B-55, with two subordinate A Teams.

B-51—the team which ran the Civilian Irregular Defense Group Training Center at Dong Ba Thin.

B-52—"Project Delta," one of the special projects units which operated directly for the overall commander of U.S. forces in Vietnam.

There were many such specially organized detachments conducting a variety of missions in Vietnam. What follows is an account of one of them, the Nha Trang Mike Force.

Prologue

It was in March 1966 that I first heard of the Special Forces detachments known as "Mike Force." At the time I was at Fort Jackson, South Carolina, undergoing the last few weeks of training which would qualify me as an infantryman.

One of my fellow trainees was a veteran of Special Forces named Mike Sherwood, who had left the Army, earned a college degree, and was now back in the Army undergoing refresher training before going on, as I was, to Fort Benning, Georgia, to attend the Infantry Officer Candidate School. From there we knew that we would, of course, be going on to Vietnam within a few months, whether we were successful at earning commissions as Second Lieutenants of Infantry or not. For that reason, we paid particularly close attention to news of the war, and when I read a report about a battle at a Special Forces camp called A Shau, I knew Mike would be interested. I sought him out and showed him the report.

"The Mike Force," he mumbled as he read about the camp's having been reinforced by a reaction element of South Vietnamese troops under the leadership of American Green Berets.

"What's that?" I asked.

"The countrywide reaction force from Nha Trang," he said. "Whenever one of the camps gets into trouble, the Mike Force goes in to help them out."

Little did I realize that I would one day find myself in the unit then engaged in one of the most desperate battles of the war.

* * *

The North Vietnamese Army soldiers moving into position to assault the isolated outpost in the A Shau Valley, in early March 1966, had every reason to feel confident that their impending attack would bring a quick and easy victory. Their target, a small triangle-shaped camp only two miles from the communists' sanctuaries in Laos, lay astride the busy Ho Chi Minh Trail. It was far from any supporting artillery, and was defended by only about two hundred South Vietnamese of the Civilian Irregular Defense Group, along with a handful of American Special Forces soldiers and their South Vietnamese Special Forces counterparts. The North Vietnamese had nearly ten times as many soldiers massing for the attack—four battalions totaling about two thousand men. And that was not their only advantage. Some of the camp's CIDG irregulars were communist sympathizers who would turn their guns on the Americans and the other defenders—many of whom were convicts sent to Camp A Shau as punishment—when the attack began.

Even the weather was on the side of the NVA. A heavy cover of cloud lay low in the valley between the steep mountains on either side of the camp, making it all but impossible for the Americans to fly aircraft into the camp's little airstrip most of the time. And even if they tried, the NVA had some twenty antiaircraft guns moving into position on the ridges above the camp to deal with any aircraft whose pilots might dare to venture beneath the thick clouds to try to assist the camp's defenders.

The massive buildup of communist forces around the camp did not go unnoticed by Captain Dave Blair, the young Commanding Officer of Special Forces Operational Detachment A-102, the team of American Green Berets who manned the border outpost and provided advice and assistance—and badly needed leadership—to the small force there with them. Since the Vietnamese Special Forces had abandoned the only two other outposts in the valley three months earlier, Blair's little force was the only one left to try to disrupt the almost constant flow of men and matériel which moved along the nearby network of trails from North Vietnam through Laos and into South Vietnam.

And now it was becoming evident that the NVA were going to mount an effort to rid themselves of this interference.

Blair radioed his increasingly troubling intelligence reports to the 5th Special Forces Group Headquarters in the coastal city of Nha Trang, and as the buildup around his camp continued, requested reinforcements from the Group's newly formed countrywide mobile reaction force— the Mike Force, as it was called.

On 7 March the commander of the Mike Force, Captain Tennis H. "Sam" Carter, flew into Camp A Shau with 143 Mike Force soldiers and their American Special Forces noncommissioned-officer leaders, to bolster the camp's defenses. His troops were smart, tough little Nungs— Vietnamese of Chinese extraction known for their discipline, tenacity, and loyalty to their Green Beret leaders. The arrival of the Mike Force troops significantly improved the chances of defending the camp, and as Blair took stock of his assets, he now counted the following numbers of people crowded into the little fortress: 17 American Special Forces; 6 Vietnamese Special Forces; 143 Nung soldiers from Carter's Mike Force; the 210 Vietnamese of his camp's Civilian Irregular Defense Group; and 7 interpreters—a total of 383 fighters. In addition, there were 51 civilians in the camp.

While the increase in the number of defenders must have caused some concern to the North Vietnamese who continued to move into position for their assault, they still enjoyed the advantages of nearly six times as many attackers, of communist sympathizers within the camp, a heavy superiority in mortars, machine guns, and recoilless rifles, and worsening weather conditions which would hamper their enemy's ability to respond with air support.

Shortly before four o'clock on the morning of 9 March 1966, the North Vietnamese opened their attack on Camp A Shau with a devastating mortar and recoilless rifle barrage, which continued unabated for two and a half hours. Forty minutes after the barrage began, the communists mounted a ground attack against the south wall of the camp with two companies of the 95th North Vietnamese Army Regiment. The defenders fought back fiercely, and enough of their machine guns and mortars remained in action at that early stage of the battle to inflict heavy losses on the attacking communists, forcing them to abandon the initial assault. But the hail of exploding mortar and 57mm recoilless rifle rounds continued to ravage the little fortress.

In addition to blasting apart many of the camp's building and bunkers, the barrage destroyed its water supply. Sergeant First Class Raymond Allen was killed by the heavy fire, and Staff Sergeant Billie Hall, the senior medic with Sam Carter's Mike Force, had both his legs blown off. In an act of the sort of extreme dedication and courage for which Special Forces medics have become renowned, the critically wounded Hall tied tourniquets on the stumps of his legs and dragged himself to others of the wounded to administer aid to them until he was carried off to the dispensary. There, he continued to give instructions for the treatment of the stream of wounded who poured into the aid station until he lost consciousness and died.

Through the thick cloud cover which blanketed the valley, attempts were made throughout the day to assist the beleaguered camp with air support. Although two light observation aircraft were able to get down through the clouds and onto the camp's airstrip, they came under heavy ground fire and were able to evacuate only one of the wounded, Master Sergeant Robert D. Gibson. Two Marine Corps CH-34 helicopters made it into the area of the camp, but one, hit by enemy fire, crashed. The other managed to pick up the downed crew and escape through the clouds. An AC-47 "Spooky" gunship attempting to support the camp with its rapid-firing miniguns was hit by the intense antiaircraft fire from the ridges above the valley, and crashed. Several attempts were made during the day of 9 March to resupply the camp with parachute drops of desperately needed ammunition and water, but because of the poor visibility, most of the 'chutes were off target and landed outside the camp. Attempts by the defenders to recover the vital supplies were met with heavy fire from the enemy, and only a small amount was retrieved.

Air Force Major Bernard Fisher, flying an A1E Skyraider,

was diverted from another mission to attempt to assist in the battle raging at Camp A Shau, and managed to get through the thick canopy of clouds and antiaircraft fire to strafe the enemy with his plane's 20mm cannons. He was to return to the camp the next day, with dramatic effect.

As darkness fell on the embattled outpost that evening, a U.S. Air Force "Jolly Green Giant" rescue chopper finally managed to get in and evacuate twenty-six of the scores of wounded defenders. Throughout the night, as the North Vietnamese regrouped to prepare for another assault on Camp A Shau, the cloudy skies above them were lit by the constant glow of flares, while Blair and Carter did their best to care for their wounded troops and reorganize the remainder to withstand the next communist onslaught.

It began about four o'clock in the morning with another brutal mortar and recoilless rifle barrage, followed an hour later by massive ground assaults against the south wall of the camp and across the runway to the east wall. While the so-called leader of the Vietnamese Special Forces team, Lieutenant Linh Van Dung, cowered in a corner, one of his men, Sergeant Yang, battled bravely beside his American counterparts. Another of the Americans, Specialist 5 Phillip Stahl, was killed during this phase of the battle.

Then, as the NVA breached the walls of the camp, the 141st CIDG Company, in an act of unbelievable treachery, joined the enemy and turned their weapons against the Americans and the Nung Mike Force troops who had come to help them hold the camp. For three hours the battle raged with the Nungs and Americans fighting desperately—often hand-to-hand—against the North Vietnamese and their traitorous new allies.

The Mike Force and the few loyal CIDG remaining in the battle managed to fight their way to positions on the north wall and in the communications bunker, where they were able to withstand another massive enemy assault at 0830.

Just as the North Vietnamese were massing a battalion near the runway to overwhelm the remaining defenders, two B-57 Canberra medium bombers emerged from the cloudy skies above the camp. Swooping down on the NVA formation, the Canberras destroyed the battalion with a salvo of deadly cluster bombs.

Captain Carter and his remaining NCOs rallied the Mike Force for a counterattack in an attempt to regain a portion of the battered camp. Two more Special Forces sergeants, Vic Underwood and Vern Carnahan, were badly wounded in the attempt to retake the area around the communications bunker and the dispensary. The situation had become so desperate that Captain Blair had no choice but to call for air strikes directly on the south and east wall of the camp, and did so.

One of the Air Force pilots responding to the call was Major Bernard Fisher in the A1E Skyraider he had used the day before to strafe the enemy surrounding the camp. This time he was joined by three more of the reliable old prop-driven fighters. As the Skyraiders plowed down through the green tracers of antiaircraft fire, one was hit in the cockpit canopy and had to retire. The others continued their attack, but Major "Jump" Meyers' aircraft was soon hit and on fire, forcing him to crash-land on the camp's airstrip as his cockpit filled up with smoke. He skidded to a halt and barely managed to escape the flames which immediately engulfed his plane. He jumped into a ditch on the camp side of the runway, but the NVA began to move toward his position. Fisher swooped down to strafe them with 20mm cannon fire, and was soon joined by two other Skyraiders which had flown to the beleaguered camp to assist in the battle.

Learning that the rescue helicopter he had called to extract Meyers from the crash site was still twenty minutes away, Fisher decided to try to land and rescue his fellow pilot himself, although the runway was badly cratered and rubbled and surrounded by the enemy. He managed to get his old aircraft down onto the torn-up strip and skid to a halt just short of a menacing fuel dump, then turn it around and guide it through the rubble to his fellow airman's position. As Meyers clambered aboard, the other Skyraider pilots, although now out of ammunition, continued to buzz the enemy to keep them down.

"You dumb son of a bitch," Meyers yelled to Fisher as his intrepid rescuer gunned the aircraft for takeoff, "now neither of us will get out of here!" But they made it, in spite of the nineteen bullet holes with which the Skyraider was peppered. For his heroic rescue, Major Bernard Fisher was later awarded the Medal of Honor.

The air strikes Captain Blair had called onto the camp put an end to the enemy's ground assaults for the time being, although the attacks by fire continued. With hundreds of the defenders dead, wounded, or deserted to the enemy, the temporary absence of ground attacks did little to improve their situation. They had been without food, water, or sleep for a full day and a half. Most of their crew-served weapons had been knocked out of action, and they were almost completely out of ammunition. At 1500 hours on the afternoon of 10 March, Blair made the decision to abandon the devastated outpost.

A fleet of Marine Corps helicopters made its way to the camp to attempt to pull the survivors out. As the choppers landed amid heavy ground fire from the communists, the Mike Force and Special Forces troops on the north wall attempted to keep the NVA pinned down while the wounded were loaded aboard. But the remaining CIDG troops, led by the cowardly Lieutenant Dung and his Vietnamese Special Forces subordinates, made a mad dash for the choppers, trampling the wounded in their panicked attempt to escape from the camp, and even pulling one wounded American out of a helicopter and onto the ground. After unsuccessfully attempting to get the panicked mob under control by beating them with their rifles, the Special Forces soldiers and Marines finally had to resort to shooting into the crowd to get the situation in hand. As a result of the unruly mob's actions, the choppers had to depart with only sixty people; only one of the wounded Americans and seven crewmen from two of the Marine Corps helicopters which had been shot down in the evacuation attempt were among them. Another helicopter full of wounded was shot down and crashed in flames, killing all aboard.

Among those left behind was badly wounded Staff Sergeant James Taylor, who was being carried to the landing zone by Sergeant First Class Donnie Adkins and Lieutenant Louis Mari. After fighting their way through the camp to get Taylor evacuated, they arrived at the landing zone, only to find that all of the flyable helicopters were gone. Taylor died of his wounds before he could be transported out. Another of the wounded Special Forces troops was more fortunate; Specialist Pointon, badly wounded in the chest and both arms, stumbled out to the landing zone. There, he was spotted by a Huey helicopter gunship crew, who jettisoned their rocket pods, landed, and rescued Pointon and thirteen more of the wounded men. They were the last ones rescued directly from Camp A Shau. That night, the remaining survivors escaped from the ruined outpost. Some were rescued from the jungle during the next couple of days; many were never seen again.

The battle at the little border camp in the A Shau Valley was a costly one—to both sides. Of the seventeen American Special Forces soldiers there, five were killed, and the other twelve were wounded. Seventy-five of the hard-fighting Nungs from the Mike Force died there, thirty-three were wounded, and another fifteen went missing in action—a staggering eighty-six percent casualty rate for the courageous Mike Force troops.

Of the 210 CIDG soldiers in the camp when the battle began, more than half were evacuated, the majority of whom had not been wounded. Many of those left behind had deserted to the enemy.

The Vietnamese Special Forces team got by with only one killed and one wounded.

For the two thousand North Vietnamese soldiers involved, the attack turned out to be anything but a quick and easy victory. Some eight hundred communists died, and hundreds more were wounded before the camp was finally taken.

Camp A Shau was the first big battle, and the most desperate, that the 5th Special Forces Group's countrywide reaction force—the Mike Force—had. But it was not the last. . . .

I

1967–1968

His imperfections flowed from a contagion of the times; his virtues were his own.

—Edward Gibbon, 1780

— 1 —

As the crowded charter airliner began its descent over the South China Sea one night in late October 1967, I awakened from an uncomfortable sleep to the taste and smell of stale cigarette smoke, and to the realization that after almost two years of training and schools and Stateside service, I was about to begin the adventure for which I had enlisted in the Army in the first place—a combat tour in the Republic of Vietnam.

The lights of the passenger cabin of the aging Boeing 707 were turned up, and the two hundred or so young men in khaki began to stir. Gone were the jokes and chatter which had characterized the earlier legs of the long flight—Seattle to Anchorage to Japan—replaced now with hushed whispers and innumerable cigarettes puffed nervously by teenage warriors whose minds were filled with secondhand tales of firefights and ambushes and helicopter assaults into fireswept rice paddies and jungle clearings. Vietnam.

The handful of aging stewardesses—relics of more glamorous flights on more prestigious airlines, but now relegated by the passing of youth and beauty to military charter flights—passed through the cabin handing out a final soggy meal of chicken, tough green beans, diced carrots, chocolate pudding, and lukewarm coffee. I refused all but the coffee, lit a Lucky Strike, and looked around me at the other young men packed into the narrow, cramped seats with which the aircraft had been fitted in order to increase the profits of the airline charter company. They were so young. Most were still teenagers, although there were a handful of older NCOs up front—some on their way back to Vietnam for a second tour. I, a first lieutenant, was one of only three officers on the aircraft, along with an Infantry Captain on his way back to the 173rd Airborne Brigade and a Quartermaster Major on his first tour. The rest were mainly privates—infantrymen bound for rifle platoons in the First Cav or the Big Red One or the Fourth Division, or another of the growing number of combat units the United States was committing to battle the increasing number of Viet Cong insurgents and North Vietnamese Army regulars. I wondered, briefly, how many of them would be going home when I would, a year from now, and how many would have already left on medical-evacuation planes or in body bags. God, they were so young.

The whir of flaps being lowered caused me to turn my attention to the window beside me, but I could see nothing except the reflection of moonlight on the sea far below. I was filthy and tired, irritated by the seemingly endless flight in the cramped seat, and the smell of two hundred men's nervous sweat, and the chill of the air-conditioned cabin. I suddenly felt lonely, a stranger to my surroundings, impatient to get off this damned airplane. I wanted to find out what assignment I would have, to be tested in battle, to see for myself what it was really like. I wanted to get on with the adventure of being a young Green Beret officer in an exotic, distant war.

A dim glow of light from the window got my attention, and I cupped my face in my hands and looked out. There it was—Vietnam; the dark silhouettes of mountains barely visible in the light of artillery illumination rounds. I assumed that the eerie, drifting flares indicated a battle in progress, and immediately my sense of adventure was outweighed by one of trepidation.

22

The stewardesses came by and collected our half-eaten meals, the landing gear came down, and we snuffed out our cigarettes and landed at the big air base at Cam Ranh Bay.

A young Transportation Corps lieutenant entered the aircraft and welcomed us to Vietnam in a manner intended to give us the impression that he had weathered a hundred attacks. It was a most unconvincing attempt. We filed off the aircraft and into buses for the short ride to the replacement depot. After handing in copies of our orders, we were issued linens, anti-malaria pills, and instructions on what to do in the event of a rocket or mortar attack: "Hit the floor and pull your mattress on top of you."

It was hot, and the mosquitoes were large. I quickly learned that sleeping nude and using the mosquito netting which hung suspended above the bunks was the only way to get a good night's sleep.

I was worried that my assignment to the 5th Special Forces Group might be changed to another unit, but the next morning my orders were confirmed, and I grabbed my duffel bag and headed for the chopper pad, where I was to catch a flight to Group Headquarters, a short way up the coast in Nha Trang.

As I waited in the already oppressive heat of mid-morning, a pair of bomb-laden Phantom fighters lifted off the runway and thundered off to the north. I wondered if they were headed out to support one of the sixty-odd Special Forces camps in Vietnam, most of which were situated near the borders of Laos or Cambodia—each a little fortress manned by a twelve-man American Special Forces A Detachment, a few hundred local Civilian Irregular Defense Group soldiers, and a handful of Vietnamese Special Forces personnel. The CIDG soldiers were usually recruited from among the ethnic minorities of Vietnam. Most were Montagnard tribesmen from the highlands of the rugged Annamese mountain chain of Indochina. I had learned quite a bit about the camps and the 'Yards, as the Montagnards were more commonly called, during the six excellent weeks of premission training I had received at Fort Bragg. The training, conducted by recently returned combat veterans

23

now assigned to the 7th Special Forces Group, was by far the best I had received in the Army.

A sergeant first class in a green beret pulled up beside the chopper pad in a jeep, to see if there were any Special Forces soldiers who needed a ride to Nha Trang. Special Forces soldiers have that tradition—they take care of each other, go out of their way to do so. I accepted the sergeant's offer, threw my duffel bag into the back seat of the jeep, and we drove out of the replacement center, past the long runways of the air base. We crossed the pontoon bridge over Cam Ranh Bay and turned north onto Highway 1—the Street Without Joy, as it had come to be called by the refugees from the North who had fled south to freedom when Vietnam was partitioned more than twenty years earlier, after Ho Chi Minh's defeat of the French at Dien Bien Phu.

The fact that the sergeant, a supply man from the logistical support center at Group Headquarters, was carrying only a .38 revolver made me a bit nervous; I had assumed that everyone carried automatic weapons in Vietnam, and carried them everywhere. In my newness to the war zone, I was still at the point at which I feared that each clump of vegetation concealed an enemy ambush. We drove past Dong Ba Thin, the home of SF Detachment B-51, which ran the Civilian Irregular Defense Group training center where cadre members for the CIDG were trained. We sped on north, past the Soui Da rubber plantation. I was very uneasy there, as I had heard many war stories about firefights in such rubber plantations.

To the east of the road were the foothills of a large hill mass, which was about fifteen kilometers in diameter and split by a deep valley. We were making a big semicircle around the area. Little did I know that I was to become very familiar with those mountains—perhaps as familiar with them as any American would ever be.

I saw the first Montagnards I had ever seen, there along the highway at the foot of the looming hills that day— Raglai tribe "lowlanders," whose main occupation was cutting wood on the slopes of the mountains.

The highway swung to the east, and we entered Dien

Khanh District, the home of Detachment A-502, "the world's largest A Team." A-502 had the responsibility for the security of the Nha Trang area, manning a number of little fortified outposts which lay in a long arc around the city. We passed within a few hundred meters of the place where I would receive my baptism by fire several weeks later.

We hadn't talked much, that NCO and I, on our speedy trip up Highway 1 from Cam Ranh Bay. I had said almost nothing, taking in all the new and fascinating sights around me. He had pointed out things of interest in a matter-of-fact manner, and now he gestured toward a small field in Dien Khanh village. When he had driven down to Cam Ranh the previous day, he said, several VC bodies were lying out in the field, laid there by the troops from A-502. While I was still wondering why they would do that, he explained that it showed the people positive results and that it gave the relatives of the dead an opportunity to claim the bodies.

It was a strange new world I had entered.

A short time later, we arrived in Nha Trang. It was not a large city, but in the heyday of French colonialism was a popular resort by virtue of its beautiful long crescent beach, abundant seafood, and lovely mountains to the west and south, as well as several hilly islands rising from the South China Sea a mile or so offshore. But now it was filled with the omnipresent stench of burning garbage, and the sight of overcrowded buses and pony-drawn, automobile-tired carts. Of three-wheeled Lambrettas and man-powered "cyclos" pedaled by wiry old men down debris-laden streets.

Most of the men were wearing either fatigue uniforms or dirty cut-off khaki shorts. The older women all wore baggy silk trousers, and the children under five had on T-shirts, or nothing at all.

The young women were beautiful—pristine creatures amid the trash-littered streets, the smoke and fumes of cheap gasoline and burning garbage, and the incessant raspy blaring of bus and truck horns. They were slender and graceful, with long ebony hair that flowed straight down their backs, and were wearing lovely silk *ao dais* which reached nearly to the ground. They looked so out of place—a riveting sight among the squalid scenes around them.

We passed a huge white statue of Buddha on a hillside, and turned south. A few minutes later we passed the end of the runway at Nha Trang air base, along a chain-link fence to a gate with a big sign arching above it: "Headquarters, 5th Special Forces Group (Airborne), 1st Special Forces."

It was a neat, tidy compound, freshly painted and far cleaner than anything I had seen on the ride up from Cam Ranh Bay. It *looked* like a military post, and the soldiers who crisscrossed the quadrangle in pressed jungle fatigues and spit-shined boots gave the place an air of professionalism—but it didn't look like a war zone.

I thanked the supply sergeant for the ride, reported in to the Group Adjutant's office, and had my records checked. I was told that I could expect to be assigned to one of the outlying A Detachment camps as the Executive Officer. That was what I had hoped for, to be one of the two officers on a twelve-man A Team, out near the border in one of the little camps with two or three companies of CIDG. The camps' primary mission was to protect the local area and its inhabitants—if there were any—from Viet Cong influence and North Vietnamese infiltration, by patrolling the surrounding area, conducting ambushes, and collecting intelligence. If a camp was effective, the enemy would sometimes mount a major attempt to overrun and eliminate it, as they had done the previous year at the SF camp in the treacherous A Shau Valley, although at a terrible price to themselves. They had tried overrunning several other camps as well, but the defenders had held on heroically, as at Nam Dong, where Roger Donlon had become the first Special Forces soldier to win the Medal of Honor, and at Camp Dong Xoai, where C. Q. Williams had won "The Big One" as well. The need for quick-reaction strike forces, under U.S. Special Forces command, to respond to such enemy attacks and to exploit intelligence reports of enemy concentrations in the camps' areas of operation had given rise to the creation of Mobile Strike Forces, more commonly called Mike Forces.

They had been formed in each of the four Corps areas, with a countrywide reaction force near the Group Headquarters in Nha Trang. Before an SF soldier was allowed to volunteer for the Mike Force in those days, he was required to serve six months in an A camp to become familiar with Vietnam and with CIDG, since, in the Mike Force, companies and platoons were commanded by NCOs, and battalions by junior officers—often under arduous conditions, far from supporting artillery and against large VC and NVA formations.

Maybe, after six months at an A camp, I could get into the Mike Force, I mused.

The assistant adjutant asked me if I preferred to go to any particular Corps area. I had thought about it previously, and responded, "Yes. I Corps." I Corps, the northernmost of the four Corps areas, bordered on Laos and the Demilitarized Zone between North and South Vietnam, and it was where, I had been told, most of the SF camp action was these days. And I was, after all, itchy for a bit of action and adventure, as I suppose all young, untested soldiers are.

As I waited for the clerk to cut orders assigning me to C Company—the one which commanded all of the Special Forces detachments in I Corps—I walked outside to smoke a cigarette and have a look around. There I saw, across the quadrangle, the man who had gotten me interested in volunteering for Special Forces in the first place—Captain Larry O'Neil. O'Neil, who had been a Special Forces NCO before he was commissioned, had been my company commander in basic training two years earlier. He was a hard-nosed Irishman, just back from a tour in Vietnam at the time, and he had driven us hard, demanding toughness and dedication, and giving us hell when we failed to meet his standards. He worked me hard enough that I ended up as the outstanding trainee of the battalion, and he felt I had the potential to be a Special Forces officer, so he encouraged me to volunteer for SF after I graduated from the Infantry Officer Candidate School and spent a year as a second lieutenant. In order to volunteer for Special Forces, an officer had previously been required to be a first lieutenant, but by the time I graduated from OCS in late '66, the need for SF volunteers was such that eleven of my classmates and I were allowed to go immediately to jump school, then straight on to Special Forces. That was probably a mistake on the Army's part—sacrificing quality for quantity—but the commanders of the Special Forces units to which we were all assigned for some experience before shipping out for Vietnam sorted us out; they fired second lieutenants by the bushel.

I called to O'Neil, and he recognized me immediately. He was commanding Detachment A-503—the countrywide Mike Force. After a couple of minutes of catching up on where I had been after leaving his basic-training company, he said, "Come with me." We walked back into the office of the adjutant, Captain Paul McCarthy, who was an old friend of Captain O'Neil's.

"Paul," he said, "I want Burruss assigned to me."

And that was that; after less than a day in Vietnam, I was in the Mike Force.

2

Start getting yourself processed in." O'Neil grinned. "Then come on over to the Mike Force. We just got out of the field, and we're having a team party tonight."

I filled out innumerable papers for much of the afternoon, then went to bed in the transient quarters. Jet lag was the excuse I used for not going to the team party that night, but the truth was that I felt too new, too much a rookie, too pale among those suntanned warriors. Hell, I didn't even have my load-bearing equipment put together yet.

I awoke the next morning and reached for my jungle fatigues to put them on. They were a well-washed pair I had brought from Fort Bragg, cooler than the new ones I'd been issued. And they didn't make me look so much like the FNG—Fuckin' New Guy—I was. I thought at first that one of the other FNGs had stolen them, but then I saw them hanging, freshly starched and pressed, from a nail in the wooden wall. And on the floor, my jungle boots, with a gleaming spit shine. Just outside, in the shade of the wood-framed hootch, were two old Vietnamese mamasans, squatting there spit-shining someone else's jungle boots. I tried to ask them, in the rudimentary Vietnamese I had learned during premission training, if they had been the ones who shined my boots and pressed my fatigues, and if so, how much I owed them. I couldn't make them understand me, though, so I gave them each a pack of cigarettes. So much for my Vietnamese. I wouldn't have much use for it in the Mike Force anyway, since nearly all the troops were Montagnard tribesmen who didn't speak much Vietnamese either.

I finished processing in at Group Headquarters, collected my gear, and walked across to the Mike Force compound to meet my new teammates and see my new home.

Larry O'Neil chewed me out for missing the party the night before, then introduced me to the team sergeant, Master Sergeant Bob Gilstrap. Gilstrap looked me up and down like an alien being, then said, "Well, at least he isn't a *second* lieutenant." Gilstrap, I quickly discerned, wasn't particularly fond of lieutenants.

Larry then took me around to show me the area and introduce me to the other members of the team.

Detachment A-503 consisted, at that time, of three officers—I made four—and about twenty enlisted men. There were four rifle companies of about 130 to 150 Montagnard strikers each, and a fifth company undergoing training. In addition, there was a Headquarters Company which consisted mainly of Nungs—Vietnamese of Chinese extraction—many of whom were survivors of the A Shau operation who had gone in to try to defend that camp from being overrun by four North Vietnamese Army battalions. A handful of the Nungs were even veterans of the French defeat at Dien Bien Phu. Headquarters Company contained 81mm and 4.2-inch mortar sections, .50 caliber heavy-machine-gun crews, and 57mm and 106mm recoilless-rifle crews, as well as an assortment of medics, cooks, tailors, barbers, mechanics, and supply personnel.

The Mike Force compound was bordered on the north by Group Headquarters, the east by the Group logistical center and signal company, the south by an American support-group compound, and the west by rice paddies which stretched out a mile or so to a small river at the foot of the hill mass we had driven around in the jeep the day before. Up past Group Headquarters lay Nha Trang air base, and beyond it, the city. Just west of the air base were the MACV recondo school, where Special Forces instructors taught a long-range-reconnaissance course for U.S. and Allied units; and Detachment B-52, Project Delta, which was a reconnaissance and exploitation unit composed of reconnaissance teams and a Vietnamese Ranger battalion used to exploit what the recon teams found.

The compound in which the Mike Force was located was shared with the remnants of Detachment B-50, Project Omega, a unit similar to Project Delta, which was in the process of moving to Ban Me Thout, in the highlands of II Corps; and with Detachment B-57, Project Gamma. B-57 developed and employed Vietnamese agents, and was later to gain a great deal of unwanted notoriety for eliminating a double agent, an act which led to the jailing of a number of Special Forces officers by General Abrams—including Group Commander Colonel Bob Rheault, who was one of the finest officers Special Forces ever had.

In late 1967 the Mike Force portion of the compound consisted of a team house, in which the team members slept; a headquarters building which held the Tactical Operations Center with its maps and radios, the team bar, and the team mess hall; three U-shaped two-story troop billets in which the strikers were housed; a mess hall for the strikers; a dispensary; and a building which served as a supply room and communications equipment shop. There was also a motor pool, shared with B-50, in which the team's assortment of jeeps, three-quarter-ton trucks, and deuce-and-a-halfs were maintained. Along the sandbagged wall next to the road which ran along the rice paddies were several conex containers, atop which were mounted machine guns and recoilless rifles for defense of the compound. In the middle of the Mike Force area were mortar pits as well.

Each of the rifle companies was commanded by an American NCO—usually a master sergeant or sergeant first class—who had two or three other SF soldiers to assist him. One was usually a medic, who served double duty as both the *bac si*—doctor—for the company, and as the platoon leader for one of the platoons, about forty to fifty men.

That's really quite remarkable, because in American units the understrength companies often fielded less than eighty men. The company commanders were captains with two years or more of experience. They had lieutenants for platoon leaders and an executive officer, and NCOs at all levels. In addition, each company had an artillery forward observer with it, and the leaders each had radio operators to relay messages and commands for them. They seldom operated beyond the comforting support of friendly artillery, and they had a battalion staff backing them up to assist with administrative, logistical, and fire-support coordination tasks. Their soldiers all had the benefit of at least sixteen weeks of training for combat, and—perhaps most significant of all—everyone spoke the same language.

The NCOs commanding Mike Force companies and platoons, on the other hand, commanded larger companies and platoons of relatively primitive young men who had only six weeks—sometimes less—of training, only a very few of whom could communicate in even the basics of the English language. They had to serve as their own forward observers during the rare occasions when they operated within the range of friendly artillery, operate their own radios, coordinate medical evacuation of their wounded, direct their own air strikes when fighters were available, while at the same time trying to maneuver their troops against the enemy and win firefights—usually getting their troops forward by their own personal example.

And unlike their comrades-in-arms in American fighting units, they seldom had long periods in the field without significant contact. For one thing, enemy units were less likely to avoid contact with the Mike Force than they were with U.S. units, whose better-trained troops and often overwhelming firepower, artillery, gunship, and tactical air support invariably led to far more casualties to the enemy than to our GIs. And the Mike Force, when committed to battle, was usually stuck directly into battles which were already under way, or into areas known to have concentrations of enemy forces, usually preparing for a major attack on one of the isolated little Special Forces camps. It was an awesome and dangerous responsibility these tough American sergeants had, and they discharged it with remarkable courage, dedication, and skill. And for a hell of a lot less pay than their commissioned counterparts in American battalions—not that those officers were overpaid.

The Australians, too, provided leaders for the Montagnard troops in the I Corps and II Corps Mike Forces, and they acquitted themselves extremely well. The bond between the Aussies and the U.S. Special Forces in Vietnam was not something new, for when the battle at Camp Nam Dong ended in July 1964—the battle for which Roger Donlon was the first SF soldier to be awarded the Medal of Honor—it was discovered that Australian Warrant Officer Kevin Conway and American Master Sergeant Gabriel Alamo had died side by side defending the camp. Before the war ended, three of the Australians working with Special Forces were awarded their nation's highest award, the Victoria Cross.

As we toured the Mike Force compound that first day, I began to meet some of those men. Eighth Company—a recently formed company of Koho tribesmen—was nearing completion of their basic training under the direction of SFC Nick LaNotte, and O'Neil told me that, once I got settled in, I was to work with Nick and assist in the completion of their training. If I had known that a few weeks later I would be with them in their first battle with the enemy—and my own—I would have spent day and night with them, and tried to pick up some of their language. In the dispensary, I met two of the medics, Sandy Saunders and Mike Sharp. They were treating everything from toothaches to recent battle wounds to pregnant Montagnard wives, assisted by a tall 'Yard nurse named K'phe Cil. K'phe had been "adopted" by a U.S. Army nurse who was the wife of a Special Forces officer, and trained by her at the 8th Field Hospital in Nha Trang, before being hired to work in the Mike Force dispensary.

From there we visited the supply room, where I met First

Lieutenant A. P. Retzlaff, the detachment XO, who was responsible for the administration and logistics of the unit. A.P. was the ugliest man I met in Vietnam, with the personality of a billy goat—but he could locate and acquire anything the team needed, and when you called for a resupply of ammo or radio batteries or chow, he got them to you almost immediately. He was a master trader, and he managed to keep the supply-room and mess-hall refrigerators full—even if it meant he had to get the Nung tailor to make him a few VC battle flags for trading material. It was surprising what he could get for the things by embellishing them with a little chicken blood and a bullshit war story.

The other officer on the team was Joe Zamiara, a hard-fighting first lieutenant who was soon to be promoted to captain. Joe had completed a normal tour, but had voluntarily extended to come to A-503 from an assignment with the III Corps Mike Force. He would be O'Neil's deputy, and I was to replace him as the operations officer. "That's the officer who goes on operations," Larry O'Neil remarked.

We went to the mess hall for lunch, and there I met many of the detachment's NCOs. All of the rifle companies were in camp at the time, so most of the team was there. The majority were senior noncommissioned officers, but there were a couple of buck sergeants, and one E-4. I recognized several of them from Fort Bragg, and had served with one of them, SSG Rittenhouse, in the 6th Special Forces Group.

Although they represented all of the military occupational specialties organic to the A Team—operations and intelligence sergeants, light- and heavy-weapons leaders, engineer/demolitionists, medics, and radio operators—most of them were, in fact, serving as infantry small-unit leaders, whose duty is to lead soldiers in combat; "to close with and kill or capture the enemy by means of close combat and fire and maneuver. . . ." The "capture" part was not something for which the Mike Force was well-known.

Eighth Company, commanded by SFC Blair Ruffaner, was going out the following morning for a three-day training operation in the Dong Bo Valley, the valley which runs through the hill mass southwest of Nha Trang, and one of the 8th Company NCOs suggested that I go along. There wasn't usually much contact in the Dong Bo—not at that time, at least; that's why it was used for training operations by both the Mike Force and recondo school. But there *were* VC out there, so for a rookie like me, visions of firefights like those which were appearing with increasing frequency on television news programs back home flashed through my mind, and the next morning I struggled onto a truck, my rucksack overburdened with ammunition and survival gear.

The trucks took us down Highway 1 to the rubber plantation I had passed a couple of days before, where we dismounted and moved out in a company file through the elephant grass at the head of the valley. The grass was about five and a half feet tall, so that the only heads which appeared above it were those of the taller Americans. Fearful of snipers, which I was certain were lurking on the slopes to the left and right just waiting for *me*, I walked for a while with my knees bent enough to bring my head beneath the level of the elephant grass. The weight of my overloaded rucksack and the smirks of the 'Yards near me soon made me abandon that tactic, if not the belief that, somewhere out there, a sniper patiently waited.

On a rough track which crossed the elephant grass, we ran across an old man in an oxcart. He seemed terribly frightened as Ruffaner's interpreter checked his identity card and questioned him about whether or not he had seen any VC in the area. One man in the point element thought he had seen a man in black pajamas with a weapon farther down the track, but the old man was the only person we encountered that first day.

For me, the day was characterized by stifling heat and chafed hips from the rubbing of my heavy ammo pouches, and the ache of my shoulders from the weight of my bulging rucksack. A few times, we moved up onto the jungled slopes of the mountains, and I was impressed by the fact that one could see only a few meters around him. How could you ever expect to find and fight the enemy in such terrain?

We formed into a night defensive position—an NDP— shortly before dark on one of the jungled hillsides, and I spent that first night huddled on a pile of rocks. But I slept soundly; a result, I suppose, of the physical and emotional strain of the previous day. I awoke for the first of many mornings to the sounds of coughing and throat-clearing by the Montagnards, the result, I later learned, of the tuberculosis with which so many of them were infected.

After a breakfast of C-ration coffee and sliced peaches—I had not yet come to prefer the sensible and relatively lightweight indigenous rations, which were mostly rice—I shouldered my burdensome rucksack, already resolving to lessen the amount of chow and ammunition and extra gear stuffed into it before I went to the field again. My trepidation of the previous day had lessened, so I asked SFC Ruffaner if it would be all right for me to move with the point element for a while. He agreed, and showed me the route we were going to follow for the remainder of the day, advising me that the 'Yards would be expecting me to point out the direction of movement from time to time.

I moved up with the point squad, indicated the initial direction of movement to the point man, and was immediately impressed by the manner in which he picked his way alertly and silently through the jungle growth ahead. He seemed to glide along effortlessly, almost invisibly blending into his surroundings, although he was just a few meters ahead. The alertness, silence, and effortless movement of the point element was comforting, and bespoke the familiarity of young men at ease with their surroundings—no surprise, as they had spent all their lives moving through such jungle. The only noise was made by me, as my gear got hung up now and then on what were appropriately referred to by us Americans as "wait-a-minute vines." The infrequency with which the point man had to stop and look back at me to verify that he was still on the correct azimuth was also impressive.

For the rest of the day we moved down the valley to a point at which it split into a Y, and set up around the stream for which the Dong Bo Valley was named. One of the ambush positions which we had emplaced a short way down the valley reported that they thought they had heard some movement to their front, so Ruffaner called for a few rounds of artillery fire from the American 105mm gun section which supported the defense of U.S. installations in Nha Trang. In less than two minutes the first round landed nearby—a bit closer in than Ruffaner had intended, but giving me a good feel for why a call for fire requested near one's own position includes the warning "danger close."

The next day, as we neared A-502's outpost south of Nha Trang, we came under fire.

It was sporadic, not really seeming to be directed at us, but the supersonic "crack" of the rounds passing nearby made it plain that it was being fired in our direction.

I hugged the ground near Ruffaner. "Goddamned M-16's!" he said, taking the handset from his 'Yard radio bearer and calling the Installation Defense Coordinator, the element which was supposed to ensure that friendly units in the area were advised of each other's locations, so that they wouldn't inadvertently come into contact.

I wondered how Ruffaner could tell that it was M-16 fire cracking nearby, and not AK-47's, which most of the communists carried. But I was later to learn the distinctive difference in sound the two rounds make when they pass close by. After one hears Soviet 7.62mm rounds searching for him a couple of times, he never forgets the sound.

It turned out that we were downrange of an area the recondo school was using for weapons training, so we got the firing shut off, moved to the bank of the river across from A-502's southernmost outpost, were ferried across in sixteen-foot fiberglass assault boats, and moved back to the compound.

I had been on a combat operation. Nothing significant had occurred, but at least I had been in the jungle, learned a few subtle lessons, and rubbed off a bit of the newness.

During the next couple of weeks I went out on short local operations a few times, but without enemy contact. I took a trip with Joe Zamiara down to III Corps to coordinate an operation which we were planning to conduct jointly with the III Corps Mike Force, Detachment B-36. Two of their companies, which were composed of ethnic Cambodians, and two of our 'Yard companies were to conduct a helicopter assault to secure a trail junction at an abandoned village called Thien Ngon, near the Cambodian border in Tay Ninh Province. A new Special Forces camp was to be built there while we secured the area.

More of the newness wore off. I began to tan, my jungle boots and combat equipment got worn in, and I began to yearn for combat so that I wouldn't have to feel like such a rookie any longer. My chance was coming soon.

—— 3 ——

A-502, the oversize A Team just outside Nha Trang at Camp Trung Dung, an old French fortress on Highway 1 in the village of Dien Khanh, deployed a number of ambushes in the area around Nha Trang each night as part of its responsibility for keeping the provincial capital secure. Often, troops from Group Headquarters would accompany these ambushes in the hope of seeing some combat action and earning themselves a Combat Infantryman's Badge. On the night of 25 November 1967, a lieutenant named Steve Cloud, from the Adjutant General's section of 5th Group Headquarters, accompanied a platoon-size ambush to a point about a kilometer north of Camp Trung Dung. They were two hundred meters or so northwest of the only bridge in the vicinity of the camp which spanned the Song Cai, a river of about 150 meters width running east to west across the coastal plain through the northern part of Dien Khanh district and the city of Nha Trang, where it emptied into the South China Sea.

Early on the morning of 26 November, Lieutenant Cloud earned his CIB. The platoon ambushed what was estimated to be a Viet Cong main-force company, and a sharp battle ensued, which lasted into the morning. The Mike Force was ordered to reinforce the ambushers with a company of 'Yards and to try to root the enemy out of the area.

Captain O'Neil and I, with 8th Company and three of their Special Forces leaders—Sergeant First Class Blair Ruffaner, Staff Sergeant Don Poncin, and the medic, Sergeant Sandy Saunders—loaded CH-47 Chinook helicopters at the air base and took off for the short flight to Camp Trung Dung. We landed at the camp, and went in to coordinate the operation with the camp commander, Major Wilbur Lee. There was a landing zone large enough for the Chinooks in the vicinity of the ambush position, and the fighting had moved some distance from there, so it was decided that we would go in there. We loaded the choppers again, and prepared to take off. Not realizing that O'Neil was doing some last-second coordination with Major Lee, we took off without him.

We landed, one Chinook at a time, in the LZ, where we were met by Lieutenant Cloud and the American sergeant with him. They explained that the VC appeared to have withdrawn east down the road several hundred meters, and south toward the river.

Ruffaner decided to move his three platoons of Koho troops down the road two or three hundred meters, then face south and sweep, on line, toward the river, hoping to trap the enemy between our line of advance and the river.

The point platoon moved out east along the dirt road, and I fell in near SFC Ruffaner between the point and second platoons. The point element had moved about one hundred meters when there was a sudden explosion some seventy-five meters ahead of me. I thought it was a mortar round which had detonated in a tree beside the road as the point element passed it.

For a moment, everything seemed to freeze—the irregular-shaped cloud of gray smoke in the treetop, leaves suspended within it, and the sudden silence, with everyone completely motionless. The only things moving were the leaves, which floated gently down, and a couple of men in the point element who collapsed onto the road.

Suddenly I was in combat. The rattle and crack of a heavy volume of automatic-weapons fire broke the silence, and I saw two more men crumple to the ground thirty or forty meters in front of me. As I dived for cover at the roadside, I saw Ruffaner dash down the road toward the point element.

It appeared that the fire was coming from our right front, from a line of coconut palms, banana trees, and two small dwellings about 150 meters to our southeast, in the general direction of the bridge.

I got busy directing the troops near me to fire into the area it appeared the enemy fire was coming from—although I couldn't really tell for certain. I hadn't known that the source of incoming fire would be so damned hard to locate.

I placed a couple of troops on the north edge of the road just short of where it had somehow become obvious that the killing zone along the road began. I don't know why it was so obvious, except that beyond a certain point, just ahead of me, people were being hit; where I was, they weren't. It was that simple.

Only a minute or so had passed since the initial explosion, and Ruffaner came running out of the killing zone, his arm hanging limp at his side. He had a clean bullet hole through the thick part of his shoulder. It surprised me that a bullet wound did so little damage to a man; it hadn't even slowed the big man down, and he appeared to be in little pain.

He said Saunders was still down there, wounded. We had too many injured people exposed along the road ahead, and the most sensible thing seemed to be to get them back behind that imaginary line where the killing and wounding stopped, regroup, and try to outflank the Viet Cong.

Poncin got Saunders on the radio, and the young medic said that he had checked on the two people up front, and they were dead. He was crawling around to check the other wounded. Poncin told him to come on out. We would get the other wounded out, who were between him and where I was. Sandy said he couldn't—"Every time I move, I get hit!" He had already sustained a bad wrist wound, and a bullet through the buttocks.

Poncin and I got the troops along the road to lay down a heavy base of fire to keep the enemy down, and Saunders and the wounded who were able to do so started out. I felt safe behind what I pictured as an outgoing wall of fire, and moved down the road to help Sandy out of the killing zone and back toward the LZ. We had a medevac chopper on the way in for Ruffaner, Saunders, and the wounded 'Yards who had made it back to the LZ.

There were four dead strikers still down the road, and several who were unhurt, and there was one sitting upright in a daze in the middle of the road, his head gushing blood. One other was trying to crawl back toward us.

Poncin made a radio call to A-502 requesting more ammunition, as the 'Yards were burning it up at a rapid rate. I couldn't find the interpreter, and in an attempt to keep up a steady volume of fire—without lulls but without burning up all the remaining ammo—was moving among the 'Yards alongside the road, imploring, "One man 'bang bang,' one man no 'bang bang,'" gesturing accordingly and having—to my amazement—some success at it.

Poncin made a daring dash for the man sitting dumbly in the middle of the killing zone about thirty meters down the road. He scooped the wounded man up and turned to make the run back to safety, but collapsed heavily almost immediately, a bullet through his belly.

Jesus. He was down, and I had to get him out. Now. He had been hit trying to save one of his troops, so how could I do less? I would probably be hit too, and there were no Americans left to come get me out. I would either be killed, or I would not, and if I waited, I might become too frightened to do what was my duty, as demonstrated to me a moment before by the brave NCO now lying wounded and dangerously exposed in the road before me.

I high-crawled rapidly down the road to Poncin, and tried to sort of swim back down the road with him, using a cross-chest carry—and got almost nowhere. So I just picked the big 220-pound man up and ran down the road with him. Somewhere along those seemingly endless thirty or forty steps, I realized that bullets were cracking all around me, that there was no outgoing fire, and that a bunch of communist sons of bitches were doing their best to kill me. I almost felt like just stopping and letting their bullets find me, so inevitable it seemed that I would be hit. But suddenly I was safe, past that imaginary line where their fire couldn't reach.

With Poncin safely at the LZ, I ran back to the edge of the killing zone to find another wounded 'Yard trying to crawl out, and still inspired by what I had seen Don Poncin do and pumped up with adrenaline from my first taste of battle, I got him out as well, in time to get him on the medevac chopper which was landing to pick up Ruffaner, Saunders, Poncin, and some of the other wounded.

And then, with the realization that I was the only American left with the company of Montagnards, with no interpreter and with a couple of wounded and several dead still in the road, the fear set in. I had a radio, but no list of call signs and frequencies. An Air Force Forward Air Controller checked in, and I passed a panicky situation report to him, calling myself "Mike Force" and him "FAC."

Another helicopter came in, this one with the ammo resupply from A-502. It was all wrong. They had sent in carbine and .30 caliber linked ammo, which was useless in the newer M-16 rifles, M-60 machine guns, and M-79 grenade launchers we carried in the Mike Force.

The NCO with Lieutenant Cloud went forward with me again, and the raw fear which had gripped me began to subside. The firing had stopped, the FAC reported that he had Cobra gunships on the way, and I had found the interpreter back by the LZ. Yet another Montagnard was crawling out of the killing zone, wounded in both legs. I crawled forward to help him out—and the damned incoming fire started again. It disappointed me, made me sick at my stomach, rekindled the gnawing fear. But we made it out unhit.

The poor injured striker with the head wound was still sitting dazed in the road—being used by the VC as bait for anyone who might dare to try to get him out. It just didn't seem right to leave him there any longer. I got the 'Yards firing again, then turned to the sergeant from A-502 and told him to get the man out. Then, "Wait a minute," I called. "I can't ask you to do that!"

I had told him to go because *I* didn't want to go in there again. I'd made it three times, but knew I was pushing my luck. I felt ashamed that I was violating that good soldierly principle of combat leadership I had first heard from my father: "Never ask your men to do anything you're not willing to do yourself."

But he was already gone. I turned and emptied a magazine into the tree line, and thought I saw a spot from which some of the enemy fire was coming. The sergeant was out of the killing zone unhurt.

As he carried the striker back to the landing zone, I took a grenade launcher from one of the 'Yards and fired at the point in the tree line where I had seen the muzzle flash a moment before. I rolled onto my side and broke the M-79 open to reload it, and some movement caught my eye. There, only about fifteen meters away, just across the road on the north side, was a man running directly toward me—a yellow-skinned man with an AK-47, wearing black pajamas and a ring of camouflage on his chest. He was running toward me, with what looked like a grin on his face, and bringing his weapon down to bear on me. He was looking at me sitting there with an empty M-79 grenade launcher in my hands, my mouth now wide open and my eyes as big as silver dollars, and the son of a bitch was grinning. He was going to bring his weapon down a few more inches, and he was going to fill my face and my chest with bullets, and kill me.

The image of the man a split second later is burned into my memory.

He is running at a tilt, like a running back turning the corner on an end-sweep. He has the face of a million other Vietnamese—memorable only by its grin. His black pajamas look neat and clean, and the camouflage ring—a circle

44

of vines with branches of leaves coming from it—is coming apart. The leaves are falling from his chest as the leaves from the tree fell from the explosion which first began this firefight. They are falling because one of the strikers I had placed facing across the road behind us to protect our rear has calmly taken aim and is emptying a magazine into the enemy soldier's chest. He continues falling in the direction he was leaning, and I know that he is dead, and dismiss him.

But I'm unable to dismiss the fact that he came from behind us, from the north, away from the direction almost all of us were facing and firing. If there was one there, then there must be others.

There was a lone, small building about thirty meters in the direction from which he had come, so I got a hand grenade, pulled the pin, and released the safety lever. I let it cook off for a couple of seconds, then threw it in a high arc toward the nearest corner of the building. Just as it hit the ground, an armed khaki-clad figure appeared from around the corner of the building, then disappeared in a cloud of black smoke and brown dust.

I had killed him. I didn't feel sad, or elated, or remorseful about that fact. I felt only that I had eliminated a threat to my life and had evened the score of the day a little.

We poured more fire into the house and into the grass and brush on that side of the road. The FAC reported that the Cobra gunships were on station, so I asked him to work them in the area from which communists' fire had swept the terrible killing zone ahead. A "dustoff"—medical-evacuation helicopter—was on the way in for the remainder of the wounded.

A group of five or six civilians, mostly women, came running up the road toward us from down where the point element had been ambushed. They must have felt that it was safe to come down the road now.

If they felt it was dangerous to remain where they had been, then it must be because the enemy was moving into the area from which they were fleeing—the village just north of the bridge.

45

The firing had ceased, and I went back to the LZ to see to the evacuation of the wounded, and to get some more ammunition in, which we badly needed by now. While I was there, several strikers went down the road to recover the dead and their weapons—and came under fire again. The killing zone was still active. Another striker was killed, and one wounded, but not so badly that he couldn't run back to safety.

O'Neil informed me that a Korean infantry battalion was on the way to the village to clear it. I was to evacuate the wounded and move from the LZ south to the river, then east to the bridge, where O'Neil and Major Lee would be waiting with some troops from A-502, who would secure the bridge. The Korean battalion would form a semicircle around the village, then close in and clear it.

A dustoff chopper called to say he was on the way in to take out the last of the wounded, so I asked him if he could take out the useless .30 caliber ammunition.

"Sorry," he radioed back, "it's against the Geneva Conventions." He was right, and I didn't protest. But then another voice broke in. "This is so-and-so. I'll take out anything you've got. Pop smoke." It was a "slick" pilot, and in he came. Out went the wounded and the useless ammo—and my rucksack, with all my chow and my poncho.

There were still five dead strikers down in the killing zone. Should I risk more lives to get them out, or leave them until the Korean battalion came in and cleared the area? I decided to do the latter, to let the Koreans police them up for us. I hadn't learned yet to place the value I later would on the bodies of dead soldiers alongside whom I'd fought. They were still strangers to me then. They were dead, and that could not be undone by sacrificing more people to recover them. I wasn't badly bothered by leaving them that first time. Perhaps it's better that way than to have others die. But later on in the war, I would have my doubts.

We moved out to the south, toward the river, the sergeant from A-502 and I the only two Americans left with the Koho company. I stayed until the last to cover the rear as the

Cobra gunships made rocket-firing runs over our heads, hearing the frightening hiss and boom as the 2.75-inch rockets passed overhead and slammed into the coconut palms and banana trees where the enemy had been. I saw no enemy trying to escape the Cobras' wrath, and moved out with the others for the river. My first firefight was over.

—— 4 ——

When we got to the bridge just south of the enemy-occupied village, we found it being secured by some CIDG from A-502. Major Lee, the Detachment Commander, and one of his officers, First Lieutenant Bob Sweeney, were there. And then Larry O'Neil showed up. I expected him to chew me out for leaving him at the camp, but he didn't. He grinned, slapped me on the shoulder, and asked me for a situation report. As I began to explain what had happened on that obscure stretch of dirt road, the reality of the death and destruction of my first taste of armed combat sank in, and my voice cracked and my eyes clouded up and spilled over.

I was ashamed of the way I had panicked on the radio at first, ashamed of the fact that we had allowed ourselves to be ambushed, and that it had cost us so many needless casualties—some of whom were still lying in the road, their young lives drained into pools of bloody mud. But battle is an imperfect art of give-and-take, and these men understood that. Like them, I had been baptized by fire now, and although they had been in other firefights, they hadn't been in this one. They listened attentively, as I had only been able to do in the past.

The Korean infantry battalion was moving into position to encircle the village on the north side of the river. I was to take 8th Company over the bridge to the south side, check out the area between the river and Highway 1, link up with an ARVN Ranger company moving in from the east, and tie in with a company from A-502 which was along the river-bank from the bridge to the west. The young sergeant who had been with Lieutenant Cloud volunteered to stay with me so that there would be more than one lone American with the company. I gladly accepted his offer, and we moved the Kohos across the bridge, extending two platoons along the riverbank to the east to prevent any of the enemy from escaping the Korean battalion's encirclement by crossing the river.

There was a flat area along the riverbank which stretched back for about fifty meters, ending at an embankment along which were trees, stands of bamboo, and several houses. I took the reserve platoon and moved out to sweep the area above the embankment and to make contact with the Rangers, who were supposed to be moving in from the east to tie in with us.

As I moved with the point element into the trees and bamboo, we came upon a fresh foxhole which I assumed to be a friendly position. I moved on east and encountered the next foxhole, and was startled to find a man crouching in it—a man in a khaki uniform.

I aimed my M-16 at him and called for him to get out of the foxhole. I was afraid he would spring up and blast away at me, or sit up and pop a grenade, killing us both—we had been warned about such suicidal attacks in training—so I held the muzzle close to his head. He didn't move, so I poked him in the back with my weapon. He jiggled. If he were dead, he would be stiff, I thought. He wasn't stiff. I shoved the muzzle under his chin and tilted his head back. It flopped back against the top of the foxhole. His eyes were open, but rolled back in the sockets, his mouth hung open, and he had a small hole in his forehead. He was dead.

I had not seen a dead man up close before, had never examined one of the enemy. The only ones I had ever seen, I saw from ten times this distance, and that had been only an hour or so before. I hadn't even been this close to the dead from my own unit. I was awed, amazed. My pulse beat rapidly, and I stood there sweating and trembling and staring at him. This was the enemy. This was what war was all about. Young men like him and me—hundreds of thousands of us—trying to kill or maim one another, until one side can no longer bear it and surrenders or just withdraws from the battlefield and goes home.

He was younger than I. He was alone. He was dead. He was a fraction of a step toward the victory we were going to win for the free world. As I stood and stared at him, and thought about these things, the sense of adventure I had felt dissipated, but the sense of duty strengthened. I did a lot of growing up that late-November day.

There was a small amount of firing some distance to the east, and I figured it was probably the Vietnamese Rangers making contact with the dead man's unit, which had apparently withdrawn in their direction. We checked a couple more foxholes, and the houses and surroundings just beyond them, finding no one.

With the Rangers in contact to the east and the Koreans moving into position to commence their attack, I decided to leave an outpost on the embankment and take the rest of the platoon to the right flank of the company, where the two platoons along the riverbank were digging in. Until the Rangers showed up, we would need to extend our position into the area where they were supposed to be blocking.

A helicopter landed near the bridge and a Korean lieutenant hopped out and reported to me. In perfect English he explained that he was the battalion liaison officer, whose mission was to ensure that we didn't fire on the soldiers of his battalion as they approached the river through the village.

The Koreans were in position now in a semicircle around the village, ready to move in and force the communists back into a small pocket against the riverbank, where they would be destroyed by the Republic of Korea troops or forced into the river and destroyed by us.

The ROKs had quad .50's—four .50 caliber machine guns mounted together on pedestal mounts—on the backs of two-and-a-half-ton trucks, and they began their attack by blasting away with them toward the center of the village. Rounds started popping over our heads, so we got down into our holes or behind the small berm at the edge of the river.

I didn't like what was going on. There were still a hell of a lot of civilians in that village. I dashed over to the depression in which the Korean liaison officer was hunkered.

"Won't a lot of civilians get killed like this?" I asked.

"We don't kill civilians," he answered without emotion, "just VC suspects."

"That's bullshit!" I retorted, and scooted back to my radio. The Koreans had a reputation for such ruthlessness, but that isn't war—it's murder. I called back to the team and asked for help in getting them to stop their attack for a while. Back at Fort Bragg, the Psychological Operations people had spoken often of loudspeaker-equipped light aircraft which could be used to broadcast propaganda messages over a broad area. I requested one of those, with a Vietnamese linguist aboard. If we could get the Koreans to stop for an hour, or even a half-hour, I'd get the loudspeaker bird to tell the villagers that the village was going to be attacked, and that anyone who wanted to get out must come to the bridge immediately.

The Koreans were reluctant to halt their attack. It was getting into the afternoon, and if they didn't clear the village by dark, some of the enemy might escape, or inflict more casualties on the ROK soldiers. But with assistance from Group Headquarters, I got what I asked for. Within twenty minutes a loudspeaker-equipped O-2 observation aircraft showed up, and the Koreans halted their attack. As soon as the aircraft began broadcasting, civilians flocked to the bridge. About two hundred came across, were checked to ensure they were "friendlies," and allowed to pass. Then suddenly they stopped coming to the bridge, and the Korean quad .50's began tearing the place apart again. I spotted a couple of figures darting around among the trees and buildings near the far side of the bridge. I believe they were

VC who were there to stop any remaining civilians from crossing the bridge. Then I saw one, wearing black and carrying a weapon, dash into a small building which looked like a country outhouse, about 250 meters from my position.

Lieutenant Sweeney was there at the time, and I asked him and the Korean lieutenant if they had seen the man. They hadn't, so I put a tracer round into the building, and the man ran out of it and hid behind a haystacklike pile of wooden stakes. I got a LAW—a 66mm Light Antitank Weapon—from one of the Montagnard soldiers and prepared it for firing. Lying down, I placed it on my shoulder, aimed, and started to squeeze the firing mechanism. Something didn't seem exactly right. Damn! I was lying with my legs directly behind the rear of the rocket launcher. The backblast would have torn my legs up.

Correcting my position, I aimed at the woodpile, placing the 250-meter tick mark of the sight directly on the center of the target, and squeezed the trigger. The LAW was a fairly new weapon at the time, and I had never had the opportunity to fire one before. It felt as if a small explosion occurred in my head. My ears hurt, and were filled with a loud ringing noise, but I saw the rocket fly straight to the woodpile, watched it fly apart, and heard a sound exactly like a strike in a bowling alley. Sweeney and the Korean were truly impressed. So was I. The next time I saw Sweeney, he called me "The Lawman," and informed me that he had checked behind the woodpile after the battle was over, and the blast of the shaped charge warhead had hit the VC in the chest, killing him.

The afternoon wore on as the Koreans pressed their attack, their quad .50's hammering mercilessly away as the noose around the village tightened. Two U.S. Air Force Forward Air Controllers in little O-1 Birddog observation aircraft were circling around to our east, where the Rangers were supposed to be. Along with the sounds of the battle being waged across the river, I could hear AK-47's firing long bursts in the vicinity of where the FACs were circling. I knew the enemy assault rifle's distinctive sound well by that afternoon. I gave them a call on the radio—Walt 30 and Walt 32—and informed them that I thought they were being fired upon. "You hear that, Billy?" I heard Walt 30 say. "They say we're being fired on. Let's go down and take a look." They swooped down in their fragile little airplanes and drew more fire, which they dealt with by firing marking rockets at the enemy. After several rockets, the enemy fire ceased.

I later came to know both those FACs well—Lieutenant Colonel "Papa" Baer and Captain Billy Boyd. The whole team came to know and love and rely on them. They never let us down.

Darkness approached, and the "friendly" .50 caliber rounds were popping more closely overhead. It had become obvious that the Koreans would not have the village cleared before dark, and the Vietnamese Rangers still had not shown up. I called back to the team to have someone check on their location, and learned to my disgust that they had done what so many Vietnamese units were doing in those days. They went home for the night. From the firing which had been directed at the FACs earlier, and the dead soldier we had found to our rear, and the absence of the Rangers, I had to assume that there were enemy to our right rear, so I ordered a squad of strikers to move back there and set up a listening post and ambush. They refused to go at first, the interpreter pretending not to understand my orders. After arguing for a while, I simply took the squad leader by the arm and dragged him back to the woodline and put him in position as the .50 caliber rounds cracked around us, and the rest of the squad reluctantly followed.

It began to rain about sunset, and my poncho was in the rucksack which had inadvertently been evacuated with the useless ammo. I was wet and cold and hungry and exhausted. I was tired of the 'Yards hesitation to go with me earlier to clear the bunkers, and to establish the OP and ambush, tired of having to place each one in his particular position, and tired of having to try to make myself understood without being able to speak their language. I got on the radio and asked O'Neil to replace them with another company. I think I really hoped he would replace me as well, and I think he knew that. Wisely, for my sake, he told me to hang in there and he would replace them in the morning. I suppose I didn't *want* to hang in there. I felt alone, still shaken from my initiation of battle and fire and death. It was getting darker, I was half a world away from my home and my family. I had only narrowly escaped wounds and death, and that realization was heavy upon me. It had been one hell of a day, and it was not at all glorious, as I had imagined it would be. I wanted to do like the Rangers had done—just pick up and go home. Larry O'Neil no doubt knew that, and knew what my faltering courage needed. "Hang in there."

Just after dark, a C-47 flareship showed up, dropping illumination flares above the village. But when the "lights" went out, the VC would throw hand grenades into the ROK positions, and immediately after they detonated, would run past the encircling troops, then hit them from behind. The Koreans were taking casualties, and many of the VC were escaping. The ROK liaison officer glared at me in the eerie light of the flares, and wouldn't speak to me. But I knew the decision to halt the battle and let the civilians escape had been the correct one, so I just glared back at him.

Suddenly a recoilless rifle fired from our rear, from the vicinity of the bunkers we had cleared earlier, where the squad of Kohos was supposed to be protecting our rear. Then a machine gun opened up on us from the same area. The rounds passed above us, the recoilless-rifle projectile exploding against the far bank of the river. The 'Yards I had positioned to cover our rear rushed back into our position, and we dug ourselves in a little deeper. All I could get them to do about the enemy weapons was to face in that direction. I made it plain that I only wanted them to fire if the enemy assaulted or if we began to take casualties. Otherwise, they would only pinpoint our positions for the recoilless-rifle and machine-gun crews. The recoilless rifle fired a couple more times from different positions, and the machine gun probed over our heads occasionally during the night, but without effect. I wanted the CIDG soldiers from A-502 on our left to try to hit the VC gun crews from the flank, but when I called the camp to get the message passed to them, learned to my dismay that they had pulled out shortly after dark. I was furious. The bastards had just gotten up and gone home. I was especially angry that the Americans who were supposed to be with them hadn't even told us they were leaving. I was losing a lot of faith in our allies.

As the night wore on, I began to feel better about things, glad that O'Neil had made me hang in there, glad that the Mike Force had stuck with it, while the Rangers and CIDG had gone home. As I reflected on the events of the day before, I realized that I had made some mistakes. But I had done some things right too. Inspired by what Don Poncin and Sandy Saunders had done, I had found the courage to go into the killing zone after them. And allowing the villagers to escape the battle had saved many innocent lives. I was only a rookie lieutenant when the day began, and now I was commanding a rifle company in combat.

By the time daylight—and the FACs—returned, I felt confident that I could do the job.

I guided the FAC, Papa Baer, to the area from which the enemy had harassed us during the night, and adjusted his white phosphorous rockets onto the positions from which I figured they had been firing. When the Rangers finally appeared, we swept the area with a few men. Lieutenant Colonel Baer's rockets had, to our mutual surprise, scored a direct hit on the VC 57mm recoilless-rifle position and destroyed the gun and its crew.

The Koreans completed the closing of their deadly noose, and counted more than sixty enemy dead. And they had recovered the bodies of our troops. Bob Gilstrap showed up with a convoy of trucks to take us back to the Mike Force compound.

I had been in a battle—not a very big one, perhaps, but very big to me. I had experienced the confusion, the fear, the disgust, and the elation of it. I had encountered emotions I had never even imagined before, and have seldom known since. I wasn't a rookie anymore. Even old hard-assed Sergeant Gilstrap treated me with a fair amount of respect.

5

The evening of 27 November 1967, I was back in the Mike Force team house—in the shower, safe and elated. I had seen Ruffaner and Saunders and Poncin. Ruffaner was pinching nurses, Saunders wasn't badly hurt, and Poncin, who was split open across his belly from side to side, was alive, though somewhat worried because they hadn't sewn him up and his gut was laid wide open. He thanked me for carrying him off that terrible piece of road, and that made me feel especially good.

Because Mike Force soldiers were directly employed by the United States government, we were able to have them treated in U.S. hospitals. I found the young Montagnard with the head wound for whom Poncin had risked his life, and was pleased to see that he was alive and lucid, and I reported that happy fact to the burly sergeant.

I went to the team bar for a beer, and to read the *Stars and Stripes* newspaper, which was delivered to us a couple of days after it was printed in Japan. The headline was "GIs Take Hill 875 After 5-Day Fight." A few days earlier, that headline would have made me think only of the glory of such a battle. Now it made me think of the suffering and fear and pain the young paratroopers of the 173rd Airborne

Brigade must have endured in that long and difficult fight, in which they had lost 158 of America's finest youth.

That night, 7th Company, which had completed training only a short time before, had a party to celebrate their graduation to operational status. Seventh Company had been recruited from among the Chams, a people who were concentrated around the coastal cities of Phan Rang and Phan Thiet. Until they were defeated by the Annamese in the fifteenth century, their Champa kingdom had ruled much of southern Indochina, extending as far west as the magnificent temples of Angkor, which they took in the twelfth century, and as far north as Hanoi, which they had sacked in the 1300's. It was only in 1822 that the last Cham chieftain had relinquished his throne.

Although they were ethnically of the same stock as the highland Montagnards, they had been converted centuries before to a combination of the Hindu and Moslem religions, which was mixed with their tribal superstitions and customs as well. They had built great temples similar in architecture to those at Angkor Wat, and the ruins of a few of them could still be found along the coast, including the ruins of two towers just north of Nha Trang. The Chams were a fairly sophisticated group, compared to most of the other ethnic minorities of Vietnam. And now they had soldiers in the Mike Force.

The Chams' priest and village chief were present with their families, and we Americans were treated as the guests of honor. They presented us with beautiful red-and-gold blankets they had woven by hand, and with ceremonial sashes. The priest made some remarks to the company, and then we were treated to one of the most beautiful sights I have ever seen. Some of the Cham soldiers began to play copper gongs, beating them with the heels of their fists, while others took up the primitive beat with hardwood sticks which they clacked together. Then six or seven girls about sixteen or seventeen years old appeared, moving gracefully to the beat of the gongs and sticks. They were dressed in white silk dresses—plain floor-length, long-sleeved, high-necked gowns. Over her shoulder, each wore a sash of the type they had presented to us, and all were barefoot. They were pretty girls, delicate in their graceful movements. Each had a conical hat, which she held in her hands and used as a hula dancer would use her hands. They moved in perfect unison, and their movements were unexaggerated, flowing smoothly to the rhythm of the dull gongs. It was sort of a cross between a ballet and a hula, and it was pure, exquisite grace. As I watched them in appreciative awe, I couldn't help but think of the contrast between what I was now seeing and what I had seen the day before, just a few miles away.

The Chams had placed cans of beer and water glasses of several types of liquor in front of each of us, and I drank deeply of them. The lovely Cham dancers performed again, this time with fans instead of hats, and I let myself enjoy the beauty of their dance as I sank into a fog of fatigue and alcohol. That dance remains as the most beautiful thing I saw in Vietnam.

During the month of December I gained more confidence in my ability to perform my duties, sharpening such field skills as the use of artillery, patrolling and ambushing in various types of terrain, communicating with the Montagnards, and selecting sites for ambushes and night defensive positions. I rode with the FACs as they directed preplanned air strikes, took part in a couple of helicopter assaults, and helped with the parachute training of the Mike Force troops.

The parachute training of the troops was done to enable us to jump into remote areas as part of the quick-reaction mission we had as the 5th Special Forces Group Commander's countrywide reaction force. It was amazing to see those small young hill tribesmen, only recently out of their loincloths, donning parachutes and boarding C-123 transports for both their first airplane ride and their first parachute jump.

Some of their actions were nothing short of hilarious. On one approach to the drop zone, which was only a short distance inland from the sea, the jump master gave the first jumper the command, "Stand in the door!"—and out the young trooper went, over the South China Sea. He landed near the beach and was picked up by helicopter almost immediately, with a real jump story to tell.

The 'Yards exited the aircraft in all sorts of unconventional ways. Some would squat in the door, some would somersault out. One stepped out of the door after walking across the back of the man in front of him, who, having second thoughts about it all, just lay down in front of the door. There were several who tried to turn around and get back into the airplane after they were already on the way out—including one who actually managed to hang on to the door frame for several seconds after he exited.

One of the Nungs got his static line wrapped around his neck and almost pulled his head off, but aside from that, the only injuries were an occasional sprain or fracture. Most weighed so little that their rate of descent was very slow, and when one managed to drift over a thermal updraft, he might hang suspended in the air for several minutes. They would land on their rear ends, their knees—every way imaginable —but they almost always walked away uninjured.

I remember seeing one parachute malfunction. A little cross-eyed 'Yard had only a small amount of his canopy inflated, and was dropping to earth quite rapidly. About twenty feet off the ground he finally pulled his reserve parachute ripcord—just in time to have the bundle of nylon fly up into his face as he plowed into the ground. He bounced off the drop zone in a cloud of dust, and the medics rushed out toward him. Somehow, the little man had escaped the incident unhurt. He stood there jabbering at the top of his high-pitched voice, pointing angrily at his reserve, apparently mad at it because he felt it had failed him.

The team had already made one combat parachute jump since they had been formed, at one of the Special Forces camps in III Corps, Camp Bunard. I could hardly imagine it, but there would be others as well.

One evening, after we returned to the compound from training, we were met by the news that we had lost the first teammate killed in action since I had come to the team— Staff Sergeant Monte Busby. He had been with one of the companies we had down at Thien Ngon, working with the III Corps Mike Force. Sandy Saunders took the news hard; he and Busby were the best of friends. We attended a solemn memorial service in the chapel at Group Headquarters, then retired to the NCO club to drink to our comrade's memory.

As Christmas approached, we found ourselves spending much of the time out of the field and in the comfortable surroundings of the Mike Force compound and the city of Nha Trang. There was to be a truce with the enemy during the Christmas and New Year holidays, and again during Tet, the lunar new year. A. P. Retzlaff managed to find an artificial Christmas tree and some decorations, and with the assistance of Miss Ling, the team secretary, had the team bar decorated for the season. At nearby Group Headquarters, the officers and NCO clubs had various rock-'n'-roll bands from Saigon and the Philippines for entertainment. We would often get them to play for us at the Mike Force compound as well, inviting the Vietnamese girls who worked for us and for Group Headquarters, American nurses from nearby 8th Field Hospital, the several wives and girlfriends of members of the team, and a sprinkling of bar girls from the Streamer Bar, Marie Kim's, or one of the other downtown Nha Trang establishments.

The Streamer Bar, while it catered to any GI, airman, or Vietnamese soldier who could afford its prices, was primarily a Special Forces watering and ash-hauling hole, and we would often end up there when we went to town. Visitors to Group Headquarters from the outlying camps often went there as well, and it was not uncommon to see one saunter in, throw a couple of hundred dollars' worth of Vietnamese piastres or military payment certificates on the bar, and say, "Let me know when it's gone, Mamasan!"

The girls were particularly attuned to the ways of the Special Forces soldier—when he went to a bar, it was usually for a session of hard drinking, country music singing, ribald joke telling, no-holds-barred fun—enlivened now and then with a hearty fistfight, an occasional shooting

spree, and an uninhibited tumble with one or more of the
girls. It was in the Streamer that I was taught the words to
what emerged as the unofficial Mike Force team song,
"Mary Ann Barnes":

Mary Ann Barnes was the queen of all the acrobats,
She could do the tricks that would give a guy the
    shits.
She could shoot green peas from her fundamental
    orifice,
Do a triple somersault and catch 'em on her tits.
She's a great big son of a bitch, twice as big as me,
Got hair on her ass like the branches on a tree.
She can shoot, jump, fight, fuck,
Fly a plane or drive a truck;
She's the kinda girl that's gonna marry me—
She's Special Forces, Ranger, Airborne Infantry—
And Mike Force toooooo!

One evening about then, when many of the team members
were celebrating rather hard, Staff Sergeant Ron Franklin
and I were on duty in the TOC when we received a call to
conduct a mission in the local area. It seemed that two
field-grade officers from Group Headquarters had been
down to the little stretch of beach about three kilometers
south of the Nha Trang military complex known as the
Coconut Grove. It was a beautiful spot just inshore from a
reef, where a little creek passed through an old coconut
plantation and emptied into the sea. They had been down
there earlier in the day to do some scuba diving, when a
sniper had taken a potshot at them, causing them to jump
into the assault boat they had taken there and flee—leaving
two sets of scuba gear and their only weapon, a .45 caliber
pistol, behind. Could we send a few troops down there to
recover the stuff?

"No sweat," I said. "We'll get a squad from the alert
company, and have the Navy guys down at the harbor-patrol
unit run them down there in one of their boats to recover the
gear."

"No way," came the reply. "This is to be strictly an American-manned operation."

When I pressed for an answer why the 'Yards couldn't be used, I was told in strictest confidence that, in addition to the two Special Forces officers, there had been two American nurses there as well. Along with the other items left behind in their hasty departure, the little group had left the nurses' purses. Ron and I went straight to the team bar and spread the word on "Operation Purse Snatch."

After the laughter died down, A.P. volunteered to lead the mission, and most of the other guys—well-oiled with holiday spirits—agreed to go along. We soon had them and their combat gear loaded onto a deuce-and-a-half and on the way to the harbor-patrol base.

We arrived there to discover that the sailors, too, were well into the holiday spirit, but would be happy to run our guys down to the Coconut Grove. As they headed down the dock to load the little assault boats, Operation Purse Snatch suffered its first casualty: one of the sailors stepped through a hole in the dock, tearing a gash in his leg. Another one—this one decked out in a karate kimono—said, "I'll take this boat," and promptly jumped for it. He missed, and ended up in the South China Sea.

They finally managed to get under way, two assault-boat-loads of America's finest, and Franklin and I returned to the TOC to monitor their progress on the radio.

When the boozy force arrived offshore of the Coconut Grove, Retzlaff decided to prep the beach with artillery fire, and called the 105mm artillery section just down the road from us. He gave a pretty good call for fire, including his direction to the target at the time, and the gun section began to shoot the mission. A.P. called in a correction from his position, but forgot to give them a new direction from which he was adjusting, as the boats steamed back and forth outside the reef. As a result, each time he called a correction from a different position offshore, the fire-direction center made their adjustments based on A.P.'s originally stated direction to the target. The rounds exploded all over the place—some in the ocean, some up on the surrounding hills—until one finally chanced to land on the beach. The little task force's commander called, "Fire for effect!" and after the rounds landed, headed his assault force in toward the beach.

As the lead craft approached the shore inside the reef, the first wave jumped over the side—most into water over their heads. A couple of them had to jettison their web gear to get back to the surface, but all managed to make it ashore. The second wave, learning from their predecessors' mistake, drove the boat in closer to shore, whereupon it foundered in the surf, swamping them. But they were all ashore. Phase I of Operation Purse Snatch was successfully completed—sort of.

Franklin and I, roaring with laughter at A.P.'s reports, could hardly wait for Phase II to commence. They soon reported that the equipment had been recovered, but since both boats were now out of commission, they would have to spend the night on the beach. Soaked to the bone and under attack from countless squadrons of mosquitoes, the men's holiday spirits began to wear off, and A.P. then reported that he had spotted sampans offshore and was about to be attacked from the sea. We had the artillery battery fire an illumination mission offshore, and Retzlaff sheepishly reported that the "sampans" he had seen were only the surf breaking on the reef.

At one point during the night, according to Staff Sergeant Ben Davan, who was one of the task-force members, someone on watch with him thought he saw something moving in the shadows beyond their little beach position. The man pulled the pin from a hand grenade and tossed it—so close that its detonation kicked sand back on them. "Damn, man! Is that all the further you can throw a grenade? Here, hand me one." Davan took it, hurled it deep into the night, and they hit the deck. It failed to explode, and his comrade asked Ben, "Did you pull the pin?"

"No," replied Davan, "I thought *you* did."

The night passed without further incident, and in the morning we sent more boats out to recover them. They arrived back at the landing site cold, wet, and miserably mosquito-bitten. The main complaint of the smokers among them was that their cigarettes had all gotten wet. As they unloaded the recovered items which had been the object of their trying task, I took the nurses' purses and examined them. In each was a dry pack of cigarettes.

Some other enterprising soul had already removed the real object of my examination—the nurses' identification cards. Operation Purse Snatch was over.

On Christmas Eve, 7th Company—the Chams—moved out to the Dong Bo, the valley through the mountains southwest of Nha Trang, to establish defensive positions at points from which we could observe the valley trails to determine if the enemy was abiding by the Christmas truce. Both sides were to conduct only local security patrols to ensure the safety of their defensive positions.

One half of the company moved to the western end of the valley, across Highway 1 from the Soui Da rubber plantation, to establish a position there. With the other half of the company, I accompanied Specialist 5 Sammy Coutts, a burly blond young ex-surfer from California, to establish a position on a hilltop where the valley split into a Y near its eastern end.

On Christmas morning, Sammy—not yet with a firefight under his belt, and antsy at having to sit for several days atop the little hill—asked if he could take a patrol around the base of the hill and over to the valley stream to get water. He did so, and soon made contact with a communist squad. At about the time I heard the rattle of small-arms fire from Sammy's location, Larry O'Neil called on the radio to ensure that all was quiet and to wish us a Merry Christmas. I wished him a Merry Christmas in return, and responded to his matter-of-fact question of, "Anything going on out there?" with a very bored-sounding reply: "Well, we're in the middle of a little firefight right now, but other than that, everything's quiet."

"What? A firefight! Do you need any help?"

We didn't need any help. I had learned from Coutts via the little HT-1 radio we used for intraplatoon communications that the enemy had quickly fled and that Coutts could find no sign of them except a trail of blood leading up the jungled slopes of the Grand Summit. But nobody likes to spend Christmas alone, so I said, "Well, yes, I suppose you *could* bring some people across the river and in toward our position."

So Larry assembled the alert Company, and I took a small patrol down the valley to meet him. We linked up, and as I wanted to show off for my boss a bit, I took the point and moved out to the area where Coutts had made contact. We saw no more of the VC that day, but we did come across a trail leading up the rocky slopes toward the summit of the big mountain—a trail we would guide on at times in the future.

The Christmas truce passed without further incident, and we returned to base. But on the night of 30 December—the night before the New Year's truce was to begin—we saw firing out across the flats near the foot of the mountains, at a small hilltop outpost manned by a CIDG squad from A-502 and three American straphangers from Group Headquarters.

We learned from the Installation Defense Coordinator radio net that the Americans felt they were in a desperate situation—and then radio contact with them was lost. We alerted 7th Company to move out and relieve the little outpost. Two UH-1 Huey helicopters were immediately available, so we loaded a couple of squads on them. The rest of the company would go up the river to the outpost in sixteen-foot assault boats.

A two-ship, night airmobile assault on an outpost from which we had last heard that it was being overrun by the enemy was not something I was looking forward to, but there were Americans out there, so I hopped onto the lead chopper and we took off. We flew over the outpost without drawing fire, so in we went. As we approached the hill, we got a call informing us that the Vietnamese Special Forces commander, General Quang, said it was too risky—that we were to wait until daylight to go in. To hell with him. There were Americans down there, perhaps wounded, so for the first of a number of times, I pulled the old "broken-radio" trick—feigning radio problems, saying that the last transmission was unreadable, and declaring that we were going in. We hovered just above the little OP and exited the chopper. There was a trench around the outpost, and I jumped into it—and right on top of a man. A dead American. There were a couple of dead Viet Cong inside the wire, and most unusually, their weapons were still beside them.

We searched the hilltop but could find no one else except a couple of dead CIDG soldiers. Then the other two Americans made radio contact with us. They were outside the wire with the remaining CIDG, unhurt. The OP was so poorly built that when the VC had attacked and penetrated the defenses, most of the CIDG and two of the Americans had simply run out through the poorly laid wire.

It was the first time the little post had ever been hit. It was very near the compounds around Nha Trang. As a result, the men manning it had fallen to one of the most deadly enemies of the war—complacency.

The VC had apparently had one mission in hitting the camp—get in, get the 60mm mortar which had been there, and get out with it. They did it well, but it cost them the lives of two men for the weapon, and they could have reaped so much more. We found, among other things, several U.S. weapons, some ammunition for the mortar, a PRC-25 radio, and what would have been the biggest prize of all—a new Starlight Scope, a night-vision device which could well have been, in late '67, the most valuable piece of equipment the VC could have captured.

They sometimes made foolish mistakes too.

The following night, we brought in the New Year by drinking a rice-wine jug filled with booze, cigarette butts, and God knows what else. We were headed for the officers' club on the headquarters compound when—thank heavens —A.P. dropped and shattered the damned thing, sparing us the need to further imbibe the vile stuff. Instead, we stumbled back to the compound, called the troops who were in the field monitoring the New Year's truce, and wished each of them a Happy New Year several times.

I had become good friends with one of them, Staff Sergeant Ron Franklin. Ron had better rapport with the Rhade troops he led than anyone I had met. He ate what they ate, drank what they drank, slept where they slept. He did his best to learn their language, visited their villages whenever he was able, and won their total confidence. Ron was a redhead, and a weight lifter who spent much of his spare time pumping his barbells, and had the arms and chest to prove it. Many of his Rhade—a tribal group of the central highlands—troops had bleached their hair so that it was red like Ron's, and they fashioned barbells out of lead pipes and big #10 cans filled with concrete, which they spent their spare time lifting in order to be like their American role model.

On the morning of 10 January 1968—my twenty-sixth birthday—I went into the dayroom for a soft drink. The dayroom, which also served as the team bar, was in the detachment headquarters building between the orderly room and the mess hall we shared with the remaining Americans from B-50. It was a single large room, about thirty feet by forty feet. The walls were decorated with captured weapons, a few photographs and plaques, and an occasional editorial cartoon. In one corner was a curved stone bar, manned usually by an old Chinese known affectionately as "Pop," or sometimes by his teenage son, Cau. All around the rest of the room were chairs and vinyl-cushioned sofas. One door led to the outside, one to a latrine, and the other to the orderly room. The room was well air-conditioned, and although I've heard people since then express surprise at the fact that the famous, tough Green Berets had air conditioners in Vietnam, it was just one example of initiative, continued improvement of their living environment, con-man abilities—and the fact that so many SF troops considered Vietnam not just a place to be suffered through for a year, then escaped from, but a second home. They made "home" as enjoyable as possible.

A couple of NCOs who had just come out of the field were there. Staff Sergeant Ben Davan was one of them, and he offered me a beer. "No, thanks, Ben," I said at first; then, "What the hell. It's my birthday."

Ben bought me a large shot of Crown Royal and insisted I accept it as a birthday offering. I did.

Other members of the team drifted in, and each, at Ben's suggestion, added another shot to the "birthday present." I decided that I needed a birthday cake, so I sought out our cook, George, and browbeat him into making a cake for me. By the time he finished baking it, I was totally plastered. George had no frosting, but he had covered the big square of cake with a thick layer of grape jelly. I dug into it with both hands, offering some to my teammates. When they refused to accept any, I made them another offer: "Eat it or wear it!" With that, I began to chase them around the building with the sticky mess. During one such circuit around the headquarters in search of my elusive prey, I spotted an irresistible target—a U.S. Navy lieutenant j.g. in an immaculate white uniform, who had arrived to coordinate some activity between the Mike Force and the Navy harbor-defense element of which he was a member. I ducked behind a jeep and laid a hasty ambush, and as the sailor passed, I let him have it squarely between the shoulder blades with a large handful of the gooey mess. I thought it was hilarious, but quickly ascertaining that the Navy officer did not, I immediately broke contact and withdrew, leaving the results of the Great Cake Ambush at Army 1, Navy 0. Some birthday.

While Joe Zamaira spent most of January in III Corps with the troops who were operating around Thien Ngon, I was out on local operations in Khanh Hoa Province, the province of which Nha Trang was the capital. We made occasional light contacts, with no more than a few casualties on either side. The Viet Cong and North Vietnamese Army elements we searched for were avoiding contact when they could.

The contacts we were making, however, were sufficient that we seemed always to have some wounded 'Yards in 8th

Field Hospital, and I visited them often. Those visits had the additional benefit of allowing us to see and chat with the American nurses there, and I became friends with a couple of them. I needed some diversion during my time off other than boozing it up in the team bar and the Streamer, and the nurses' companionship filled that void and drove away some of the loneliness I felt for my wife, Karen.

Diane, a first lieutenant who seemed always to be there attending our wounded, seemed very much interested in the Montagnard and Cham cultures, and I spent some enjoyable time with her, explaining what I knew about their customs and way of life. I invited her to the compound for one of the Rhade celebrations, at which they ceremonially slaughtered a water buffalo, consumed copious amounts of rice wine, which was sucked through reeds from big earthen jars, and honored their guests with the presentation of brass brace-lets. Diane got along very well with them—helped in part by the fact that Montagnard soldiers, like all others, tend to fall in love with the nurses who attend them. I began to see Diane at every available opportunity, sometimes sharing drinks with her in the hospital officers' club, sometimes taking her to one of the two French restaurants which still thrived in Nha Trang, and once convincing her to visit the Streamer Bar. The bar girls loved it. I bought them all a Saigon Tea—Diane included—and they sat talking enthu-siastically to her about girlish things, asking innumerable questions of the first young American woman they had ever met.

I began to have feelings for her that went beyond friend-ship, and I made a few romantic passes at her, but never got past a good-night kiss. Not wanting to risk losing the companionship which was so welcome after beating around the boonies with the 'Yards, I let it go at that.

January also saw the arrival to the team of an officer with whom I soon became best friends, Lieutenant Bud McBroom. I had met Bud at Fort Bragg, not long after he had been commissioned. Bud was an experienced Special Forces soldier who had spent years as an SF medical NCO, scuba instructor, and military free-fall parachutist, and had the distinction of being one of a handful of men who had been "skyhooked"—snatched off the ground by an aircraft which snagged a long lift line held aloft by a big balloon, then reeled it in as it soared along five hundred feet above the ground.

We had been alerted to prepare for an operation to reestablish a Special Forces camp in the dreaded A Shau Valley up in I Corps, which the North Vietnamese Army had ruled unchallenged since they had overrun the old camp there nearly two years earlier. The last time the Mike Force had gone into the A Shau, they had been overwhelmed and decimated, in spite of the courageous efforts of our predecessors, who had fought heroically against terrible odds. Larry O'Neil was anxious to go back in to avenge that defeat and reopen a camp there from which patrols could interdict the vast numbers of enemy troops and supplies which flowed down the nearby Ho Chi Minh Trail. Bud would be a welcome addition to the team for that operation.

McBroom's first operation with the Mike Force was a "routine" airmobile assault into the big hill mass southwest of Nha Trang.

There were a number of well-used trails on the back side of the Grand Summit, and the Mike Force company patrolled the area during the day without contacting the enemy. But that night, they ambushed the trail network, in one case using what is called a "mechanical ambush." A mechanical ambush is actually a series of booby traps set up temporarily along a route the enemy might be expected to use. It is particularly useful in situations where the trails are too numerous for the ambush parties to cover all avenues. Bud and Sergeant Todd Seaver had their 'Yards emplace one such mechanical ambush on a trail near their night defensive position. A hand grenade was placed in an empty C-ration can, which was anchored alongside the trail. (The pin was pulled from the grenade, but the safety lever would remain in place until the grenade was pulled from the can, at which time the fuse would be activated and—after a 4 1/2-second delay—the grenade would explode.) A small vine was then attached to the grenade, stretched across the

70

trail at shin level, and tied to a tree on the other side. Thus, if someone came along the trail and hit the vine, the grenade would be pulled from the can and explode among the members of the patrol behind the point man.

Shortly before daylight the next morning, an enemy patrol hit the mechanical ambush. When McBroom and Seaver heard the explosion—and the ensuing firing from the enemy, who apparently thought they had hit a manned ambush—they took a patrol to the site, arriving about twenty minutes later, just at daybreak. They found small pools of blood and bits of enemy uniform, and followed a trail of blood spots to some freshly dug earth a short distance away. There they were amazed to find that the communist patrol, ambushed only about twenty minutes earlier, had already—in the darkness—buried two of their comrades in shallow graves and fled.

McBroom and Seaver followed their trail down into the valley, where they encountered an old man piling up some brush. As they were questioning the old Vietnamese to find out if he had seen the enemy patrol, AK-47's opened up on them from a knoll they had passed shortly before. As the old man continued to work calmly at the pile of brush and Seaver and several 'Yards returned fire, Bud called to several more of the strikers to follow him, and ran around to the side of the knoll, then uphill through the jungle toward the sound of the enemy weapons, to hit them from the flank. As he approached the enemy position, he turned to the 'Yards to tell them to get on line for the assault—and discovered that he was alone. It was a valuable lesson to him about ensuring that the strikers understand what you mean for them to do.

Bud's second operation was a rather unusual one. For several days the Vietnamese Navy had been tracking three Chinese Communist trawlers down the coast of Vietnam. The boats, of about sixty-foot length, were suspected of being supply ships headed for some remote stretch of South Vietnamese coastline, but because they were in international waters, the Viets couldn't bother them unless they made a run for shore. Eventually, one of them made a dash for a rocky, mountainous peninsula not far north of Nha Trang, Hon Heo Peninsula. The boat was standing in a little bay about fifty feet offshore, unloading ammunition, when the Vietnamese Navy jumped it with gunboats, causing it to explode with such force that its cabin was blown off, and up onto the shore.

Bud went with a company of strikers, traveling aboard a South Vietnamese Navy ship to the peninsula, where they secured the shore for several days as the sailors recovered what was left of the cargo. It was the first time any noncommunist forces had operated on the Hon Heo Peninsula since the French had been there in the 1950's.

They made several light contacts, but the real value of the operation was the recovery of enough weapons and ammunition to supply a Viet Cong battalion for a year, according to the Navy's estimates. The ironic thing, though, was that some of the weapons recovered by the South Vietnamese Navy were again retaken from the communists after a patrol was ambushed by an element from A-502, sometime—and some distance—later. More Vietnamese corruption, no doubt.

As January drew to a close, we were looking forward to the return of our troops from their operations in III Corps to celebrate the lunar new year with us, for there was to be another truce during that Tet holiday period. They got back on the twenty-eighth, and on the evening of January 29 we celebrated with a dinner at La Frégate, the best French seafood restaurant in all of II Corps. After a feast of lobster and wine, Joe Zamiara and Larry O'Neil decided to stay in town and celebrate the midnight arrival of Tet with the locals, while the others of us returned to the Mike Force compound. We were going to sit out on the sandbag walls and watch the Vietnamese bring the New Year in by lighting the sky with tracers and parachute flares—the wartime version of a fireworks display.

—— 6 ——

We sat there as midnight approached, listening to the stories our comrades had to tell about the fights around the trail junction which they had helped build into another of the little border fortresses which dotted the maps of Vietnam.

Their favorite tale was about Al Efird, the NCO who commanded one of the companies of strikers. They were under heavy mortar attack from across the nearby border with Cambodia one night, hunkered down in the bunkers they had built to protect them from such fire, when Efird suddenly exclaimed, "Oh, shit!" and dashed out into the rain of iron fragments. While his bunker mates were still wondering at the cause of his sudden decision to abandon the safety of the bunker, Efird dived back in with them, his little transistor radio in his hand. It was eight o'clock on a Saturday night, and Al Efird was not about to miss the Armed Forces Vietnam Network broadcast of *The Grand Ol' Opry!*

Another story they had to tell was about a Cavalry major who arrived from the east with a tank and several armored personnel carriers one day, and asked if anyone had been down the trail to the border of Cambodia recently. The Mike Force troops explained that they had not—they were having a tough enough time keeping the enemy out of the 1,500-meter radius around the trail junction they were trying to keep secure while the camp was being built. "You people are chickenshit," the major declared. "We're going to the border!" And with that bold pronouncement he mounted up and struck out west down the little trail toward Cambodia. He got about 1,500 meters before the communists hit him, destroying most of his vehicles and engaging him in a sharp battle for most of the day before he could break contact and limp sheepishly back to the trail junction and the "I-told-you-so!" smirks of the Mike Force troops.

Midnight arrived, and we turned our attention toward the city, where the air was suddenly filled with long bursts of orange tracers, parachute flares, and red, green, and white star clusters, as well as conventional fireworks. It was quite a spectacle, and continued for some time, then slowly died down to a trickle. Then, gradually, it seemed to increase again. There were fewer tracers and a greater number of dull explosions. The tracer rounds were no longer directed high into the sky, but were ricocheting wildly around the horizon, and many of them were green. The explosions were more deep-throated, larger than the firecracker sounds of before. Something was wrong, we knew, as the alert siren at Group Headquarters began to wail in confirmation of our suspicions. The communists' massive Tet offensive of 1968 was under way.

We were to learn only later of the extent and magnitude of the enemy's desperate offensive, and that it had begun there in our "hometown." For the moment, we figured it was only a limited local attack. Our standing operating procedures directed the alert company to move to the perimeter wall with their combat equipment when the siren sounded, and SFC Musgrove had his company there and ready almost immediately. We were informed that the attack was apparently directed against the MACV Sector Headquarters compound, right across the street from La Frégate restaurant, where we had enjoyed our lobster feast just a short time before. There were some Americans trapped by the enemy in the command bunker at the sector headquarters compound, and our initial mission was to effect their rescue.

We loaded the alert company onto the two-and-a-half-ton trucks, and Bud McBroom and I jumped into a three-quarter-ton truck with a sergeant from the Installation Defense Coordination element to lead the convoy downtown. We moved through the Special Forces compound to the air base and across it to the gate which opened onto Beach Road, the broad palm-lined avenue which ran along the crescent beach the two miles from the air base to the northern edge of the city. About a half-mile up the road toward town, we were halted by some American Military Police who said we couldn't pass.

"There's fighting going on down there!" one of them nervously explained.

"No shit!" McBroom answered, gesturing to the several truckloads of armed strikers behind us. "Why do you think we're going down there?"

We continued up the avenue until we reached a point a block east of our objective, where we dismounted, then moved west along both sides of the street until we were across from the sector headquarters compound, at the main gate on the corner of the block. Musgrove deployed his troops behind the wall of a villa on the southeast corner of the block, directly across from the gate. On the southwest corner of the intersection, within a meter-high brick wall, stood La Frégate, and on the northeast corner was the Nha Trang post office.

I had been calling the Installation Defense Coordination Center—IDC—in an attempt to ascertain the locations of other friendly units in the city, but, caught off guard by the appearance of enemy soldiers in the middle of town during the biggest holiday of the year, in the midst of a supposed period of truce, they had no idea. We would have to sort it out on our own. I managed to get hold of the Americans who were trapped in the bunker of the compound across the street from us. They felt that they were the only ones left alive, with the possible exception of a Lieutenant Ross, another of the sector advisers, who was still out on the compound somewhere. In spite of their panicked efforts to explain their location to me, I couldn't tell exactly where the bunker was in which they were trapped.

Behind us, in one of the outbuildings of the villa which Musgrove had cleared, he had found a large number of woven-bamboo-covered satchel charges, which the enemy had either brought along for their attack or which their communist comrades had cached there for them. The ground floor of the villa was on fire, and across the street in the Sector Headquarters compound, one of the buildings was burning furiously. Hand grenades and small-arms ammunition were exploding in the fire, and it was difficult to determine if we were being fired on or if there was a firefight taking place inside the compound, or just what was going on.

It soon became evident that we were taking fire, though, as the distinctive snap and ricochet of Soviet 7.62mm rounds began crackling around us. It appeared to be coming from two sources: a rifle from the vicinity of the restaurant, and an RPD machine gun from up the block at the northern corner of the compound. The most immediate threat was the RPD. Bud McBroom and one of Musgrove's platoon leaders, young Specialist 4 Gary Swanson, were trying to find cover behind one of the eighteen-inch-wide concrete columns at the entrance to the post office. Somehow, they both managed to squeeze behind it, as a steady stream of bullets chipped away at it. We poured fire back at the enemy machine gun, and it became silent for a while after that.

While SFC Musgrove and I stood there behind the villa wall, still trying to ascertain where the trapped Americans were, there was a sudden explosion at the top of the concrete electrical pole above us. Musgrove began to scold the 'Yard grenadier who was firing his M-79 grenade launcher from a position beside us, when I suddenly realized that it couldn't have been a round from his weapon—he was too close to the explosion for the round to have armed, so it must have been either an enemy B-40 rocket or a round from a captured M-79.

At about that time a couple more truckloads of Mike Force troops showed up, driving north right up the road between our position and the restaurant! As they approached, I hurled a grenade into the restaurant complex to try to keep the sniper who had been firing at us from there from taking the newly arrived reinforcements under fire as they quickly unloaded. As they joined us behind the villa wall, I threw another grenade in the direction of the hidden sniper, but it bounced off a tree and landed beside the lead truck. Fortunately, the troops made it to cover before the grenade exploded—but it blasted the front tire of the lead truck, flattening the tires on the left side. Specialist 5 Menard, the Group Commander's driver, who had been pressed into service to drive one of the truckloads of troops to the battle area, suddenly found himself immobile, and began joking about the ass-chewing he was bound to get from the crusty old Group Maintenance Officer, Chief Warrant Officer Hardy Batchelor.

There wasn't much firing in the compound now, so Musgrove sent Swanson and a few of his troops over to secure the gate of the compound, while the remainder laid down covering fire or secured the area behind us.

The machine gun a block north of us opened up again, and Swanson was hit in the hand, nearly taking off two of his fingers. McBroom and I dashed across the intersection to his assistance—Bud to engage the enemy machine gun with an M-60 machine gun he took from one of the Montagnards, and I to attend to Swanson's wound. As I dressed the young soldier's wound, I could hear Bud dueling with the North Vietnamese gunner. He would unleash a rattling burst of fire at McBroom, who would return a six-round burst back at the enemy position. Back and forth, they traded deadly streams of lead, until finally I noticed that the enemy gun had fallen silent, as Bud's continued to bark its angry message. McBroom had won the duel—we heard no more from that enemy weapon that night.

As I finished tying the dressing on Swanson's hand, I rolled over to look at Bud, five meters away on the other side of the gate. Lying right between us was a satchel charge, which hadn't been there before. It had been placed there while our attention was drawn to other tasks—placed there to blow us apart. I yelled, "Satchel charge!" and helped Swanson scurry behind a nearby three-quarter-ton truck, where McBroom and several 'Yards quickly joined us. As we huddled there waiting for the deadly charge to explode— fortunately for us, crouching behind the vehicle's gas tank, it never did—I suddenly realized that whoever had placed it there had to be right on the other side of the compound wall, a few feet away! Quickly I tossed several hand grenades over the wall, and as soon as they exploded, we scurried back across the street with Swanson. As the smoke cleared, we could see someone in the concertina wire atop the wall behind which I had just thrown the grenades. The 'Yards unloaded several magazines of rifle ammunition into him. The man who had nearly killed a bunch of us, including three Americans, ceased to exist.

We still hadn't been able to get to the three trapped Americans, but I decided that since *they* knew where they were, maybe we could get them out without stumbling into another bad situation. I got them on the radio. Was their bunker near the main gate? Yes. If we threw a bunch of grenades into the compound, and covered them from the gate, would they be able to make a dash for it? Yes, they thought they could make it. We secured the gate again, threw several hand grenades into the compound, and as soon as they had detonated, gave the command to "Go!" The three men scurried to safety immediately—from a bunker just inside the gate.

It was about that time that a little girl on a bicycle came riding up the street toward us. Several of the 'Yards leveled their weapons at her, and we frantically yelled, "No shoot! Baby-san! No shoot!" When she was about ten meters from our position, she hurled a grenade at us. It rolled up against the wall we were behind and exploded harmlessly. The Montagnards immediately cut her to shreds with rifle fire. I can second-guess allowing that to happen, and probably will for the rest of my life. Could I have jumped the wall, run her down, and captured her? I don't know. That kind of question can drive you mad. Probably not, though, because she lived only a couple of seconds after she threw the grenade.

I found the Vietnamese interpreter, asked him how those communist bastards could motivate a child to do something like the little girl had just done. He thought it was a very simple thing—you had merely to hold pistols to the parents' heads, tell the child that if she didn't pedal up and throw a grenade at the enemy, you'd kill the parents. And, of course, off she would go.

I had heard of such brutality, of the communists sending children out to pick up unexploded cluster-bomb projectiles to use for booby traps, knowing that many would explode when the children picked them up, maiming or killing them. I had seen them trying to keep the inhabitants from escaping the embattled village of Dien Khanh a couple of months earlier, as the Koreans pressed their attack. I was to learn of their deliberate attack on Montagnard dependents at Song Be, when they burned two hundred women and children to death with flamethrowers. But I still didn't want to believe it was true. From then on, I hated them. They had, as far as I was concerned, forfeited their membership in the human race, and I wanted them all to die.

Sometime later, another bicyclist, a grown man, pedaled madly toward our position. We saw him coming, and opened up on him with eight or ten weapons. On he came, untouched, until he was about twenty meters away, when he slung a satchel charge in our direction, then whirled and pedaled back down the street. As far as I know, the son of a bitch is *still* pedaling.

Later, when a three-wheeled Lambretta scooter-bus came puttering up the street from the same locale, the 'Yard grenadier at the wall didn't bother to ask what to do, nor did he hesitate. He fired a 40mm high-explosive round into the windshield, killing the driver immediately.

Meanwhile, as the villa to our rear burned, someone came running out of the restaurant gate toward our position, carrying a long object. One of the Montagnards put a round between the man's eyes, and it was not until after daylight that we discovered he was the maître d' of La Frégate. The long object he was carrying was a ladder. All I can figure is that he was going to rescue someone from the burning villa, although we never saw anyone there.

It was a mad, surrealistic night.

Daylight approached, and we still had not secured the Sector Headquarters compound. We didn't know how many friendly or enemy soldiers were still in there, nor where they were.

There were a few dead NVA inside the gate, casualties of my earlier hand-grenade barrage. The one in the wire above the wall was only half a body; there was nothing left of him below his rib cage. He must have been carrying satchel charges on his belt, which one of the hand grenades had caused to detonate, blowing his body apart. Perhaps he had even jumped on one of the grenades in an attempt to shield his comrades, though I didn't want to believe that at the time.

We were taking no more fire from within the compound now, and the burning building had burned itself out, so we began to clear the rest of the buildings. We did it John Wayne–style—kicking doors open and hoping to blow away any remaining enemy before they blew *us* away. I started on the long building on the left, just inside the gate, a series of single rooms with doors to the outside. In the third room, I found an ARVN soldier hiding under a low bunk. I just looked at him in disgust and moved on. From then on I began yelling for anyone inside to come out, before kicking the doors open. I found no one else in that building, but at the end of it there were about twenty 55-gallon drums. I looked in among them and found a couple of ARVN uniforms. As I searched farther in among the drums, I discovered two soldiers who had crawled back in among them and removed their uniforms, cowering there. They pointed to their uniforms, and to themselves, indicating that they were ARVN soldiers and that I shouldn't harm them. I have never seen such cowardice before or since, and I guess I should have done something with them. But there was no one to turn them over to, so I just threw their uniforms at them and left them crouching among the barrels.

Bursting into the door of the next building, I was startled to find a man in black pajamas, standing at a radio. He had on a "Hoi Chanh" patch, indicating that he was a former communist who had changed sides under the South Vietnamese government's "Open Arms" policy, whereby defectors were taken into the South Vietnamese Army and employed against their former comrades. He calmly explained, in English, that he was a radio operator, so I moved on.

It wasn't until days later, when I was reflecting on the battle for Nha Trang, that I realized the man *must* have been VC. The NVA had been all over that compound, but they hadn't bothered the man at the radios. Surely that would have been one of the first places they would hit, in order to sever the Sector Headquarters' link with the outside. I don't know how I could have missed that point at the time.

We found several more NVA bodies in the compound, some with large numbers of weapons on them. There were M-1 rifles, Browning automatic rifles, and M-2 carbines, as well as their own AK-47's. They had obviously taken them from the armory and were trying to escape with them.

On one of the enemy soldiers we found a cigarette lighter inscribed with Lieutenant Ross's name. We never did find the lieutenant or his body during our stay on the compound.

The fighting had moved a couple of blocks north, to the Khanh Hoa Province headquarters building, so I sat down and leaned against the wall of a building near the gate to encode a situation report to send to IDC, not noticing that one severed leg of the NVA soldier who had been blown into the wire atop the wall was lying nearby. The mutilated corpse was still hanging there, and several dead NVA lay around the area. I was talking on the radio when O'Neil and Zamiara showed up. They had been trapped downtown when the attack began, and had been able to make their way back to the Mike Force compound only a short time before.

It was a gory sight which greeted them, with bodies lying all around, one building burned to the ground, and the others shot to hell. Larry O'Neil listened to my situation report, then said, "Bucky, we've got to take Province Headquarters now." He made it sound like such a simple thing to do—like, "Bucky, we've got to go to lunch now."

We stacked the NVA weapons and the ones from the Sector HQ armory into the jeep that O'Neil and Zamiara had brought, and fell in behind them and the troops with whom they had already moved out toward the Province Headquarters building, which lay north a block, and east toward Beach Road. There was a large shrine in the open area between the buildings at the north end of the Sector compound and Province Headquarters, and we kept ourselves masked as we moved in behind it. From there we dashed the thirty meters to the south wall of the Province Headquarters compound, drawing fire from a couple of enemy weapons as we crossed the open area. The wall was about five feet tall, the bottom half solid concrete, the upper half slotted—four-inch concrete pickets, then four-inch vertical slots—along its entire length. From the entry gate directly in front of the main entrance of the headquarters building, the wall angled away toward the shrine we had passed. O'Neil, Staff Sergeant Norman, Zamiara, and a couple of strikers led the way along the wall from the corner nearest the shrine toward the gate, and drew fire from the headquarters building. We got low along the wall, thinking we'd be masked from the enemy fire, but a portion of the wall was visible from the second-floor windows. The 'Yard immediately in front of me took a round in the chest. I crawled forward to help him, heard the unmistakable crack of a round passing very close by, and felt something sharp strike my back. At first I thought I'd been hit, then realized it was just concrete from the wall being splattered against me. I got the hell out of the way just before the next round cracked nearby. Spec 5 Menard, the driver whose truck I had accidentally immobilized with a hand grenade earlier, was directly behind me along the wall, and I heard the sickening "thunk" as a bullet struck him. He was motionless, lying on his back, when I turned back to him. Taking hold of his web gear to pull him to me, I heard—and felt—another round hit him, this one in the chest. But he was already dead. The first bullet had hit him in the brain.

Dai Uy Hung, the captain in charge of the Vietnamese Special Forces team assigned to the Mike Force, was moving toward the same spot along the wall. I yelled for him not to come, but he kept coming anyway, and took a bullet in the arm. It was only along that short stretch of the wall that the sniper could hit, but it was a deadly spot.

We started trying to blast the communists out of the building with rifle, machine-gun, and grenade-launcher fire. Sergeant Norman stuck his head and shoulder around the gate of the compound in an attempt to locate the source of fire—and took a bullet in the shoulder. The wounding of Norman angered Joe Zamiara, and he jumped into the middle of the gateway to loose a burst of fire at the enemy, but crumpled to the ground almost immediately. We really poured it on then, McBroom blasting away through one of the slots in the wall with his M-60 machine gun, and others of us emptying magazine after magazine into the house. We managed to get a few people through the gate and up against the west wall of the building. That wall was louvered for about a foot of its width, where a stairwell climbed along the inside wall of the building. One of the strikers was standing in front of the louvers, and one of the enemy stuck the muzzle of his weapon through the narrow slot and blew the 'Yard's head apart. We still couldn't get into the building.

Norman, hit in the shoulder, was still up and moving, and *Dai Uy* Hung had only a flesh wound. But Joe was still down, in bad shape. The round had entered near his solar plexus and exited from the middle of his back. We had to get him out of there, and the jeep back at Sector Headquarters seemed the best way. As the others continued the assault on the building, I ran back to get it. Some of the Vietnamese Rangers from Project Delta's 81st Ranger Battalion were moving through the area. I noticed one with a carbine and one spare magazine of ammunition in his hand. He had no web gear, but under his arm he had a chicken he had "liberated" from somewhere. When I got to the jeep, the weapons and the radio we had put in it were gone—also "liberated" by the Rangers, I supposed. But no matter; I would need the room for Joe anyway.

I hopped in the jeep and started up the street toward Province Headquarters, sliding low in the seat as I passed the shrine—so low, in fact, that instead of looking through the windshield, I was peeking around the outside of the jeep in order to see where I was going. I sped up beside the wall near Joe. The medic and I crawled with him toward the jeep, and he seemed to be trying to help by crawling himself. When I put my hand to his back to help him into the jeep, my fingers sank into the gaping exit wound in the middle of his spine. I hadn't realized until then how badly he was wounded. The lower half of the jeep was masked from enemy fire from the building, so with Joe and the medic on the floor in back, I jumped in and made a dash across the open area. We took some fire, but all they managed to do was flatten one front tire and put a couple of rounds in the frame of the jeep. It was hard to steer with the flat tire, but I went as fast as I could on the rim down Beach Road to the air base and across to 8th Field Hospital. When I tried to turn in to the hospital gate, I hit the wall. There were several medical people standing by the emergency room who thought it was funny. I didn't, and pulled up to them cursing mad, telling them to get a goddamn stretcher, and get it now! They saw Joe then, and became strictly businesslike, handling him with practiced efficiency.

Joe didn't look at all good when they put him on the stretcher. He had turned ashen gray, and I suppose he was already dead by then. If not, he died shortly afterward.

The United States Army lost one of its finest when Joe Zamiara died. He had served well, fought hard for more than a year of his young life, turning down offers of safer jobs than leading Mike Force soldiers into combat. But while his civilian peers in the States were taking to the streets in protest of a war they understood far less than he did, Joe had extended his tour in Vietnam to carry on with what he saw as his duty as an American. The moment of his fatal wounding may not have been a glorious one, but his whole tour of combat in Vietnam had been marked by courage and dedication, as were the tours of so many young Americans of all ranks who died that fateful day.

Poor is the country that has no heroes, but beggared is that people who, having them, forgets.

—Unknown

7

Back at Province Headquarters, the attempt to dislodge the enemy was not going well. Larry O'Neil, fed up with the casualties his team was suffering from the communists inside the building, courageously assaulted it single-handedly. As he entered the big room at the front of the building, he saw movement on the stairwell to his left, turned, and fired a burst from his CAR-15 assault rifle at the enemy figure there. He killed the NVA soldier, but not before the man got a burst of fire off at him. A bullet smashed into the crusty Irishman's thigh, shattering his femur. Bud McBroom saw to his evacuation to the beach, having him carried there sitting in a chair, like the glorious old warlord he was.

As I left the hospital on the air base, I noticed one of the Air Force Forward Air Controllers' O-1 Birddogs taxiing out. Maybe the FAC could help us root the bastards out. I intercepted the little airplane in the crippled jeep, pleased to find Papa Baer in the pilot's seat. I climbed in with him, and he took off for the north end of town. I pointed out the contested building, and he circled it once as we called McBroom and ascertained that there were no friendlies inside. Then he swooped down toward it, bearing in until I was afraid we would crash into it. From just meters away, he launched a single white phosphorous marking rocket—straight through the window on the west side of the building. Good shooting, Papa. The building began to blaze almost immediately. That would get the bastards out.

Lieutenant Colonel Baer landed to get some rockets with high-explosive warheads from the Army aviation unit at the air base, as the Air Force FACs were supposed to arm their little observation airplanes with marking rockets only. Papa Baer was going hunting.

Since early morning, 7th Company had been deployed to the west side of Nha Trang to defend the ARVN signal-corps compound which was under attack there, so I wished Colonel Baer good hunting, stole an unsecured jeep, and headed there to see how Sergeant First Class Ken Roberts, Sammy Coutts, and their Chams were making out.

The signal compound was located on the dirt road at the western edge of town, just north of a jail which we had learned sometime earlier was to be a VC target at some point in the future.

Roberts and Coutts had been told that the signal compound had been probed, and the fat U.S. Army major who was the senior adviser there wanted reinforcements to help secure the place. When they arrived and unloaded the trucks, Coutts went in search of the major to get further instructions. He walked around the corner of a building, and there, sitting in a hole right in front of him, were five North Vietnamese soldiers. He ducked back behind the building and, before they had time to react, dumped two fragmentation grenades into the hole with them, killing all five.

They had then rooted a few more out of the compound, and began to clear the village of tin-roofed huts and small concrete dwellings which lay between the signal compound and the rice paddies to the west—paddies which stretched for about a half-mile to the foot of the mountains from which the enemy had come. In addition, they had been fighting all morning with some enemy in the houses to the north, up toward the big statue of Buddha beside Highway

1, where that highway entered the city from the west. One
ARVN soldier who had been holed up in that area saw an
opportunity to escape to safety in the early hours of
daylight. He jumped on a bicycle and pedaled furiously
toward the Mike Force troops at the north gate of the signal
compound. Just as it seemed he would make it to safety, one
of the Chams—whether it was because he felt the man was
NVA, or was abandoning a wife or girlfriend, or had been
hiding when he should have been fighting, or just because he
hated ethnic Vietnamese—for whatever reason, he leveled
his machine gun at the man and blasted him off the bicycle.
An ARVN officer who witnessed the incident immediately
began loudly protesting the Cham gunner's actions, until the
young striker placed the hot barrel of the weapon under the
officer's chin, ending the protest and causing the officer to
withdraw.

On the way up the dirt road from the air base to the signal
compound, I passed a large number of American soldiers
facing east and northeast along the road, toward a civilian
fuel-storage yard and the cluster of hootches adjacent to the
air base known as the Turkey Farm because of the gobbling
which occurred in the dirty little whorehouses there. The
soldiers were headquarters types from 5th Group Headquarters, and they were blasting away with rifles, M-79's,
and hand grenades. The fuel depot was burning with
great clouds of black smoke, and although there seemed
to be no incoming fire from that direction, the clerks
and jerks continued blasting away, suffering occasional
wounds from their own grenades, picking up those CIBs
and Purple Hearts, and generally having a good time
of it.

By the time I reached 7th Company's location, Ken and
Sammy and their troops, along with a couple of Americans
from A-502, had rooted the enemy out from around the
compound and had them backed up to the edge of the
village with their backs toward the open rice paddies—
where it would have been suicide for them to try to escape.
In fact, prior to daylight, an AC-47 "Spooky" gunship had
caught some of them under its flares while they were in the

open rice paddies trying either to escape the village or to reinforce it. The groaning old gunship had killed scores of them in the rice paddies with its crackling miniguns.

We learned from IDC that some of the enemy captured during the fighting were indicating they were from the 7th and 8th battalions of the 18B NVA Regiment. The ones we had been fighting in the northeast part of town were part of the 7th Battalion, as were the ones who had attacked the Korean and U.S. Military Police compounds in the center of town. The ones around the signal compound and their dead comrades in the rice paddies beyond were from the 8th Battalion. Their VC guides had apparently gotten them lost on the way in from their mountain staging area, or we might have had an even tougher battle in that part of town.

When I reached the signal compound in search of Coutts, Roberts, and their troops, I found the weird spectacle of the fat American Signal Corps major standing in front of a CBS television news crew, rattling on about what a fine job he was doing in defending his compound. He had a steel pot jammed down onto his head, beneath which only his nose and chin emerged, and he wore a flak jacket which came high up around his neck to the bottom of his helmet. He looked amazingly—and comically—like a turtle standing on its hind legs.

Waiting impatiently until he finished his war story for the benefit of the American public, and the news crew departed, I asked him where our people were. He wasn't really sure, but he gestured to the southwest and said he thought they were "over that way." I found Ken Roberts and some of his troops, and moved with them down among the tin shacks to the area where the communists were holed up. Two Americans from A-502 were carrying a gut-shot teammate out of the area on a poncho. We were discussing the situation with them when an AK-47 took us under fire, killing one of the Chams. We backed off a way and got out of sight.

The enemy had their backs to the wall, and we both knew it. It was either stand and fight where they were, or get chewed up trying to escape across the rice paddies to their rear. A cornered man is a desperate, dangerous animal, and rooting them out was going to be costly, especially since nearly every house in the area had a little bunker in it, in which the occupants would huddle during mortar attacks on the nearby military installations. While small-arms fire would get through most of the tin huts in that part of town, the bunkers and scattered concrete houses were another matter.

We had—understandably—been unable to get any air strikes approved for targets within the city the night before. We had not even been able to get approval for the use of artillery illumination rounds above our objectives.

We hadn't encountered any civilians in the area since I'd gotten there—they had fled the fighting there, and most were now gathered over near the air base and the MACV Recondo School—so we felt that an air strike along the edge of the village would be the only way to clear the cornered enemy out of it without suffering excessive casualties ourselves. I called IDC, gave them our assessment, and asked for some close air support. They had to clear it with General Quang, the Vietnamese Special Forces commander who was also the senior government official in the provincial capital. He finally gave his approval, and shortly afterward a FAC in an O-2 push-pull observation plane arrived overhead. I passed the details of our air strike request to him, and we pulled back to give the fighters the necessary separation between ourselves and the target area. The fighters checked in, and the FAC called to clear the strike through his channels. He was refused clearance—General Quang had apparently had a change of heart. The fighters were canceled, and we got no air strike.

The FAC offered to do what he could. He had a minigun pod mounted on his aircraft—the only one I ever saw on an O-2—so we marked our positions for him and cleared him in. He made his run in over our heads in order to attack the target at the enemy's front, and we heard the supersonic crackling of the stream of bullets passing overhead, followed instantly by the combined sounds of the weapon firing and the rounds striking their target—and then came the most god-awful rattling I've ever heard, and something hitting all around us. We jumped like scared rabbits for cover, and I thought we were taking minigun fire ourselves. Then we discovered—to our delight and chagrin—that it was only the spent cartridges from the FAC's minigun hitting the tin roofs and landing among us. It scared the hell out of us, but did no damage.

After the FAC had expended his ammunition, we began moving back toward the positions we had occupied earlier, but made contact almost immediately. The NVA had moved in close to us when the aircraft arrived overhead, hugging as close to us as they could get to deny us the separation necessary to employ air-delivered munitions. It was a technique they put to good use throughout the war.

Another O-2 aircraft showed up and the pilot asked if he could help, indicating that he had "two-eight" rockets. The Forward Air Controller aircraft I was accustomed to were O-1 Birddog aircraft with four 2.75-inch, white phosphorous marking rockets, and I thought "two-eight" rockets were just a different kind of marking rocket, of which he carried four. We had moved back in toward the enemy some distance, and didn't want to pull back and give them a chance to retake more ground, so I told him, "No, thanks." It was only later that I learned he was carrying four rocket pods, each with seven 2.75-inch high-explosive rockets—twenty-eight in all. We could probably have put them to good use. A failure to communicate.

Ken Roberts was really angry about giving up the ground his troops had fought all day to gain in order to put in the air strike, only to have it canceled after it had initially been approved, and about the delays which had given the NVA an opportunity to regain much of the ground.

Some Vietnamese field-grade officer from VNSF Headquarters came up and ordered us to retake the area we had relinquished in order to put in the aborted air strike. Perhaps we would have, except that, in the first place, it was getting dark and the troops were worn out from fighting all day, and in the second place, no goddamned Vietnamese officer ordered the Mike Force around in those days. Someone uttered the sentiment we were all feeling at that point:

"If General Quang wants the goddamn village taken back, let him come take the son of a bitch."

It had been a long day. We were all tired, we had done a lot of fighting, and we had lost a lot of good men in the process of recovering most of the city. And we had killed a large number of communists, without much help at that. So we dug in where we were to hold on to what we had, consolidated and resupplied with ammunition, fed our troops, and rested some of the people.

Compared to the other cities and towns the communists invaded that day, we had recovered Nha Trang quickly. The NVA prisoners who were captured that day attributed their rapid defeat to the fact that we had reacted to their attack so quickly. We caught them by surprise by jumping into the middle of them before they could consolidate any of their gains. That's the Mike Force for you.

Also, they had expected the civilian populace to welcome and support them. They had made all sorts of plans about how they were going to run things once they took over—but they had no withdrawal plans, no orders as to what to do in the event they got their ears boxed. And we had boxed their ears badly.

There were sporadic fights in and around Nha Trang for the next couple of days. An AC-47 "Spooky" Gunship caught a few more of the 18B Regiment's survivors trying to escape back to their mountain hideout, but for us, the battle for Nha Trang was over; we were put on alert to "put out the fire" at several other locations the next few days, but ended up only running a few operations in the local area during that time.

I continued to stay awake throughout the second night of the offensive, with the help of a couple of "green hornets," as we called the Dexedrine capsules we used to stay alert on ambushes and at other times we found it necessary to remain awake for extended periods.

When I got back to the compound, I learned that SFC Nick LaNotte, who was supposed to have gone back to the States the previous day, was still there. He had been injured evacuating some nonambulatory patients from our dispensary at about the time the attack began, when some fool, celebrating Tet or for hateful reasons, had thrown a tear-gas grenade into the dispensary. He had then spent the rest of the battle downtown in a two-and-a-half-ton truck, making runs into and out of the embattled area, picking up civilians and ferrying them to safety—especially the children. Nick loved kids, and he got a lot of them out of danger that night. He could have chosen to do nothing, or he could have chosen to do less. But he was not that kind of man, so he risked his life to ensure the safety of others. We put him in for a medal for his actions.

The next morning, I had to go to the morgue to identify Joe Zamiara's body. Some unconcerned mortician mumbled a couple of questions, then pulled out a big drawer, and there was Joe—young and cold and waxen and dead. I wept at the sight—and the loss—of him.

Then I went to the ward—Diane's ward—to see Larry O'Neil. He was really hurting badly from the wound which had shattered his femur. He was in a cast which ran from his waist to the toes of his injured leg, and to the knee of his uninjured one. They were going to evacuate him to Japan on the first available aircraft for further treatment. He asked me to request the nurse to give him something for the pain, but she had given him something just a short while before.

There was an aircraft inbound to the air base for patients, and the medics were going to load him into an ambulance to take him there, so I stayed to help. It was painful for him when we moved him onto the stretcher, and when we carried the stretcher to the ambulance, and when we put it into the ambulance. No sooner had we gotten him into the vehicle than the commies mortared the air base, and we had to take the wounded out of the ambulance and carry them back onto the ward. Then, after a while, we put him back into the ambulance—and the airfield got mortared again. He pleaded for us to just leave him in the ambulance, the pain of moving him was so severe, so we did. Finally they took him away. I didn't see Larry until some seven years

later, when he came to Fort Bragg to visit his son, who was a
Special Forces medic in my company by then. Small world.
Larry had been medically discharged from the Army as a
result of his severe wound, which had still not completely
healed after years of treatment.

Diane wasn't on the ward, so I went to her quarters to
check on her. She and her hootchmate, Judy, were asleep,
getting some well-deserved rest after being swamped with
fresh casualties from throughout the region during the
previous day and a half. For a few minutes I sat there in the
peaceful quiet of the place, which had the look and the smell
of a home shared by a handful of young American women. I
thought of the death and carnage I had seen—had been part
of—the previous couple of days. I remembered my hand
sliding into the hole in Joe's back, still warm and wet from
the blood which no longer flowed from his young heart. I
thought of the little girl blasted from her bicycle to save the
lives of her parents, and of the Group Commander's driver,
and of the 'Yard boy whose brains lay splattered on the
ground outside Province Headquarters. And I remembered
the NVA soldier who had tried to kill McBroom and
Swanson and me, blown apart now by grenades from my
own hand, and I was glad about that. But if I had seen a few
dozen dead and wounded lying around, what must these
girls have seen? Hundreds, I supposed. Hundreds of young
men, torn and bleeding and moaning with relentless pain,
far from home and wondering if they would ever *see* home
again. I could imagine their eyes, searching the eyes of these
nurses for a sign of hope as the young women's hands
worked to keep their lives within their torn bodies. Sometimes, I knew, they failed to stop what we had started on the
battlefield, and the soldiers died. How many had they
treated the last day or so? How many had they saved, and
how many had they been unable to save, and what did all of
that do to the souls of American girls who should have been
skiing in the Rockies or sunning themselves on a Florida
beach?

I would, at that moment, have given anything to be able to
just lie down beside Diane and hold her to me as she slept.

But she would not have allowed that, so I kissed her on the cheek and went back to the team.

I had been awake for nearly two and a half full days, under considerable strain. I had taken several Dexedrine tablets during that time, and I was burnt out. I crashed on one of the little two-seat sofas in the team bar, lying on my back with my legs hanging over the arm at one end. It was some eighteen hours before I awoke, having slept through a couple of mortar attacks without realizing it. My legs were nearly dead from hanging over the end of the sofa, and it was many long and painful minutes until the circulation to them returned enough to enable me to get up from there.

By the time I got cleaned up and into the TOC—Tactical Operations Center—enough intelligence had come in from various sources to confirm the severity of the defeat we had dealt the 18B North Vietnamese Army Regiment. We sent the Psychological Operations aircraft out to the mountains to which they had limped, and dared them—begged them —to come back for more; and when they didn't, we went out after them, but they were gone.

I got a letter off to Karen, my wife, elated about the blow we had dealt the enemy and about the victory which had been won by our side all across the country. We had met the bastards nose-to-nose all over Vietnam, and we had whipped them soundly. The war was as good as over, and I had visions of getting home before my full tour was over.

And then the press and the politicians took over, the former making it sound, somehow, as if *we* had been defeated, as if the fact that the communists had infiltrated the towns and cities under the cover of a truce—only to be rooted out and slaughtered in unprecedented numbers— meant, somehow, that they had won a great victory. And the latter—the politicians—joined their ill-informed constituents in clamoring for a withdrawal from the war, and refusing us the authority to invade the enemy's cross-border sanctuaries, to which they had crept to lick their terrible wounds. And so the communists were given a morale boost by their enemy's institution of a free, if not always accurate or responsible, press. And that institution's own defenders

95

were, meanwhile, being demoralized by its insanely inverted assertions.

For the communists, there was new life from the propaganda victory; new resolve. And the opportunity to refit, regain strength, and return.

For the American forces, the period of the Great Rot had begun.

8

Since shortly before the Tet offensive was launched throughout Vietnam, the Marine combat base at Khe Sanh, in northwestern I Corps, had been under intensive bombardment from North Vietnamese artillery, rockets, and mortars. Across the border in Laos, Special Forces long-range reconnaissance teams from the highly classified Command and Control Detachment, North—CCN—were reporting a large buildup of NVA forces, including the unusual presence of tanks, Soviet-built PT-76's. B-52 bombers delivered air strikes into the area in an unsuccessful attempt to destroy them.

In the meantime, several miles to the southwest of Khe Sanh, at Special Forces Camp Lang Vei, a Laotian Army unit, the 33rd Royal Laotian Elephant Battalion, had crossed into Vietnam and made contact with the Americans at Lang Vei. They indicated that they had been forced out of the area across the border by the large buildup of North Vietnamese forces there. Several Special Forces NCOs attached to A-101, the team at Lang Vei, were assigned as liaison to the Laotian unit, which was bivouacked just up the road from the Lang Vei camp at the abandoned site of an earlier SF camp.

At the new camp, an element of the I Corps Mike Force had been sent in as reinforcements in response to the enemy buildup, and Lieutenant Colonel Dan Schungle, the commander of C Company, 5th Special Forces Group, which was responsible for all of the SF camps in I Corps, had gone to the camp to assess the situation there.

Early on the morning of 7 February 1968, the NVA armor attacked Camp Lang Vei, quickly overwhelming the I Corps Mike Force outpost near the camp and arriving in the camp's defensive wire before the occupants realized they were there. The camp's defenders engaged the PT-76's with 66mm LAWs, but with little effect. Their two 106mm recoilless rifles, however, had considerably more success, and at one point in the battle, Lieutenant Colonel Schungle was manning one of the guns, and was credited with several kills. He was later awarded the Distinguished Service Cross for his actions in the battle.

The defenders placed a frantic call for assistance to the Marines at Khe Sanh, but for some reason, the only help they got was some eventual artillery support, which came too late to be of much assistance. The camp was overrun by the North Vietnamese, with most of its occupants killed, captured, or escaping into the surrounding jungle. Schungle and several other people were holed up and hiding in the dispensary and mess hall, but most of the remaining survivors, including the camp commander, Captain Willoughby, were trapped in the command bunker, which had a PT-76 atop it. The last that Group Headquarters knew of the situation, the camp had been overrun by some eleven enemy tanks and supporting infantry, and communications with the survivors had been lost.

It was at that point that we received an order which scared me out of my wits. We were to conduct a parachute assault with our Mike Force troops directly into the enemy-occupied camp!

It was madness, and I was so frightened that I quickly agreed when Bud McBroom volunteered to lead the initial company and its American NCO leaders and Montagnard strikers in the initial assault. I would come in with the

98

second lift of assault forces. I have always been disappointed in myself for not insisting that I go in with the initial assault. It was my responsibility, not Bud's, but my courage faltered. Bud McBroom's, and that of the NCOs with whom he was going to parachute into the teeth of the enemy, did not.

Thank God the planners at Group soon saw the suicidal futility of such a plan, and changed their decision; we were to fly into Khe Sanh on C-130 transports, and either chopper in or move overland to the beleaguered camp from there. We moved to the airfield, boarded the C-130s, and took off for Khe Sanh. An hour or so later, when we were on descent for landing, I looked out the window and saw that we were not landing at Khe Sanh, but were over the South China Sea, on final approach for landing at Danang. The plan had been changed again.

Out at the ravaged little camp, the NVA had been trying to force their way into the command bunker. They demanded the surrender of its occupants, and the South Vietnamese soldiers within it did so, leaving the handful of Americans to fend for themselves. The Special Forces soldiers managed, somehow, to keep the NVA out, although the enemy was able to toss grenades and satchel charges into the air vents, wounding everyone inside.

Meanwhile, the NCOs with the nearby Laotian battalion —Sergeant First Class Eugene Ashley, Sergeant Richard H. Allen, and Specialist 4 Joel Johnson—were trying to get them to assault the camp in an attempt to dislodge the North Vietnamese, or at least distract them enough to enable the trapped Americans to escape. Five times, Sergeant First Class Ashley courageously led the reluctant Laotians in assaults against the camp, but each time, the Laotians broke, until finally the intrepid black warrior was severely wounded by machine-gun fire, and unable to lead them anymore. After one of the most courageous displays of battlefield gallantry in the history of Special Forces, he was carried away to the site where the original Camp Lang Vei had previously been located, where the Laotians were bivouacked. There, he was lying wounded in a jeep, awaiting evacuation, when he was killed by incoming artillery.

Courage, above all things, is the first quality of a
warrior.

—Clausewitz

By now, thanks to Ashley's efforts and air strikes which
had been delivered onto the camp, Schungle and the others
managed to escape, evade to the outside of the camp, and
link up with the Laotians.

In Danang, where we had assembled with the I Corps
Mike Force on their compound, we learned that a thirty-
man team from CCN was going in to extract the survivors
from Lang Vei. Our mission was now to form a task force
with the I Corps Mike Force and Project Delta's Ranger
battalion and, under the command of Delta's Major Everett
Baker, the senior adviser to the Ranger battalion, move out
and wrest the camp from the North Vietnamese. But after
the element from CCN linked up with Schungle and the
other survivors outside Old Lang Vei and got them safely to
Khe Sanh, the decision was made to abandon the battered
camp and hammer its new occupants with rumbling, earth-
rending "arc lights," as the devastating air strikes from B-52
bombers were known.

Friendly casualties in the battle at Lang Vei included ten
Americans dead or missing, and eleven of the remaining
fourteen wounded. About two hundred of the five hundred
strikers were dead or missing, and seventy-five wounded.

We returned to Nha Trang soon after, bumming rides on
C-130's headed in that direction. On one occasion, we
managed to cram 175 troops onto one of them, placing them
ten abreast on the floor of the aircraft and tying them down
with nylon cargo straps.

While we were back in Nha Trang, our new Detachment
Commander, Major Richard A. Clark, arrived. He brought
the news that we were going to be expanded into a B
Detachment, with two subordinate A Teams, whose mem-
bers would provide the leadership for the two battalions of
Mike Force strikers into which we would be organized. Each

battalion was to have three rifle companies and a Combat Reconnaissance Platoon. I was going to be allowed to command one of the A Teams, and thus become the commander of 1st Battalion, 5th Mobile Strike Force Command. A first lieutenant with only a year and a half of commissioned service, I was going to command an infantry battalion of more than five hundred men in combat. I was elated. The other Americans in the battalion would be Jack Cheatham, a newly commissioned second lieutenant who had been a Special Forces NCO, SFC Rich Reilly, SSG Ron Franklin, SSG Bob Skinner, SSG Ben Davan, SSG Sam Coutts, SGT Todd Seaver and a young medic named Baribeau.

As we were authorized an additional company, I sent Franklin to the highlands to recruit the Montagnards to fill it, expecting the task to take him a couple of weeks. Two days later, he called to ask that a couple of aircraft be sent to Pleiku to pick up him and his new recruits. When they arrived, I told him to take the company, many of whom were still wearing loincloths, and move them to the supply room to pick up uniforms, blankets, and eating utensils. We would issue them the rest of their equipment the following day. Ron told his interpreter to march them to the supply building, and as I watched in amazement, the 'Yard barked a series of commands in French, the recruits snapped to attention, faced to the left, and executed a file from the right, column-right movement to the supply-room door.

"Where in hell did you *get* these guys, Ron?" I asked. Franklin grinned and explained that they were all members of FULRO, the Montagnard underground liberation movement. They had just finished training together as a company in Cambodia, away from the scrutiny of the Vietnamese government. Instead of the six-week training plan I had intended to put them through, they were ready for combat only two weeks later.

One night soon after, I walked into the team house and encountered an American GI whom I had never seen before. He was opening the doors to our rooms and peering into each, as if he were looking for someone. I asked whom he was looking for, and he said, "What fucking business is it of yours?"

"I happen to live here," I answered. "Who the hell are you?"

"None of your fucking business," he replied.

I laid him out with a right hook, breaking my hand in the process. O'Neil would have been proud of me. Before he had gotten himself shot assaulting Province Headquarters, he would call me over some evenings and tell me to put on my Mike Force shirt—a rather gaudy affair which Retzlaff had gotten made for each member of the team. On the back was embroidered a big dragon wearing a green beret and carrying an M-16 rifle. It was ugly. Anyway, Larry and I would put our Mike Force shirts on and head for town. The object was to go into one of the bars frequented by REMF's—"rear-echelon mother fuckers"—and wait for one of them to make a rude remark about our shirts, whereupon the feisty Irishman would initiate one of his favorite sports—the barroom brawl. Fortunately for us, the officer in charge of the U.S. Military Police in Nha Trang was Ron Paliughi, who had been in O'Neil's basic-training company when I had, and was an OCS classmate of mine. We got hauled in once, when we couldn't convince the MP patrol that showed up during the fight that it was all the REMF's fault, but Ron took care of it, and kept our names off the blotter.

Dick Clark was from a different mold than the "work hard, fight hard, play hard" mold from which Larry was cast, and saw little humor in my handling of the team-house intruder. Nor did he think my response was funny, not long after that, when he issued an edict that no one would come into the team bar without socks on. I suppose it was some sanitary thing, because troops with a lot of time in the bush developed foot sores, so when they were in the rear, they would air them out by wearing shower shoes. Hell, many of us didn't even wear socks under our jungle boots, for that matter. I thought it was foolish, and indicated my feelings one night when some of Clark's friends from the Group staff were in the bar with him, by marching in wearing a steel helmet with no liner, my web gear, and socks. Nothing else. I walked up to the bar and said, "Pop, give me a whiskey," and, gesturing to my exposed penis, "Oh, and one for my horse, here." Most of the team thought it was hilarious, but Clark didn't, and asked me to leave.

That wasn't the first incident resulting from the new team leader's new rule, either. Just after he had issued his guidance about wearing socks in the bar, two members of Detachment B-57, who shared the compound with us, came in. One of them, First Lieutenant Barry Buzzard, was wearing only shower shoes on his feet. I told him he couldn't come into the bar without socks on, and when he protested too vigorously—we had both had a bit to drink—I invited him outside. He promptly knocked me into the sand and was whaling the hell out of me, with my teammates standing around yelling for me to get off the ground and deal with him. I wasn't making much progress; in fact, he was pounding my head into the sand so far that I could feel it running into my ears. Finally, though, I seemed to get in a lucky blow. He rolled off me, stunned, and I got up and pushed him back toward his team's area, throwing his shower shoes after him and warning him not to come back without socks on or he'd get more of the same.

I sauntered back into the bar, bragging to my buddies, "Well, guess I sure showed *him!*" McBroom looked at me, laughed, and said, "Hell, Bucky, he'd *still* be whipping your ass if Coutts hadn't drop-kicked him in the head."

My hand was still in a cast when we were tasked to attach a company to Project Delta for an operation—code-named Samurai IV—up in I Corps. They were going into the A Shau, and Major Chuck "Bruiser" Allen wanted a Mike Force company to be a reaction force for his recon teams in case they got into trouble. Their organic 81st Ranger battalion—commanded by Vietnamese officers—reacted too slowly in such situations. We were pleased to oblige.

I flew with 7th Company up to Phu Bai, where Delta was establishing their Forward Operations Base, and we set up on the perimeter in an old Chinese cemetery.

Delta's recon teams were inserted, and soon began sending back reports of hearing heavy vehicle traffic, so 7th Company was given the mission of going into the area to conduct a reconnaissance-in-force.

As the company prepared for their mission, the elderly Cham who was designated as the indigenous company commander sought out Ken Roberts and told him that he had had a dream the previous night, and that if he went in on the first lift, as he customarily did, he would be killed, because the landing zone was going to be "hot"—opposed by enemy fire. It was neither the first nor the last time that we were to hear of accurate premonitions from the Chams.

Roberts had been replaced as the U.S. commander of the company by Ross "Pete" Potter, by virtue of Potter's seniority in rank, so he and Sam Coutts loaded up with the first lift and took off.

As the old Cham had predicted, they made contact immediately on landing. Roberts and the remaining Chams prepared to go in either to reinforce the small element on the ground with Potter and Coutts or to assist in their extraction. I cut the plaster cast off my arm and got ready to go in as well, but because their reconnaissance-in-force mission had been compromised, Bruiser decided to extract them, and they got out with their wounded without further casualties.

Delta inserted additional recon teams into the area, and they discovered a major NVA engineering feat: they were building a vehicle-bearing road pointing directly toward the old imperial capital of Hue. In addition, the recon teams spotted a number of Soviet-built trucks along the road, only twenty-five miles from the defenses of Hue, where the Marines were still mopping up pockets of NVA who had occupied the city during the Tet celebration.

Because the Tet offensive had disrupted our logistical chain, we were short of combat rations, so we had been given funds to purchase food from the local economy to feed our troops when they were at the Forward Operations Base, and with the troops now safely back at the FOB, Sammy and I went to Hue to buy poultry and fresh vegetables for the company. We found a terribly inflated economy, because food was scarce in the town at the time, and we were having to pay ten times the amount for the ducks we bought than the going price had been for them back in Nha Trang. Our shopping trip was interrupted when a sniper opened up on the marketplace—to which the Marines responded with an Ontos, a tracked vehicle with six 106mm recoilless rifles mounted atop it. The vehicle roared in, spun toward the area from which the sniper had fired, and unleashed a salvo of the big antitank rounds into the huts, not only destroying a number of them but also scattering food and merchants around the square with the weapons' powerful back-blasts. The civilians were angry as hell at this massive and harmful overreaction to the sniper, and appeared about ready to riot. Though we would have agreed with them, some appeared ready to take out their anger on us—after all, we were "roundeyes" like the Marines. Wanting no further part of the volatile situation, we returned to the FOB.

Bruiser Allen alerted us to prepare to go in to attempt to capture some of the trucks, promising that whoever could drive one out and back to the FOB would be awarded a DSC and a thirty-day leave anywhere in the world. It was an inviting offer, but before anyone could attempt to take him up on it, the First Cav, learning of the trucks' presence from Delta's intelligence reports, dispatched Cobra helicopter gunships to the area. They found the trucks and destroyed seven of them.

Because of the increasing indications of large NVA forces in the area of operations, Major Allen decided to commit his Ranger battalion into the area, leaving our Chams to secure the FOB while they were gone. I took the walking wounded from 7th Company's earlier engagement—stopping by the Navy hospital to have my broken hand recasted—and hitched a ride back to Nha Trang on an Air Force MC-130 Blackbird, the specially configured version of the aircraft, which had the capability of "skyhooking" a man from the ground, as Bud Mc-Broom had experienced on training missions back at Fort Bragg.

Back in Nha Trang, I learned that Delta's Ranger battalion had gotten into a major battle when they went into the area of the NVA road. Several of the Marine CH-46 helicopters which took them in were hit by rocket-propelled grenades as they flared for landing, and there were heavy casualties. One of those killed was Specialist 5 John Link, a fine young demolitions specialist who had been on my first A Team at Fort Bragg. He was killed while rescuing a wounded comrade from the fire-swept LZ, shielding the other man with his body when he was taken under machine-gun fire, for which he was posthumously awarded a Distinguished Service Cross. John Link had been one of my favorite soldiers, a good-hearted kid who had no business amidst the death and destruction of war, but who believed strongly in what we were doing. Confronted with the twisted reporting of the week-old newsmagazines and their photos of Link's civilian peers protesting the war in their all-too-similar "individual" hippie uniforms, I sat down in my hootch and wrote about my young friend in a poem:

> Look here.
> Have you ever seen a soldier cry?
>
> I weep
> Because I lost a friend today—
>
> Not some "comrade-in-arms"—
> But a fine, young friend.
>
> You'll never understand
> Why he died,
> Nor why I grieve for him,
> Because you never even understood
> Why we came.

I knew. He knew.
Perhaps someday, like you,
I'll forget—
If I live that long

Link
KIA—1968
Ranger Valley, RVN

Before they were replaced by 5th Company, Coutts and the Chams went back into the Delta area of operations, capturing a large cache of NVA ammunition. For their actions on Operation Samurai IV, Project Delta and our 7th Company received the Valorous Unit Award.

—— 9 ——

One day, that spring of 1968, a letter from my kid brother arrived with the surprising news that he, too, was in Vietnam. I knew that he had gone into the Army, but had no idea that he was in country. Tommy didn't have to be in Vietnam, as there was a regulation at the time which stated that a soldier whose other brothers were in Vietnam was not required to go. But when his First Sergeant had informed him of that fact, Tommy had said, "So what?" and shipped out with his buddies. He was an M-60 machine-gunner in a straight-leg infantry battalion, the 5th Battalion, 46th Infantry, of the Americal Division—the same division our father had served with in the Pacific in World War II.

I went straight to Sergeant Major Maddox, the Group Command Sergeant Major, and said, "Sergeant Major, I notice you have a number of legs here. How'd you like to have another good one?"

"Who is it?" he asked, and when I said, "My kid brother," Maddox asked me for his name, service number, and unit, and it was done. We joined the number of other families with more than one member serving together in 5th Group in Vietnam: the Adams boys, the Dovers, the Hodgeses, the Terrys, and a number of others. One of the most notable families was the Batchelors. Chief Warrant Officer Hardy Batchelor, a veteran of three wars who had more time on jump status than anybody else in the Army, and who had been General Westmoreland's First Sergeant in the 187th Parachute Infantry Regiment before the Korean War, had two sons with him in the 5th Group at the time: Sergeant Tommy Batchelor, who was in the Mike Force with me, and Hardy junior, a lieutenant in Detachment A-502, where my brother ended up being assigned.

A couple of weeks after my conversation with Sergeant Major Maddox, I got a call from Tommy. He was at Cam Ranh air base, awaiting a flight to Nha Trang the next day. Cam Ranh was only a short distance south, so I told him to wait where he was, and called the FACs to see if, by chance, one of them could pick him up from Cam Ranh. Captain Billy Boyd was in the air, so I asked him if he could drop into Cam Ranh and pick up a passenger. "Who is it?" he asked, and when I answered, "Same last name as mine. Spec 4," Billy said, "I'm on the way in there now."

When the public-address system squawked, "Specialist Burruss, your aircraft is waiting—tail number 555," Tommy went out to the flight line, and looked at the tails of all the big C-130 and C-141 transports, but none bore the number "555." Finally he noticed the little O-1 Birddog sitting there with the pilot waving him aboard. He jumped into the back with his duffel bag, and off they went. In order to ensure that my young brother's first flight with a Forward Air Controller was more than a routine hop, Billy took him out over the jungle and put in a preplanned air strike—giving him a taste of the stomach-churning maneuvers which occur when the little airplane swoops and dives over the jungle canopy to mark the target for the fighters.

He landed at Nha Trang air base a short while later, and my kid brother—a little green around the gills—climbed out from behind the grinning FAC.

One of the 'Yards with me took his duffel bag, and the other handed him a cold beer, and I gave him a big hug, noticing the Combat Infantryman's Badge he had already won—and the absence of a Parachute Badge.

Our dad was a paratrooper, and it would never do for one of his sons to stay a "leg," so a short while later he was down at the training center at Dong Ba Thin, undergoing basic airborne training. McBroom and I went down to make a jump with him, and he promptly showed off for us by having a parachute malfunction, while I yelled frantically at him until he deployed his reserve. Mom would never forgive me if he ended up biting the dust on a drop zone in Vietnam.

Thus qualified, he was assigned to A-502 for on-the-job training as a Special Forces soldier.

One night not long after that, Papa Baer and I were sitting in the Mike Force bar having a few beers with our teammates. We considered Baer and Boyd members of the team, and occasionally joined with them in singing "The Friendly FAC and the Green Beret," a song which one of their fellow pilots in the 21st Tactical Air Support Squadron, Captain John Myer, had written to the tune of "Wabash Cannon Ball":

Friendly FAC, oh, friendly FAC, this is Green Beret,
We see you flying high above, out of danger's way.
If you can spare a moment to help your fellowman,
I wish you'd try to find me, and tell me where I am.

Green Beret, oh, Green Beret, this is your friendly
    FAC,
You see me flying overhead while you're still in the
    sack—
Still, I'll try to find you, and set you people straight,
But hurry, 'cause it's steak night, and I don't want
    to be late.

Friendly FAC, oh, friendly FAC, this is Green Beret,
We appreciate your helping, and you'll send us on
    our way,
But I really wish you'd think about our danger on
    the ground—
Tromping through the jungle, while you just "fac"
    around.

110

MIKE FORCE

Green Beret, oh, Green Beret, this is your friendly
   FAC,
If you no longer need me, I'm going to head on
   back.
I'll settle for a sourvenir—whatever you can bag:
An AK forty-seven, or a bloodstained VC flag.

Oh, friendly FAC, oh, friendly FAC, we've just come
   under fire!
And if you cannot help us, we'll join the angels'
   choir.
It's automatic weapons, we're really getting hit,
So hurry with the fighters, 'cause we are in deep
   shit!

Green Beret, you were cut out—I read you
   "numbah ten";
The C Team's telling dirty jokes, so please transmit
   again.
If you've got Charlie cornered, please don't let him
   get away.
I've sent a call for fighters—though it may take all
   day. . . .

Friendly FAC, oh, friendly FAC, please get your
   finger out,
We've tangled with a regiment, of that there is no
   doubt.
If you can get us out of Charlie's fierce and dreadful
   grip,
We'll give you FACs a grateful square in our comic
   strip.

Green Beret, oh, Green Beret, this is your friendly
   FAC.
Let me take some photos, in case you don't get
   back.
Turn this way a little. Hold it. That's the style!
You're on *Candid Camera,* so let me see you smile.

MIKE FORCE

Green Beret! Hey, Green Beret! They're shooting at
    this FAC!
I hear the bullets whistling by, I hear the rifles' crack
I'm missing my siesta, and I need a taste of rum,
If you no longer need me, I think I'll head for home!

Oh, thank God; our fighters now are circling
    overhead!
Charlie's going to wish that he had stayed at home
    in bed.
He's going to meet his maker in the Land that is to
    be—
We're going to blow his body up, and set his spirit
    free.

Friendly FAC and fighters, I hope you see our
    smoke—
That first strike came too close to us; it really was no
    joke!
Green Beret, we're holding high—the FAC, he got it
    wrong;
He thought that you were marking the position of
    the Cong!

Fighters, this is friendly FAC, please hold it high and
    dry.
We can get this straightened out, if we all really try.
It really doesn't matter if I mark the friend or foe,
'Cause you can't hit a cow's rear end, no matter
    where you go!

Fighters, you're cleared in again, just do the best you
    can.
The situation's all fouled up, beyond the help of
    man—
Just bomb the general area, and when the smoke
    clears out,
Well, we'll just count the bodies, and let God sort
    'em out!

Now most of us are safe at home; we beat the
    dreaded Cong,
We simply let it all hang out to help the war along.
The friendly FAC and fighters will always save the
    day—
Killing off the Charlies, to the last damned Green
    Beret.

The duty NCO stepped into the bar and reported that an
element of A-502 was in contact at the foot of the mountains
to the west. "What call sign?" I asked, and when he told me,
I exclaimed, "Oh, shit! That's my kid brother!"

Papa Baer jumped up. "Let's go!" he said, and we jumped
in his jeep, sped to the airfield, and hopped in the little
Birddog aircraft. As we taxied out for takeoff, he put in a call
for a "Spooky" gunship, and we were soon over the area of
the firefight, watching the tracers from my five-year-younger
brother and his CIDG troops fly at the enemy positions. We
got him on the radio, and he activated a strobe light to mark
his position, giving us the range and direction from there to
the enemy positions. "Spooky" showed up soon after,
illuminating the earth below with his parachute flares. Papa
Baer swooped in, marked the target with a "Willy Pete"
rocket, and the old reliable AC-47 gunship was soon raining
tracers from its rapid-firing miniguns, which made a sound
like a cow mooing, as they unleashed 7.62mm tracers at a
rate of three thousand rounds a minute.

As I have mentioned, we were having a few beers when we
learned of the firefight, and now Baer found himself with a
terrible need to relieve himself. "Hand me the stick from
back there, Bucky," he called. "What?" "The control stick.
Take the cotter pin out, pull it off, and hand it up here.
Quick!"

I did so, and he proceeded to urinate into the hollow
control stick, dumping it out of the window of the airplane
as he refilled it several times.

"Wham!" Something slammed into the little aircraft,
causing it to shudder, and opening a hole in the skin of the
fuselage beside me.

"What was that?" I shouted, wondering if Papa Baer had been hit, and if I would have to try to fly the Birddog back to Nha Trang, then realizing the impossibility of that, since he still had the backseat control stick up front with him.

"Oh, shit!" he exclaimed. "We snagged a burned-out flare!"

Fortunately, we had hit it with the wing strut, causing no damage except the hole beside me. A few inches to the right and it would have entangled in the propeller, and we would have been in a hell of a mess.

Flying with the FACs was always a fun diversion from patrolling in the jungle, and I often did so while we waited in Nha Trang to react to our next mission.

Sometimes we would fly low across the jungle while, high above us, a radio-intercept aircraft scanned the airwaves for enemy radio transmissions, fixing the enemy's communications site with its direction-finding equipment. He would pass us the coordinates of the site, and we would buzz around the location, looking for any signs of the enemy. If we spotted anything, and there were fighters available, the FAC would mark the site for them to strafe and bomb. It must have made the lives of the communist radio operators exciting.

At other times, we would search some area of the sector where intelligence reports indicated the presence of VC or NVA, occasionally spotting enemy troops and calling for fighters to attack them. If no fighters were available, we would deliver what we came to call "mini-strikes." I would sit in the back seat with a case of fragmentation hand grenades and my little 5.56mm CAR-15 assault rifle, and if we spotted an enemy position, Papa or Billy would fly low over the area, and we would rain hand grenades down on it, or swoop by and fire a magazine of ammunition at them from my weapon. The first time we tried that, we had to change our tactics slightly, as we swooped past with the target on our left. I poked my weapon out of the window on that side and let loose with a long burst—and the hot expended cartridges ejected from the weapon and went straight down the neck of the pilot's flight suit. From then on, we delivered our mini-strikes from the *right*-side window.

Once, we spotted the VC unloading some sampans far up one of the small rivers near Nha Trang, and Colonel Baer decided to try to engage them with his rockets before they escaped. He bore in, and as the enemy soldiers blazed away at us with their AK-47's, he dived on and on, down toward the sampans, unleashing a volley of rockets just above the treetops, and destroying both of the boats. It was amazing how accurate he was with those marking rockets, considering that his only aiming device consisted of a grease-pencil mark on the windshield.

I noticed that an increasingly large number of the radio direction-finding intercepts were being made in the vicinity of the Grand Summit, the tallest of the rocky, jungle-covered mountains southwest of Nha Trang, which rose to a height of some three thousand feet.

Additionally, our companies were making more frequent contacts with enemy patrols at the base of the mountain.

During one such contact, I was out with a recently arrived NCO, SFC Snyder, and his company, which was moving across the valley floor below, when the point element spotted two of the enemy a couple of hundred meters away. The 'Yards took them under fire, and one of the communists turned and unleashed a burst of rifle fire as he fled into the jungle. One round from the burst struck Snyder in the heart, killing him almost instantly, and leaving a wife and six children to survive him.

Every time our troops would try to pursue the enemy up the treacherous slopes of the mountain, they would be met with a barrage of hand grenades on their badly channelized avenues of approach, inevitably taking a number of casualties, and having to withdraw to evacuate them.

One day I was out in the area with Sammy Coutts and the new medic assigned to 7th Company on a local security operation near where Coutts had made his first contact and where Snyder had been killed. The idea struck me that it might be possible to walk past the mountain along the valley floor, being very conspicuous as we did so, as if we were headed for the outpost on Highway 1 at the far end of the valley. Then, when we were well down the valley, and the enemy figured we were gone, we would sneak up the slope at the end of the mountain, hide for a day, then try to double back high up along the mountain's steep face. In this way, we might be able to hit them from above or from the flank, instead of trying to fight our way uphill to them.

We moved a short way up the valley along the Dong Bo stream, and set up for the night there, building cooking fires to ensure that the enemy was aware of our presence.

The new medic, a buck sergeant who had prior service as a Navy corpsman and had served as a medic with the Peace Corps in Malaysia, and who had the same name as the actor who portrayed television's famous Dr. Kildare—Richard Chamberlain—hung his hammock up between two trees near where I slept on the ground.

He was still asleep at dawn the next day, and I was making some breakfast coffee, when suddenly there was an explosion at the perimeter of the company about twenty-five meters away, followed by a few rounds of incoming AK-47 fire, and several long bursts from one of our machine guns.

Chamberlain put on one of the most remarkable displays of speed I have ever seen. In what seemed to me no more than two seconds, he was out of the hammock, had it down, rolled, and in his rucksack, and was crouched there with his weapon, his eyes as big as hubcaps, ready for action.

I had to stop laughing before I could even check to see what had happened on the perimeter. A couple of enemy, probably checking to assure themselves of our location, had bumped our perimeter, had a Claymore mine fired at them, fired a burst in our direction, and took off—apparently without being touched by either the Claymore or the rounds from the machine gun the Cham had loosed at them.

No sweat—it would serve to reinforce the impression that we were being lax—that we were just out there for a quick sweep through the valley.

After chuckling for a while about Chamberlain's hammock-evacuation act, we formed up and moved a bit farther up the valley, then turned ninety degrees to the left and started up the slopes of the Grand Summit, now rigidly enforcing noise discipline. When we got about halfway to the top of the ridge, we again made a ninety-degree turn to the left and began our movement back toward the area we had previously been unable to penetrate.

It was rough going. Beneath the jungle canopy, the mountain comprised huge boulders, many as large as houses, and was cut by sharp, deep crevasses, many just too wide and deep to cross. When we got to such places, we would have to back the company up, and search uphill until we could find a place to cross. We did that all day, and got only about two-thirds of the way back toward our objective. But as it began to turn dark beneath the jungle canopy, we started finding signs of recent enemy occupation—a couple of areas where the sparse dirt between the boulders had been leveled, apparently for sleeping places, and a few footprints from "Goodyear go-betters," as the enemy's sandals, fashioned from tire treads and held on by straps made from inner tubes, were known.

We set up there for the night, and there was no problem getting the Chams to observe noise and light discipline. The next morning as dawn broke and we quietly formed up to move out, Chamberlain whispered to me, "You know, sir, I think I'm going to earn my CMB today"—referring to the Combat Medical Badge which medics are issued in lieu of the Combat Infantryman's Badge. He was right, and then some. . . .

We had moved for a short distance when the point man spotted an enemy soldier fleeing from in front of us. Neither man fired, and we moved on in pursuit. A short while later, we made a light contact. Coutts and I pushed up to the front, and soon we had a hot little firefight going between our point element and a few of the enemy. I radioed Chamberlain and told him to maneuver his platoon around us, uphill to our right, then sweep down and try to hit the enemy on the flank from above.

The amount of enemy fire from our front increased about then, and as I looked at Coutts a few feet away, the leaves next to his head rattled and fell, and his radio operator, sitting right next to him, tumbled over backward, a bullet in his chest. As so often occurred in terrain such as that, the bad guys were just a short distance away—maybe twenty meters—but we couldn't see them. We tried inching toward them, but their fire just ate up the trees and rocks around us, keeping us down. I started raining hand grenades into the area from which the fire was coming, and the shooting slacked off for a while, so we began to push forward again. But then the fire *really* started pouring in, so heavy that I thought it *must* be Chamberlain's platoon, even though it sounded predominantly like AK-47 fire. I grabbed the radio handset and told him to hold off, that he was apparently disoriented and firing into us. It wasn't his people, he said. They were pinned down from three sides and hardly able to get a round off without taking casualties. They already had five wounded.

I could hear firing then from a fairly long distance—about two hundred meters, I estimated—and told him when the fire slackened to fire three rounds slowly. Shortly after, during a relatively quiet moment, I heard his three shots. He verified over the radio that the three shots were his. I tried maneuvering some people to the left then, but we ran into more of the NVA, and took additional casualties.

We were fighting at least a company, and on their own ground, at that.

The one side of his platoon from which Chamberlain was not yet taking fire was his downhill side, so I told him to move on down before he became surrounded—he was already cut off from us, with no other American to take over if he got hit. He had a wounded man who was about to die on him, so we got a dustoff cranked up, and called for a FAC as well. Chamberlain ran into punji pits as he moved downhill, and we were taking an increasing amount of fire, including M-79's and rocket-propelled grenades. It became increasingly obvious that we had stepped into something big.

We had several critically wounded strikers who needed to be evacuated before they died, too, and good ol' Billy Boyd was on station with a set of F-4 Phantoms, so I decided to pull out, evacuate the wounded, try to link up with Chamberlain, and let Billy work the enemy over with his fighters. Anyway, we were short of ammunition by then.

We got a good mark on our locations, and Billy started in with the fighters. The NVA tried to hug close to us as they had during Tet, so when we got across a big backbone of rock, I had him put the stuff right on the other side. Boyd and his fighters did a magnificent job, putting five hundred-pound high-drag bombs just fifty meters behind us—so close that we could hear the cries of their wounded. The concussion of the exploding bombs nearly knocked our hats off, and the napalm, although a little farther away, was close enough for us to feel its heat on our faces.

The Chams who were carrying the wounded must have been afraid that I was going to bring the stuff right in on top of us. They dropped their wounded comrades and ran. It was a disgraceful thing. Had I known it at the time, we could have gone back after them, but whether from fear or shame or for whatever reason, they didn't tell Coutts and me until we were back on the valley floor.

Chamberlain, meanwhile, had called the dustoff chopper in, and standing on a rock in a small open place, nakedly exposed to the enemy he knew to be nearby, hoisted his seriously wounded strikers out. He was near the floor of the valley, so we moved both elements down to rendezvous. It was when we reached an open area for a pickup zone big enough to get a dustoff chopper into that we discovered that some of the wounded had been left behind. I was sick. We had put air strikes all over the area where they had been left. I had gained a deep distaste for leaving people behind by then, and though they were almost surely dead by now—or if not, captured by the NVA—I considered going back up the mountain after them. I didn't want to, but I would have, except that only a few of the strikers, including Coutt's superb indig platoon leader, Khoe, and of course Sammy himself, were willing.

It had been that tough a fight up on the rocky mountain—the Chams seldom balked, but they would have no part of going back up the enemy-infested Grand Summit that day.

When we finally linked up with Chamberlain, I had been so fearful for his life during the time he had been cut off from us and nearly surrounded, that my eyes brimmed over at seeing him alive and well, and we greeted each other like long-lost brothers. The young medic had, as he had predicted that morning, earned his Combat Medical Badge that day. And more. I put him in for a Silver Star for his gallantry in action.

In retrospect, I have to wonder if the NVA—all around him as he stood on the bare rock up on the treacherous mountain—hadn't been so impressed by his courage, as he put man after man onto the hoist to be lifted into the chopper, that they chose to let him live. We shall never know.

10

In April 1968, while draft-exempt students in the United States were engaging in their latest protest fad—the "sit-in," which consisted of occupying public buildings and sitting there on their asses for days or weeks while the news media fawned on them, broadcasting their demands for cutting off support to Vietnam—while they were making a party of that sort of activism, their uniformed peers in the First Cavalry Division were slogging and slugging their way to Khe Sanh, finally relieving that beleaguered garrison and destroying more than a thousand of the North Vietnamese enemy in the process. A week later, they recaptured nearby Lang Vei, where the NVA had been conducting an armed version of the "sit-in" since they had overrun the place with tanks two months earlier.

Detachment A-109 at Camp Thuong Duc, west of Danang out near the Laotian border, was under siege. We had sent some troops up there to reinforce them. We had a Combat Reconnaissance Platoon which had just finished training down at the CIDG Training Center at Dong Ba Thin, and although I was due to go on R&R—Rest and Recuperation—I decided to take them up to I Corps and out to Thuong Duc. Once I got to the C Team in Danang, I saw

Lieutenant Colonel Schungle, and when he learned that I had a platoon that needed to get out to the camp, he directed me to use them to take a convoy of supply trucks out there. I went down to the I Corps Mike Force to borrow a radio for the trip, and when the major commanding our sister unit heard of the plan, he paled. They had just tried to get a heavily armed convoy out there themselves, and it had been destroyed, with a number of his Australian and American leaders killed or wounded. He was incredulous that Schungle expected a lone American and a lightly armed platoon to make it through, and he stormed up to the C Team to talk some sense into them. He returned a short time later to say that he had gotten them to change their minds, and we would be taken out to the camp in Marine helicopters.

As it was, we got mortared on the landing zone below the camp, and had a brief skirmish with some communists in the village beside the LZ before we could even get up to the camp. While I was there, a Marine convoy headed out to the area, escorted by tanks and armored personnel carriers. It was hit and badly mauled by the enemy, and I wondered if I would still be alive if I hadn't stopped by the I Corps Mike Force to borrow a radio.

It was terribly crowded at Thuong Duc, which was under almost constant mortar or rocket attack. It was so crowded in one of the bunkers that a guy knocked a shotgun off the wall and it discharged, killing him. Staff Sergeant Eulis Pressley took his 'Yards out and captured an 82mm mortar, which he promptly turned around and used on the enemy, but even that didn't take much of the pressure off. Then the Marines committed a large force into the area, and the attacks subsided. When I learned that a chopper was on the way out with a television news crew, I figured it was time for me to go, so I caught the bird back to Danang.

After I got back to Nha Trang, I caught a flight to Hawaii for R&R. Karen met me there, and we spent a blissful week in Honolulu, as so many young couples did during the Vietnam war. It was a wonderful week for us. We had spent only about three months together in the year and a half we had been married, and much of that time she had been pregnant with our son, Jeff. It was our honeymoon, and we spent more time in our hotel room than we did swimming and seeing the sights, making love with the desperation that only a soldier on a short break from war, and a young wife who wondered if she might ever see her husband again after the brief week passed, could know. Sammy and Linda Coutts were there at the same time, but we saw little of them—to the surprise and dismay of none of us.

The times that we did see each other, the first thing each of us wanted to know was whether or not the other had seen anything on the news or read anything in the paper about the Mike Force. We were two members of the Mike Force brotherhood now, and the team was never too far back in our minds.

Then, suddenly, the brief week in paradise was over. Sam Coutts and I found ourselves back in the team house in Nha Trang.

We soon learned that the 403rd Special Operations Detachment, 5th Group's signal intercept element, had reported that the NVA unit we had attacked on the Grand Summit a couple of weeks earlier had taken over fifty casualties that day—most, no doubt, from Billy Boyd's expert air strikes. They had asked their higher headquarters for permission to withdraw. It was the rebuilt 18B NVA Regiment we had attacked with our Mike Force company of Cham strikers, the whole goddamned regiment, and we had dealt them a severe enough blow to cause them to ask to be withdrawn to a safer base area.

Their request was denied.

I saw Diane again. She had been spending a lot of time with one of the physicians with whom she worked, and they were becoming romantically involved. One day, when Major Lee, the team leader out at A-502, was having a going-away party at Camp Trung Dung, five of us—Diane, her doctor, the two FACs, and I—drove out to the camp in Papa Baer's jeep. We had a hell of a good time, but stayed a bit too long. It was nearly dark when we left for the return trip to Nha Trang. To make things worse, we took highway

421 to the northeast as we left the camp, instead of turning east onto Highway 1. By the time we realized our mistake, we were well into the Koreans' area of operations, out in no-man's-land. Luckily, we didn't run into one of their ambushes—or one of the enemy's—before we got back to the road to Nha Trang.

Papa Baer was driving, with Diane and the doc crowded into the seat beside him, and Billy Boyd and I were in back. As we rounded the curve on the bumpy dirt road at the end of the runway of the air base, we hit a bump. The doc fell out of the jeep, grabbing Diane in an attempt to keep from falling out. As a result, she went out of the jeep behind him—and sat square on his head. The poor doctor suffered such a severe concussion that he had to be medevaced to Japan for treatment.

A streak of violence had surfaced in me during my time in Vietnam, that I had not had before. I was trying to solve every disagreement with my fists, and it wasn't just an attempt to emulate the brawling ways of my Mike Force mentor, Larry O'Neil. To him, fistfighting was a sport; to me, it was the surfacing of something deeper. Whether it was a carryover of the boiling hate I had developed for the enemy, a release of the frustration of not being able to defeat them once and for all, a response to the alienation from the American people we were starting to feel, as story after story in magazine after newsmagazine told us that we were wrong to be there fighting, when we knew we were right—whatever the reasons, it was there.

One night a young radio operator from the B Team, after receiving a "Dear John" letter, had gotten hold of an AK-47 and made some halfhearted threats. When it was reported to me, I had gone to find him, and when I did so, managed to get the weapon from him, then beat him unmercifully—going far beyond what was necessary to subdue the kid. It was a disgraceful display for an officer.

On another occasion, I had blind-sided A.P. over some minor disagreement, and beat his face up quite badly. I was getting out of control, and Major Clark warned me to get hold of myself.

124

Then, one summer night, I went to the hospital to ogle the roundeye nurses. As I took a shortcut through one of the wards to get to their little MASH-like club, I was confronted by the ward nurse, a cute little second lieutenant, who told me I couldn't go through. "Oh, yes, I can," I said cutely, and we began flirtatiously sparring with words. Then the hospital Staff Duty NCO happened in, and took our little confrontation seriously. He ordered me to leave, and I told him to buzz off; I was having too much fun with the nurse. He grabbed me, and I decked him. But on the way down, he drew his pistol, and I soon found myself being marched before the hospital duty officer.

When the incident was reported to Clark, he called me in and told me to find a new home. He'd had enough of my rabble-rousing.

He was leaving and I figured that when he was gone, I could come back over to the Mike Force, so I went to the Group operations section and asked Master Sergeant Bill Edge, a good friend and supporter of the Mike Force, if he could find me a job for a while. He did, and I was reassigned as the 5th Group Assistant Training Officer, working with a young Spec 4 named Roger George.

A week later, Clark was gone, replaced by Major John Borgman, and I began spending my spare time back at the Mike Force, waiting for an opportune moment to ask for reassignment back to the team.

Bud McBroom, with two companies of strikers, made another attempt to penetrate the NVA base on the Grand Summit not long after Borgman's arrival, but—no surprise to those of us who had been there—was unable to do so.

I was there when they returned to camp, sympathetic with their frustrated attempt to get into the deadly area. Major Borgman was less sympathetic, as his NCOs stood there in the team bar, attempting to explain the difficulty of the terrain and the degree to which the place was infested with the enemy. He began to make remarks which I felt were disparaging to the fine NCOs under his command, so I joined in their efforts to explain the difficulty of an assault into the tenacious enemy's home ground. Apparently

Borgman hadn't been privy to the radio-intercept report which indicated the size of the force on the mountain—those were highly classified and compartmented—and he made a remark to the effect that we had been run off the mountain by "a highly mobile squad."

My anger rose, and I protested loudly. When he retorted, "You can't tell *me* that; I'm the *commander!*" I lost my cool.

"Oh, is that right?" I yelled, getting in his face. "Well, let me tell *you* something, motherfucker! If you want to command *this* bunch of hard-dicked sons of bitches, you'd better get your ass up on that fucking *hill* and command them!"

Some of his cronies from Group Headquarters were there, and one of them made a move toward me. Coutts stepped in front of him and suggested that he sit back down. Wisely, he did so. Another of them was shouting, "Don't let him talk to you that way, John! Court-martial him! Run him out of the Army!"

"Oh, yeah?" I yelled. "You *can't* run me out of the Army—'cause *I* fuckin' *quit!* Because of assholes like *you!*"

The situation was well out of hand, and someone—I think it was Bud McBroom—could see that it was about to get worse, and got us out of there.

I was in big trouble, and knew it. I had blown any chance of going back to the team, and what was worse, might be faced with a court-martial. Since I *was* nearing the end of my obligation of service—I had less than two months remaining in the Army, although I had put in the paperwork to extend my active-duty status indefinitely—I decided to quit when my time was up. I withdrew my request for voluntary indefinite status.

Bill Edge told me later that, shortly after that, Borgman had indeed intended to have me court-martialed, but Major John J. Manolakis, the Group Assistant Operations Officer, had said that I worked for *him* now, and since I was leaving the Army anyway, and he had the Mike Force to run, why didn't he get back over there and run it?

None of this changed a damned thing on the Grand Summit, though, and the Mike Force went back in, this time with four companies, with the same result: they couldn't root the NVA out of their cave-riddled stronghold. Among the casualties was my replacement, Dick Wright, who got his thumb shot clean off.

Then, after an unsuccessful attempt to burn the enemy out with an air strike consisting of fighters with high explosive bombs and C-130's dropping pallets laden with barrels of jet fuel and gasoline onto the area, I found out that another attempt was to be made—this time with four of our companies supported by two companies from A-502.

I was short by then, with only eighteen days left in country, but I went to the Group Operations Officer, Lieutenant Colonel Eckner Panzic, and asked for permission to accompany my old teammates on the mission. He reminded me that I didn't work for the Mike Force anymore, but when I told him I had a leave approved to go to Australia during that time anyway, he asked me if I really wanted to go that badly. I said that I did, and he shook his head in amazement, but gave me his permission.

I didn't even bother to ask for Borgman's permission, as, once again, he wasn't going anyway, and wouldn't know until I was already on the ground, if then. I simply got my gear, went to the airfield, from which the helicopter assault would be launched, and linked up with McBroom, Sammy Coutts, and my other Mike Force buddies.

We went in at the peak of the steep boulder-strewn summit, the choppers hovering above a small clearing from which the trees had been blown by air strikes, while we jumped to the ground. I was standing atop one of the rocks when the next lift came flaring in. The rotor wash from the helicopter blew me off my perch, and down I tumbled, striking my head against a rock and momentarily knocking myself unconscious. I had also sprained my wrist in the fall, and, woozy from the blow to my head and unable to hold my weapon properly, I got back on one of the choppers and returned to the air base.

The companies on the mountain pressed their attack, but try as they might, they couldn't overwhelm the enemy defenders. Again the "highly mobile squad" of NVA held firm as the friendly casualties mounted, until, once more, our troops were withdrawn.

It was only after I was safely back in the States that the mountain was finally taken. An entire Korean regiment was committed to the operation, supported by tactical air strikes and heavy eight-inch howitzers delivering direct fire into the enemy stronghold. The Koreans ringed the entire area with troops, employing tear gas against the NVA as they slowly closed the circle. They suffered heavy casualties, but in the end, annihilated my old foe, the 18B North Vietnamese Army Regiment, killing more than four hundred members of that "highly mobile squad."

The Mike Force ran two more missions to Special Forces camps under attack by the communists before I left for home in early September.

Camp Duc Lap, just inside Vietnam near the easternmost point of Cambodia, came under attack by a large force of the North Vietnamese Army in mid-August, and was in danger of falling to the enemy. Our sister unit from Pleiku, the II Corps Mike Force, committed a battalion to the battle on 23 August. In spite of valiant fighting by the American and Australian leaders and the Montagnard soldiers of the battalion, the NVA launched a strong assault on the twenty-fifth and captured the north hill of the kidney-shaped camp.

Additional elements from Pleiku were called in, and the Nha Trang Mike Force was given a simply stated—if not so simply executed—directive: "The NVA have the north hill at Duc Lap. Go take it back." They did—J. C. Cooper and Walt Hetzler and all the others—wresting it from the deeply entrenched North Vietnamese soldiers bunker by bunker.

Sergeant Woody, a young medic, assaulted one of the NVA-occupied bunkers alone, charging it with his pump-action shotgun blasting away to keep the enemy down until he could get to the bunker and kill them with a hand grenade. Another of the Mike Force medics, Walt Hetzler, crawled to another of the bunkers as his company commander, J. C. Cooper, blasted away at it with a machine gun. Once he reached the bunker, Hetzler signaled to Cooper to cease fire, then rose and dumped a hand grenade in among the enemy. Another NVA position was taken. And so it went, bunker after bunker on the camp's north hill, until once more it was back in the hands of its rightful occupants. The camp's CIDG defenders, and the Mobile Strike Force soldiers from Pleiku and Nha Trang, supported by devastating air strikes, counted nearly 650 NVA dead during the three days of fierce fighting.

Less than a week later, Camp Ha Thanh was partially overrun by the communists. They were in dire straits, as a 122mm Katusha rocket had scored a direct hit on the team house as the A Team was conducting a meeting to discuss the camp's defense. Most of the team was killed or wounded, and the Mike Force was rushed into the battle.

Stan Dubiel, recently having taken command of one of the battalions after a stint as operations officer, was wounded in the assault to retake the camp, but his company commanders—Talley and Pressley and Reilly—carried on with the assault and retook Camp Ha Thanh from the enemy.

While I processed out of Group Headquarters Company for my return to the States, an order was issued which made me sad for my comrades and fearful for the well-being of the Montagnard and Cham troops I had come to love: an order which directed the "Vietnamization" of the Mobile Strike Force units throughout the country. Beginning at the lower levels of leadership, the Vietnamese Special Forces were to eventually assume command of the Mike Forces. I doubted, with good reason, that it could ever work.

—— 11 ——

By the time the troops returned from the battle of Ha Thanh, I was gone. Bud McBroom and I left together, flying down to Saigon and the out-processing center at Long Binh. We had to stay there for several days, as the chartered aircraft which was to take us "back to the World," to "the Land of the Big PX," was broken down in the Philippines. Planeload after planeload of GIs who were manifested on later flights left before us, as we sat in the little replacement-center officers' club, sipping Crown Royal.

It was during that wait, I believe, that Bud bought himself a watch to replace the one his wife, June, had sent him earlier in the year. Sometime before that, A.P. returned from R&R and presented me with a present—a big wrist-watch with about four hands on it, and several bezel rings around the face which were supposed to tell the reader everything from the time in Timbuctu to the hours left before his combat tour was up. I was mighty impressed with the thing, until about the second day I wore it, when it rained. The crystal clouded up, and the various hands ground to a halt. I was sitting at the bar examining the thing in disgust when Bud said, "Let me have a look at it." He looked it over for a moment, then smashed it to pieces on the stone bar.

It was several months later that June sent him a watch—a beautiful thing, crafted in Switzerland. He was proudly showing it off, and I said, "Hey, that's nice! Let me see it." Before he realized what he was doing, Bud handed it to me. I grinned evilly at him and said, "Remember what you did to *my* watch?" Too late, he remembered, as I smashed it down, the little gears and springs flying everywhere. "Payback is a mother . . ."

Finally we were called to report for boarding for the flight home. We bought a bottle of Crown Royal to see us through the long flight, which I smuggled through customs without getting caught. An airborne infantry lieutenant in front of me was not so fortunate. He was carrying a big plaque on which was mounted a captured AK-47, its barrel chromed and wooden stock shellacked. The Air Force customs man took it from him, ripped the weapon from the wooden plaque, and laid it aside. "Sorry, sir," he said. "No automatic weapons, demilitarized or not."

The poor lieutenant protested vehemently, but there was nothing he could do about it, and tears fell from his eyes as he passed on through with the ravaged plaque, now bearing only a little brass plate declaring, "To the best damn platoon leader in the U.S. Army."

We boarded the Freedom Bird and lifted off the runway of Bien Hoa air base, to the cheers of all aboard.

Nearly a day later, after refueling stops in Japan and Alaska, we touched down at Travis Air Force Base, California. We were home.

Bud and I parted there, he for home and I for the out-processing center where I would be mustered out. We hugged each other, and went our separate ways with the standard Special Forces parting comment of the day: "You sweet motherfucker, don't you never die."

Out-processing was not a glorious affair; no band, no praise for a job well done, not even a handshake or a "good luck" wish, just paperwork, and "do this, do that" from a REMF Spec 6.

The mood was no better at San Francisco International. Between the shootings at Kent State and those at My Lai, it seemed that anyone wearing a uniform was assumed by many to be a murderer. Glares of disgust from well-dressed businessmen led me to wonder how many of them were making a living from companies selling war matériel. There were occasional remarks about my uniform, although they were usually mumbled behind my back, and I quickly learned that such remarks could quickly be ended by staring into the man's eyes and taking a step or two closer. I hoped a nurse would show up in uniform and be subjected to some derisive comment, so that I could beat the shit out of the commenter, but none did. It was a bad feeling, and left me feeling somewhat lonely until I ran into a sergeant first class I knew from my tour in the 6th Special Forces Group. He was heading back for his third tour in Vietnam. I bought him a drink, brought him up-to-date on news of the war, then wished him luck and headed home.

I transferred to another flight in Chicago, marveling with undisguised delight at the latest fad in my homeland, as woman after braless woman jiggled past, breasts swaying and nipples pressing against the fabric of their blouses.

I linked up with a major headed for Fort Eustis, near my home, and when we got to National Airport to await our flight to Newport News, I said, "Man, I gotta straighten up. My wife and family are going to meet me at the airport, and I'm so tired and hung-over, I can barely keep going."

"I know just the thing," he replied, and ordered us each a redeye—beer and tomato juice. It didn't help much. By the time we got to Patrick Henry Airport, I was about to go under, but the sight of my wife and son, and my parents and my sister, brought me back to life for a while. Karen had rented us a motel room in Williamsburg, a cold bottle of champagne beside the bed. I showered, lay down on the bed, and waited for her to join me and consummate the homecoming—and the next thing I knew, she was shaking me and saying, "Wake up, dammit! It's time to check out." Some homecoming. She got even with me by preparing me a home-cooked meal of rice.

For the next several months we led an idyllic life in my parents' old house in Gloucester County, Virginia, while I tried to figure out what I was going to do with the rest of my life. Should I use the GI bill benefits I had earned to get a master's degree, become a schoolteacher or a reporter? I devoured the morning paper each day for news of the war, watched every television newscast I could. The Mike Force had conducted a parachute assault near Nui Coto, I learned, and had again gone to the relief of another besieged Special Forces camp in II Corps. The U.S. units were suffering from a new enemy—drugs. And there I sat. I put in an application with the CIA, hoping to go back to Southeast Asia and work with the army of Meo tribesmen they were running in Laos.

While I waited for my application to be processed, I did a bit of substitute teaching, played with my baby son and his mother, and wrote a few pieces of poetry.

I learned that Larry O'Neil's wound had not healed well and that he was to be medically discharged from the Army, so I wrote a poem for him:

> Limp
> For the rest of your life
> Proudly.
>
> It is your award for valor
> Your badge of courage
> The Purple Heart you'll wear
> Long after the uniform
> Is put away.
>
> It is the symbol of the sacrifice you've made
> For freedom's sake.
>
> You
> Who offered your life
> In freedom's name
> Were made a living monument
> To those who died
> For freedom.

Limp
For the rest of your life
Proudly.

We went to see Karen's parents in Kingsport, Tennessee,
and were invited to a party that one of our college friends, a
fraternity brother of mine named Jerry Beck, was giving.
Like Jerry, many of his guests were lawyers, and I expected
some lively debate about the war and politics and the like.
But most of the conversation centered around the cost of
groceries and of their children's braces. Only Beck seemed
concerned with the *real* issues of the day. Finally, one of his
guests brought up the subject of the distant war, talking
about some friend of his who had refused to go on an
assault, and how wise he thought that was. I excused myself,
collected Karen, and went home.

One day not long after that, Karen came to me and said,
"You're not happy, are you? You sit in front of the television, tearing yourself apart over the news and complaining
about the leadership the guys you love so much are getting
—or not getting. Why don't you do something about it?"

I'll always be grateful to her for that. I went to Washington, D.C., to the Military Personnel Center, and requested a
return to active duty.

"Sure. Where do you want to be assigned before you go
back to Vietnam?"

"Fort Bragg. Special Forces."

"Bad idea. All your time has already been in SF. You need
to go to a conventional unit."

"Look, I'm here because I want to be. I've already fulfilled
my active-duty commitment. If I can't get back into SF, I'll
just take my paperwork and go home."

"Well, all right, then . . . Special Forces it is."

And that was it. I was back in the Army, back in SF.

I went back home and wrote another poem:

My strength returned to me today
I heard a cry from far away—
I think it was a child.

134

MIKE FORCE

I don't know if he called to me
Or cried out to the enemy
But for a while
I heard him weep,
Then something woke me from my sleep.
I fear it was a shot.
I wasn't sure—I woke up fast
And thought I heard an echoed blast
And thought I heard the weeping stop
And heard another awful shot.
My strength is back, and I must run
Toward the sound of that far gun.
I must go there and see.
I must go find the child who wept,
Who called out to me while I slept
Or called the enemy.
It makes no difference whom he called,
Nor yet whose bullet made him fall,
But I must go and stop the gun
And if he lives, show someone cares
For if he's ours or if he's theirs
The child who wept was someone's son.
His cry awakes me, makes my heart
Beat strong, tear petty thoughts apart
His cry disturbs my peace,
Yet gives me strength to do what must be done;
To fight, when all else fails, hot gun to gun,
Till all the world finds peace.

I dug out my uniforms and my green beret, and just after
New Year's Day 1969, we packed up and headed down the
new interstate highway to Fort Bragg.

II

1969–1970

Only the dead know the end of war.

—Plato

—— 12 ——

Fort Bragg had changed little in the year or so since I had left there for my first trip to Vietnam; I had changed considerably. It was not just the way in which I saw myself and the Army and life in general which had changed, but the manner in which I was treated, as well. As custom required, I reported in to the 6th Special Forces Group Headquarters in dress greens, now with the Special Forces patch—a blue arrowhead with a gold sword and three lightning flashes superimposed on it—on the right shoulder of my blouse. This indicated that I had served with Special Forces in combat, and together with the Combat Infantryman's Badge and ribbons above my left breast pocket, brought a degree of respectful treatment which I had not known during my last tour at Fort Bragg.

A few days after I returned to Company B, 6th Special Forces Group—the same company I had served with during my previous tour on Bragg's Smokebomb Hill—I was promoted to Captain and given command of Special Forces Operational Detachment B-64. B Teams are normally commanded by majors, but there was a shortage of officers volunteering for SF, so many of us were assigned to duties which normally would be held by officers of higher rank.

Many of the members of B Company were the same ones I had served with before. Lieutenant Colonel Lancelot Kreuger, a crusty old veteran of World War II, Korea, and Vietnam, with two stars above his CIB, was still the company commander. Many of his senior NCOs were the same ones I had served with before, as well.

A young staff sergeant named Drew Dix, who had left for Vietnam at about the same time I had, was back, and not long after my return, he came to me and asked me something about the special uniform allowance which Medal of Honor winners were authorized.

"Oh, I don't know, Sergeant Dix. I think there *is* some such thing they're given. Why? Do you know someone who's getting a Medal of Honor?"

"Well, yes, sir," Dix answered sheepishly. "I am."

It turned out that he was being awarded the coveted medal for his actions at Chau Duc during the Tet offensive, when time and again he had sortied out to various parts of that city to rescue nurses and others who had been captured by the communists, often taking on groups of enemy soldiers single-handedly.

There were quite a few soldiers at Fort Bragg with whom I had served in Vietnam. Just before Valentine's Day, I was in the PX shopping for a present for Karen when I noticed a very pregnant woman, her head turned mostly away from me, standing at the counter. Something about her reminded me very much of Diane. I had turned back to speak to the saleslady, when I heard a familiar voice say, "Bucky?" It *was* Diane. I stood and looked at her, remembering the Tet offensive, and her troubled sleep the day that I had wanted to slip into bed with her and hold her close to me. But that was a million miles away and a thousand years before, it seemed. And here we both were, in the post exchange at Fort Bragg. We shook hands as if we were two used-car salesmen who had sold cars across the street from each other, then spent a couple of minutes catching up on each other's news. She had married Doc Vargas, who was now stationed at Fort Bragg. He was going to leave the Army soon, and they were going to move to New York and make babies and money.

"Just don't screw it up by sitting on his head," I remarked. We laughed, and said goodbye with the inevitable, "We'll have to get together for a drink." But we never did. That was the last time I saw her.

I did see her hootchmate from 8th Field Hospital, though. Judy had married an OCS classmate of mine, and lived just down the street of the housing area from us. Small world.

For the next few months, much of my time was taken up with the task of training the lieutenants and junior NCOs who continued to report in after graduating from the Special Forces Training Group. As I had done, they were there to spend a while in a Stateside unit before shipping out for the war. Sometimes, after they had been gone for what seemed no time at all, we would get word of the death of one of them, and we would go to one of the NCO clubs or the Green Beret Sport Parachute Club after work to drink to his memory, saying, "Boy, it's a damned shame. That guy really had his shit together," or, "No surprise. The crazy son of a bitch acted like he thought he was going to go win the war by himself."

News of the Mike Force continued to filter in too. They had gone back to the Seven Mountains area of IV Corps, and, with the IV Corps Mike Force, had finally wrested the Nui Coto stronghold from the communists. The operation didn't receive much attention from the news media, which was no surprise, as only a relatively few Americans were killed or wounded in the battle, compared to the number of Americans lost in major battles fought by U.S. units. But for the handful of Special Forces soldiers leading the Mike Force troops in the battle on the rocky slopes of the mountain, the "relatively few" constituted heavy casualties.

Nui Coto had long been in control of the communists under the ethnic Cambodian leader of the VC in the region, a man named Chau Kim. The villages around the base of the two-thousand-foot-high pile of granite were populated by VC sympathizers of Cambodian extraction, lured by Chau Kim into the communist camp with promises that the region would become a part of Cambodia if they assisted his cause. They kept Chau Kim and his soldiers well-supplied with food and information on government troop movements in the area.

For nearly a year, ARVN units had been trying to wrest the mountain away from the enemy, but the huge granite boulders of which Nui Coto was formed, riddled with deep caves which were impervious to artillery and air strikes and infested with snipers and booby traps, had thwarted their efforts. In March, the Nha Trang Mike Force was called upon to fly to IV Corps and take the mountain from Chau Kim's troops.

Most of the enemy troops were concentrated in the ravines and caves of Tuk Chup Knoll, a promontory of Nui Coto rising some 750 feet above the surrounding rice paddies, and during the first half of March, local allied forces conducted operations to seal off access to the knoll to preclude resupply and reinforcement of the communists hidden there.

On the sixteenth, after preparatory strikes by artillery and air which lasted for an hour, the two Mike Force battalions began their assault, with SFC Richmond Nail and the troops of 6th Company leading the way, followed by 4th Company, led by Sergeant John Talley. Initially, they received only sniper fire, but as they worked their way onto and between the giant rocks of the hillside, the enemy unleashed a hail of rifle, machine-gun, rocket, and grenade-launcher fire. In spite of the mounting casualties, the Mike Force troops pressed on toward their objective atop the deadly hill, with the lead elements reaching the summit in just over three hours.

The plan called for them to form a solid line from the base of the hill to its crest. Once that was accomplished, they would sweep around the mountain, rooting the enemy out of their caves, tunnels, and ravines as they went.

Reaching the top was accomplished at no small cost to the Mike Force troops—they had lost seven men killed and forty wounded, many from the devastating fire of a Honeywell hand-cranked automatic grenade launcher the communists had captured from an American mechanized infantry unit. A number of others were wounded by enemy troops hidden fifteen or twenty feet down in the deep crevices between the rocks—shots to the groin delivered as they crossed from one rock to the next.

The combined effects of the torrent of exploding grenades from the Honeywell and the hidden riflemen blasting them from below dealt a severe psychological blow to the strikers, and their American leaders had difficulty getting them to continue the assault. As fragmentation grenades, during previous attempts to capture the mountain, had proved ineffective in the rocky crevices of Nui Coto, the Mike Force troops were carrying concussion grenades. By dropping these into the gaps between the rocks before crossing, they managed to preclude any further casualties from the hidden enemy below them, although the concussion grenades stirred up clouds of persistent, powdered tear gas which had been dropped from the air in prior efforts to discourage the enemy from using the caves and tunnels in the mountain. The gas was an irritating nuisance, and hampered the strikers' efforts to aim their weapons. Fed up with the slow progress, Nail and Talley decided to make a dash for the summit. Calling to their Montagnard troops to follow them, they began hopping from rock to rock, dangerously exposed to sniper fire, but moving quickly enough that they managed to reach the top unhurt.

With 4th and 6th companies now protected by the boulders atop the hill, the enemy snipers turned their weapons toward the troops of SFC Stan McKee's 1st Company, at the base of the mountain.

First Company had been formed of ethnic Vietnamese troops and a cadre of Vietnamese Special Forces leaders, with only two Americans assigned to them. It was part of continuing attempts to "Vietnamize" the Mike Force. It didn't work. After being committed to the continuing assault and beginning to take casualties from heavy sniper fire and rocket-propelled grenades, the Vietnamese strikers became reluctant to move forward. While McKee was preoccupied with trying to reach 2nd Company's Sergeant John Greene, mortally wounded as he attempted to drag one of his injured troops to safety, about half his company sneaked away to the rear, deserting the battle. Even the litter detail McKee had organized to try to help him recover Greene fled. Later, they further disgraced themselves when they were assigned the task of carrying supplies forward to the Montagnard troops fighting on the knoll; instead of taking the badly needed ammunition and supplies forward, they threw them down among the rocks and went back to the safety of the rear.

The snipers, hidden deep within the rocks in well-chosen shaded positions, were taking a heavy toll of the other companies as well. Hearing a call for help from one of 3rd Company's Americans who was pinned down by a sniper, Sergeants Nail, Blanchard, and Talley moved downhill to assist him, followed by a camera-bearing representative from the IV Corps Public Information Office. As they reached the position, the cameraman decided to film the action—and promptly took a round through the chest. From his position nearby, Sergeant Hamp Dews slid down the face of the rock to administer first aid, the sniper's rounds ricocheting off the rocks beside him. The five men, now crouched low in a depression in the rocks together, found themselves pinned down, while Dews worked feverishly to save the wounded man.

Attempting to get into position to fire on the sniper, Rich Nail became his next casualty. A bullet tore through the bridge of his nose, knocking one of his eyes out of the socket. As he grabbed his face and spun, another bullet struck one of his ammunition pouches, setting off two rounds which blasted into his kidney. Having lost in his efforts to revive the dead cameraman, Dews turned his attention to Nail.

"Something's wrong, something's wrong!" Nail kept repeating as he lay beside the dead man while Dews attempted to convince him that his wound was not serious, and kept him from feeling the wound with his fingers. "Something's wrong," he repeated, his unwounded eye looking at Dews. "I see your face, but I see another face too!" His other eye, although blown out of its socket, was still functioning, and Dews soon realized that it was lying on Nail's cheek, looking into the face of the corpse beside him.

In an attempt to find out if the sniper still had their position under observation, Talley reverted to the old trick of placing his helmet on the end of his weapon and raising it above the edge of their hiding place. The sniper drilled the helmet immediately. Above them, their comrades were trying to locate the deadly sniper, moving toward the report of his rifle each time he fired. Staff Sergeant Ben Davan took an M-60 machine gun and crawled on top of a boulder in an attempt to engage the communist marksman. The sniper sighted him first, however, and shot once, hitting Davan in the head and killing him instantly. But Sergeant First Class John Maketa heard the enemy's weapon fire from a position directly beneath him. Strapping a flamethrower on his back and fashioning a harness of rope, he had the flamethrower team from whom he had gotten the weapon lower him to a position beside the point from which he figured the sniper had fired. Once in position, he swung himself out in front of the enemy, killing the deadly sniper with a stream of burning fuel from the flamethrower.

And so it went, with the Mike Force troops slowly but surely rooting the enemy out of the previously impregnable stronghold, until on 26 March they discovered and cleared the main cavern deep within the mountain.

More than two hundred Mike Force troops became casualties in the battle of Nui Coto, including three of their American leaders killed and fourteen wounded. But, as the official After Action Report stated, "After twenty years of enemy domination, the impregnable Tuk Chup Knoll had fallen to government forces. The VC boast of invincibility had been destroyed by the aggressive and audacious fighting" of the Mike Force.

Shades of nearby Nui Khet in April 1970.

In addition to the fifty-three communists known to have died on Nui Coto, ten were captured, and twenty-three more surrendered. More than five hundred weapons and ninety thousand pages of documents were yielded up as well.

That summer, we learned at Fort Bragg that Ben Het was under siege again, with two thousand North Vietnamese, supported by heavy artillery, vying with the camp's CIDG for control of the little fortress. As usual, the Mike Force was called in to hold the enemy off—the II Corps Force's 'Yards deploying there to keep the communists at bay, while the enemy pounded the camp with almost 450 rounds of artillery fire in one day. One thing was different about the siege of Ben Het in the summer of '69, though; it was ended by a relief force of South Vietnamese soldiers arriving at the camp in armored personnel carriers in early July. Perhaps Vietnamization was working, after all.

Meanwhile, though, the Great Rot was eating into the American forces. In August, Colonel Bob Rheault, the 5th Special Forces Group Commander, was thrown into Long Binh jail with seven other members of his command. He didn't have to be there. He could easily have allowed the blame for the "termination with extreme prejudice" of the Vietnamese double agent whose elimination led to the charges of murder and conspiracy against his subordinates and him, to be laid where it belonged—on the head of the civilian official who had ordered it. But that would have been out of character for Rheault. He would rather suffer the indignity of being thrown into jail than allow his troops to be railroaded by the contagion of the times—an attitude among our countrymen that it was all right, somehow, for the enemy to slaughter whomever they wished, but that we Americans had to respond to their ruthlessness with kid-gloved restraint—or at least not get caught at acting like the enemy.

General Abrams may have been well-intentioned in his scapegoatish handling of the "Green Beret Murder Affair," but he destroyed one of the most capable and dedicated officers ever to shit between a pair of jump boots. Colonel Bob Rheault, whom most of us would have followed into hell, resigned his commission and left a void in both leadership and character which must have made Abrams' mentor from World War II, General George Patton, twitch in his grave.

My father died that summer, his last battle a manly fight

with cancer. He fought back hard, holding off its relentless assaults with courage and dignity, until he realized the battle was lost and that its remaining result would be only emotional strain for his wife and family. He surrendered quietly to it then, and was gone. Two more weeks, and he would have lived from the time man first flew until he landed on the moon.

We dressed him in his uniform for the last time, his breast bedecked with campaign ribbons from two wars and more than thirty years of service to his country, and then we buried the old war-horse in the Hampton National Cemetery amongst his kind—American soldiers who had fought in every war from the Revolution on.

Not long after my father died, Ho Chi Minh did too.

I recalled a photo of Daddy taken when he was off killing communists in Korea, standing beside a sign that expressed his sentiments about the death of Joe Stalin. I paraphrased the sign and displayed it in the headquarters of the 6th Special Forces Group not long before I left to go back to Vietnam: "Ho's dead, so they said. Hurrah, hurrah!—that's one less Red."

Orders to Vietnam were waiting for me when I got back to Fort Bragg from my father's funeral. En route, I was to go to Fort Benning for a two-week course entitled "Infantry Officers' Vietnam Orientation Course." I dutifully attended the course and learned that during the ten months I had been away from Vietnam, the VC had remained communist, the NVA still infiltrated down the Ho Chi Minh Trail, the mosquitoes still carried malaria, and the Vietnamese continued to subsist on a diet mainly of rice.

Even the songs the Infantry Officer Candidates were singing were old news, such as the one they sang, as we had, to the tune of "My Bonnie Lies Over the Ocean":

They promised us wings of silver.
They promised us bars of gold.
They made us all second lieutenants,
To die when we're twenty years old.

Ah, yes, TS, to die when we're twenty years o-o-old,
Ah, yes, TS, to die when we're twenty years old.

They told us to go out patrolling.
They said no VC were around.
We found an entire battalion—
They shot every one of us down!

(chorus)

They said Vietnam was exciting,
They said Vietnam was a gas.
Please tell me what's so damned exciting
'Bout punji stakes stuck up your ass?

(chorus)

They said what I learned at Fort Benning
Would make me as smart as a fox,
But Charlie's a little bit smarter—
They're shipping me home in a box!

By then, I had about decided to make a career of the Army, and since I was going back to Vietnam to fill an allocation to Special Forces, I went to the Infantry branch representative at Fort Benning and requested that I be assigned to a conventional American unit; after all, it was the Infantry-branch people who were insisting that it was detrimental to an officer's career to spend more than one or two tours in SF, and I had already spent three. Besides, I wanted the experience of leading American soldiers in combat.

"No sweat," the branch rep declared. "We have to send you back on this SF allocation, since we don't have enough Special Forces qualified officers to send. But since you're on your second tour, you'll be able to get your choice of units when you get in country—if not your first choice, then certainly your second."

Sure enough, when I got to the replacement center at Long Binh two weeks later, I was given a preference statement to fill out. In order of preference, I listed the First Cav, the 101st Airborne, the 173rd Airborne Brigade, the 11th Armored Cav, and 5th Special Forces Group. Within the hour, my orders were posted: Burruss, Lewis H., Jr., 05331711, Captain, Infantry; assigned to 5th Special Forces Group (Airborne), 1st Special Forces.

Well, to hell with career development. If I was needed in SF, so be it. That's where my buddies were anyway, and four straight tours in Special Forces couldn't be much worse for my career than three. No problem.

I did have one small problem, though. I had caught a cold during my trip back to the war zone. Also, I had decided that, unlike my last time in country, I would be prudent about taking antimalaria pills. The big orange ones, until the user's system got accustomed to them, had a most unpleasant side effect—diarrhea. For the next several days, every time I was unable to stifle a sneeze, I shit in my trousers.

While I waited at Bien Hoa air base for a flight to Nha Trang, with damp, chafing trousers I had rinsed out after one such sneezing episode, I ran into Tommy Batchelor. He was assigned to the Mike Force again, and he had good news: the team needed officers. They were on an operation back down at Camp Thien Ngon, and both battalion commanders were scheduled to leave soon. Maybe I could get my old battalion back.

When I reported in to the assistant adjutant at Group Headquarters in Nha Trang, he took my records, stepped into the Adjutant's office, and returned a moment later to inform me that I was to be assigned as the Public Information Officer. Bullshit. I pointed out to him that I was a Mike Force officer, that I knew the team had vacancies, and that—goddammit—I was not going to be the Group PIO. He went back into his boss's office and returned to say that I could go back to the team—Detachment B-55, 5th Mobile Strike Force Command.

When I got over to the Mike Force compound, I discovered that Major John Nix, who had been my faculty adviser in the Special Forces Officers' Course, was the team leader, but that he would be leaving soon. His replacement, Lieutenant Colonel Sid Hinds, was already on board. But Nix gave me the news I wanted most to hear: after the Thien Ngon operation, I would be taking over A-503—1st Battalion, 5th MSF.

Before getting completely processed in, I flew down to Thien Ngon to see what was going on and to see my old teammates and meet my new ones. I was picked up at the landing zone by one of my favorite strikers—a Cham named Khoe, who had been the indigenous platoon leader of Sammy Coutts's platoon in 7th Company. Khoe was one of the bravest soldiers and best leaders I have ever met. He was a deeply religious man, and he believed that his faith made him impervious to enemy bullets. I recall seeing him in firefights, running up and down the line of his platoon, getting his troops firing and up into the assault, with people all around him being hit and Khoe never being touched. I found it hard to believe that he had ended up as a truck driver in Headquarters Company, so I found a Cham interpreter and asked him how that had happened. It seemed that he had gone to the new American commander of 7th Company and informed him that he felt he needed to go back home for a few days to see his village priest and get himself right with his God. The new American, not understanding the depth of Khoe's faith, had refused his request —something Coutts and Ken Roberts would never have done—but Khoe had, of course, gone home anyway. So he had been fired from 7th Company, depriving the Chams of their best leader. I resolved to rectify that situation as soon as possible.

As I wandered around the Mike Force positions to see my old teammates again—John Talley and "Nick" Nicholas and Tommy Batchelor and the others—I came upon a group of Koho strikers. "Oh, Dai Ui Buc-Key! 'One man bang-bang, one man no bang-bang!'" one grinning 'Yard said, reminding me of my first firefight nearly two years earlier, when I had tried to control their rate of fire with that simplified phrase. It had been the young Koho's baptism by fire as well, and we both remembered and shared a hug.

Then he led me over to another Koho striker, and I recognized him as the one who had been wounded in the head that day and had sat stunned in the road until Don Poncin went into the killing zone to get him, showing me what an American Mike Force leader was expected to do for his troops. And here the young man was, back on the battlefield. I shared an embrace with him.

I also met some of the Americans who had come to the team since I had left: Sergeant Major "Jaw" Taylor; Master Sergeant Paul Soublet, the Intelligence Sergeant; Joe Halligan, one of the medics; and the Intelligence Officer, Captain Frank McNutt. I took a liking to McNutt immediately. He was serious about his job, but had a sense of humor, and he got along well with the NCOs. He had been with the team since their tough battle on Nui Coto earlier in the year, and had won a Bronze Star for valor in that action.

I flew back to Nha Trang, finished in-processing, drew my weapon and equipment, and returned to Thien Ngon to go to work. While I was gone, the B Detachment Logistics Officer (S-4) was bitten by a poisonous spider and evacuated to the hospital. As the whole force was to move to the Special Forces camp at Katum to conduct operations there within the next few days, Colonel Hinds directed me to take over the S-4 duties temporarily. I was to see that a fire base was built there and that the team's equipment was moved in. He had decided to leave Lieutenant Burt, who was doing a good job of running the battalion, as the CO for the remainder of the operation in III Corps.

The last of the troops to leave Thien Ngon for Katum, Sergeant First Class Sam Huggins and his Combat Reconnaissance Platoon, had one more contact before leaving. The enemy had drawn them to the trenches of a former French position by baiting them with light contacts. Instead of occupying the abandoned trenches, however, Sam had his troops occupy new positions nearby. It was a good thing; as they settled in for the night, the enemy fired a massive barrage of mortar fire onto the old French position, assuming that the Mike Force troops had occupied the ready-made trenches there. They then followed up their mortar attack with a ground assault on the position, but were driven off by Huggins' troops, while his battalion commander responded with artillery counter-battery-fire onto the enemy mortars.

It felt good to be back at work where the results were always so obvious, and I worked hard at it. We got the fire base set up, put in bunkers and defensive wire, and built revetments for our ammunition and for the aircraft of the FACs who were working with us. Once we got set up, I went out with Frank McNutt on helicopter-borne "sniffer" missions to try to locate enemy concentrations in the area. "Sniffer" was the name given to a device mounted on the chopper which was supposed to be able to detect the presence of human beings by collecting and chemically analyzing the air over which it passed. The helicopter would fly at treetop level over the jungle, and where there were high concentrations of ammonia—a product of human perspiration—the indicator needle of the sniffer would jump, supposedly pinpointing the location of troops. It never did meet with much success in its intended mission— especially as a few ounces of bird shit gave as high a reading as a platoon of troops. Even McNutt's idea of dropping *Playboy* centerfolds into the area to make the VC sweat more probably wouldn't have worked.

They were exciting flights, though, as Red Stevens, the young warrant officer flying the Huey helicopter, skimmed the treetops with the skids of his aircraft. On one occasion, we scared up a large deer and, hoping to put some venison on the mess-tent tables, we opened up on him with three automatic weapons. He was last seen crossing into Cambodia untouched, dragging numerous jungle vines which had become entangled in his antlers.

There wasn't much action stirred up at Katum that trip, although we got mortared a few times. The residents of the camp—which they had nicknamed "Kaboom"—seemed to think that there was a VC mortar gunnery school across the border in Cambodia, and that the enemy used their camp as a target for beginners. When a mortar attack would start, some of the team members would run up on top of the team bunker to show their contempt for the enemy gunners.

During one such attack, I went up with Larry Jackson and John Talley to watch the show. Suddenly there was a loud boom from a short distance outside the wire, and an object which looked the size of a 55-gallon drum came arching out of the jungle toward us, detonating within the camp in a huge cloud of dirt and black smoke. Jackson, Talley, and I were back inside the bunker a few short seconds later.

Martha Raye came out to Kaboom to visit us one night. Maggie was no stranger to the Mike Force—she spent much of the war visiting "her" Green Berets, and was always a welcome break from such news as Jane Fonda manning the antiaircraft guns of our North Vietnamese enemies, and students rioting in the streets in protest of our presence in Vietnam. So when it was discovered that there was no vodka in the camp—Maggie had a fondness for a taste of vodka from time to time—we were more than pleased to dispatch Red Stevens and his Huey to Tay Ninh to pick up a jug for her.

Stevens was not unlike many of the young chopper pilots who flew in the Vietnam war—full of skill and courage and a boldness which led often to the accomplishment of impossible missions, but all too often to untimely deaths.

There was an enemy antiaircraft position on the approach to the airstrip at Katum, and it had scored hits several times on aircraft landing at the camp. A Cobra gunship pilot from a nearby unit decided that he would go find the position and solve the problem. He found the position, all right, one day when McNutt and I were out with Stevens on a sniffer mission, and promptly got himself shot down. Stevens swooped in and picked him up. About a week later, the Cobra pilot went back for revenge. The enemy shot him down again. Stevens, his crew chief, Paul Soublet, and I were near Red's Huey when the Mayday call came, so Red hopped in the pilot's seat, his crew chief jumped into the copilot's seat beside him, and Soublet and I climbed into the back to ride along as door gunners. As soon as the rotors were turning fast enough to get us off the ground, Red "pulled pitch," and flying at treetop level, sped to the rescue. We spotted the burning Cobra and landed nearby.

The downed pilot said that he and his copilot gunner were being pursued, so when they appeared from the tree line with their pistols drawn, I decided to pull the minor-hero bit and ran to the tree line to cover their dash to the chopper. They ran by me, pointing to the jungle behind them, where I saw movement in the vegetation. I flipped my M-16 onto automatic and squeezed the trigger to loose a burst at the pursuing enemy—and a single round popped off. Oh, shit. My magazine had fallen out. I took what I felt was appropriate immediate action—and beat the gunship crew back to Red's Huey.

I felt like a damned fool, but I must say that the poor gunship pilot who had gotten himself shot down by the same antiaircraft position twice in one week must have felt like an even bigger fool. The problem of the AAA position was solved shortly after that, however, by a flight of B-52 bombers.

The relative lack of enemy contact around Katum at the time made it no place for the Mike Force, so we packed up and moved back to Nha Trang to await our next mission.

—— 13 ——

Back in Nha Trang, Lieutenant Colonel Hinds complimented me on jumping in and doing a good job as the S-4, adding, to my disappointment, that he was going to leave me in that job for a while and allow Lieutenant Burt to finish the short time left in his tour as the 1st Battalion commander. I could take over the battalion when Burt left, he said. But at about the time that was to have happened, Hinds left to take command of A Company, the SF company in charge of all the camps in III Corps.

His replacement was Lieutenant Colonel Homer Lynch, whose on-the-ground style of leadership gave us the feeling that we would do well under his command. But he ran afoul of the Vietnamese Special Forces commander, and they managed to get him transferred away not long after his arrival.

Lynch was replaced by Lieutenant Colonel Charles Black, a Military Intelligence Corps officer who had been serving as head of the 5th Group Intelligence Section (S-2). Black decided that he, too, would leave me in the S-4 job "for a while," until he had a chance to evaluate the team. I began to wonder if I would ever get the opportunity to command a Mike Force battalion again.

One morning I awoke shivering, with a splitting headache and with my bed soaked in sweat. In a daze I wandered over to the dispensary, where K'phe, the Montagnard nurse, sat me down and popped a thermometer into my mouth. Discovering that I had a burning temperature of 105 degrees, Joe Halligan rushed me over to 8th Field Hospital. There the medics immediately put me into a tub of ice water to bring my body temperature down, as a 105-degree fever can quickly lead to brain damage. I've never been so miserable in my life as I was for the next week or so. After the ice-water bath got my temperature down to a safe level, it was still necessary for me to lie on a refrigerated pad to keep it there. The doctors were unable to determine what strain of malaria I had contracted, and time after time for the next several days the medics came by and drew vials of blood from me for testing, as I lay there shivering. I was so miserably ill that I didn't care if I died or not.

Finally the fever broke and I was able to eat and drink again, and they pulled the intravenous feeding tubes out of me. I had lost almost twenty pounds from my already slight body. So much for the religious taking of malaria prophylaxis.

Before I left 8th Field Hospital, I stopped by to see another guy from the team who had been hospitalized, to see how he was doing. "I'm doing fine," he remarked, "but see that poor bastard over there?" He pointed across the ward to a young paratrooper from the 101st Airborne Division, who was lying there with his head encased in a thick layer of bandages. "Guess what happened to him?"

"I give up . . . what happened to him?" I asked.

"You'll have to ask him. You wouldn't believe me if I told you."

A nurse came by about then, so I said, "Excuse me, Lieutenant, but could you tell me what happened to that guy over there with the bandages on his head?"

She looked over at the trooper from the 101st Airborne, then back at me, and said, "Him? You wouldn't believe me if I told you. You'll have to ask him yourself." She went about her duties.

My curiosity had the better of me now, so I walked over to the soldier and said, "I'm sorry to bother you, trooper, but would you tell me what happened to you?"

He looked up at me. "You wouldn't believe me if I told you," he answered.

"Aw, come on," I implored. "It couldn't be *that* unbelievable. Now, tell me, what the hell happened to you?"

Reluctantly he explained that he had been outside his company perimeter with another soldier on a listening post, to provide early warning to the company in the event the enemy attempted to probe the perimeter. In the middle of the night, he thought he heard something to his front, and he craned his neck forward in an attempt to hear better. The next thing he knew, something clamped onto his skull and began to shake him violently about. It was a tiger, and if his buddy hadn't killed the giant cat with his rifle, no doubt it would have dragged the young American off into the jungle and made a meal of him. As it was, the animal's big teeth had punctured his skull in four places.

"You gotta be kidding!" I exclaimed.

"See?" the trooper retorted. "I *told* you you wouldn't believe me!"

Christmas was approaching by the time I returned from the hospital, and we began to get into the spirit—wondering, however, if we would be called out to react to some flagrant communist violation of the truce, as usual.

With the Christmas season came the singing of Mike Force Yuletide "carols," such as "Rat-a-tat-tat," which was sung to the tune of "Jingle Bells":

> Rat-a-tat-tat, rat-a-tat-tat,
> Mow those bastards down,
> Oh, what fun it is to have
> The Mike Force back in town.
>
> Driving through the streets
> In a black Mercedes Benz,
> Killing all the dinks,

Saving all our friends,
Machine guns all ablaze,
Oh, what a glorious sight!
Oh, what fun it is to have
The Mike Force back tonight!

Oh, mortar rounds, hand grenades,
VC in the grass,
Take your "Merry Christmas"
And shove it up your ass!

That would soon be followed by another "carol," such as
the Special Forces version of "The Twelve Days of Christmas":

On the first day of Christmas the VC gave to me
A sniper in a palm tree.
On the second day of Christmas the VC gave to me
Two hand grenades and a sniper in a palm tree . . .

I was anxious for news from home, for Karen and I were
expecting another child around Christmastime. Finally, on
New Year's Eve 1969, the good news arrived: Karen had
given birth on the twenty-ninth to a healthy baby girl,
named, as my dad had suggested on his deathbed, after my
mother, Frances Charlotte. That was something to celebrate
in addition to the New Year, and we did so.

Frank McNutt was going home on extension leave the
next day, and I had agreed to drive him down to Cam Ranh
Bay to catch his flight. I stayed up all night celebrating the
New Year and the new daughter, and when I went to Frank's
room to wake him up, he didn't seem to want to get out of
bed. Frank was suffering from an infestation of ringworm,
and his anus had been itching him so badly that he had
gotten into the habit of rolling up a towel and sawing it back
and forth between his legs in an effort to relieve the
maddening itch. His butt was raw from this improvised
treatment, and now he lay there on his bunk facedown,

158

naked, and asleep. There was a can of Manpower spray deodorant on the table beside his bunk, so I took it, spread the cheeks of his buttocks, and gave him a long burst from the spray can. He was up in a flash, mad as hell and ready to fight, and dancing around at the burning pain in his rear end. But we got him off to Cam Ranh air base, and he reported, when he returned from leave, that the ringworm hadn't bothered him since.

The 1969–70 truce period was fairly calm, for a change, and with both battalions in camp, our sergeant major, Ben "Jaw" Taylor, had his hands full trying to keep his somewhat rowdy subordinates in hand.

There was a curfew in effect, and everyone not on official business had to be off the streets of Nha Trang before midnight. Bill Llewellyn got stopped by a young Military Policeman while heading back to the team from town after curfew. For some reason, he had his socks—white ones—around his neck, so when the MP halted him, Bill put his finger to his mouth and said, "Shhh!" Pointing to the socks around his neck, he whispered, "White-sock alert. I'm on white-sock alert." The MP looked at him quizzically, and Llewellyn added, "You *do* know what a white-sock alert is, don't you?"

Not wanting to seem uninformed, the cop answered, "Well, sure . . . white-sock alert. Carry on." Llewellyn winked, and went sneaking off into the shadows as if on a mission of great importance. When he spotted an American crackerbox ambulance passing by, he flagged it down and asked the driver if he could catch a ride back to the hospital.

"I'm not going back," the driver answered, "but I'll tell you what . . . for ten bucks, I'll sell you this thing." So Llewellyn paid the soldier ten dollars and drove the brand-new ambulance back to the compound. It was in the motor pool several days later, its identifying bumper numbers and red crosses being painted over en route to becoming the Mike Force beach buggy, when a couple of Criminal Investigation Division agents showed up to reclaim the stolen vehicle. "We found it abandoned near here," I explained to the skeptical CID men. "We were just repainting it to keep the guys in the motor pool busy until somebody showed up to claim it." They took our would-be beach buggy away.

In the team house during such slack periods, practical jokes were the order of the day. Shaving-cream ambushes were sprung on unsuspecting passersby, toilet bowls were covered over with nearly invisible plastic wrap, and teammates who liked to use such periods to jog around the area were liable to pull on their jockstraps to discover that the inside had been smeared with analgestic balm or insect repellent, which produces severe, if temporary, inflammation and burning on sensitive body parts.

But perhaps the classic joke was pulled on Sergeant Major Taylor by Sergeants Bill Scruggs and Jack Tobin. Taylor's room had an overhead fan on the ceiling, which was controlled by a switch beside the door. When he entered, he would switch on the fan to create a cooling breeze. While he was out one day, Tobin and Scruggs taped smoke grenades to the blades of the fan and tied the straightened safety pins off. When the sergeant major returned and switched on the fan, the blades turned, the pins were pulled, and the room was soon filled with thick, acrid clouds of yellow, green, and violet smoke. The resultant powdery residue covered everything in the big, mean Taylor's room. Jaw was furious, and devoted countless hours to trying to figure out who had laid the smoke-grenade ambush. But—until now, at least—he never discovered who the culprits were.

But then the holiday truce ended, and it was time to return to the business of killing communists. Captain Chuck Randall, now commanding 2nd Battalion, took his troops to the swamps of IV Corps and took on the Viet Cong who were in almost undisputed control of the Ca Mau Peninsula —the southeastern tip of the Republic of Vietnam. He gave them hell, and supported by Navy boats and helicopter gunships, set the enemy 'way back in what had been one of their sanctuaries. On one occasion, he and three of his subordinate leaders, Sergeant First Class Sam Huggins and Staff Sergeants Clark and Thompson—two of Huggins's platoon leaders—were conducting a visual reconnaissance of an area they were going to patrol the next day. The pilot of the helicopter from which they were conducting their VR spotted three sampans that had been pulled up into a mangrove thicket beside one of the many canals in the area, and camouflaged. Deciding to seize the moment and check the boats out with the lightly armed leaders of Huggins's company, Randall directed the chopper pilot to fly them to a small field a short distance across the canal from where they had spotted the suspicious sampans. On the way in to the landing zone, the chopper came under automatic-weapons fire from a position near the boats, but Randall and his three NCOs jumped off the chopper and moved toward the enemy location as the helicopter flew away to avoid battle damage.

They approached the canal bank across from the VC sampans and, as they crossed the small canal, came under enemy fire. Huggins and Thompson returned fire, while Clark and Randall continued on to the sampans and climbed into them. As the enemy fire increased in intensity, Clark discovered that the sampan he had boarded was loaded with cans of gasoline and enemy weapons and equipment. It was a welcome discovery, because the little party, with only a few magazines of ammunition among them because of their aerial-reconnaissance mission, were running low on ammo from their fight with the much larger Viet Cong force. The impromptu raiders seized the enemy weapons and held the communists at bay while they ransacked the sampans, capturing four or five pounds of valuable documents and a number of weapons, including two rocket-propelled grenade launchers and a quantity of rockets. After half an hour they withdrew with their booty and boarded the chopper which had returned to pick them up. It was an incredibly productive raid, as the documents included photographs of virtually all of the VC infrastructure in the province.

Randall called for an air strike on the enemy position, but when he was told that no tactical air support was available, decided to send two of his platoons to the position under Huggins's command. As Huggins and his force approached the area that evening, they learned—the hard way—that higher headquarters managed to find some tac air after all. Just as Sam was about to launch an assault on the enemy position, a set of fighters arrived and, without being aware of the Mike Force presence nearby, delivered a devastating strike on the communists' location. The Mike Force troops were so close that, had it not been for the fact that the bombs bored into the mud before exploding, they would have taken casualties from the bombs' fragments. "Close only counts in hand grenades and horseshoes." And air strikes in the mud of IV Corps.

A few days later, Randall's troops were out on another operation, and ambushed another group of sampans on one of the canals. In one of the sampans was a child—a little girl—who ended up floundering in the muddy canal. The Mike Force medic on the ambush, Specialist Green, dived into the river with the enemy around her, and rescued her. It was one of those enigmatic situations that American soldiers faced in Vietnam, where the enemy—and the CIDG and South Vietnamese soldiers as well—sometimes took their dependents with them. The actions of young Specialist Green in that confusing and difficult situation, as those of Nick LaNotte's were when he rescued children in Nha Trang during the Tet offensive of 1968, were not isolated examples of the sort of gallantry displayed by American soldiers in that war. But they were, unfortunately, examples of acts of bravery which were ignored only because there were no television cameras present to record the spectacular footage. The recorded footage of a burning monk or of a VC assassin being summarily executed by an official in Saigon was, after all, much more salable than video pictures of some country boy like Sam Huggins standing in front of the camera explaining how his young medic had saved a little Vietnamese girl from drowning in the middle of a firefight. But then, there never *were* many television cameras out where such actions took place.

Huggins's company had one more notable action down in the swampy Ca Mau Peninsula before they were replaced by another of Randall's companies. One evening, while sweeping through the enemy-infested swamps, he dispatched a squad to establish an ambush position some distance away, under the command of Sergeant Brown. En route, the squad bumped into a communist unit's bunker complex and, jumping into a narrow canal for cover, got pinned down. Huggins and another of his NCOs, Sergeant Johnson, responded to Brown's call for assistance with a platoon of strikers. They reached the pinned-down squad's position, where Huggins found that their main problem was that they couldn't get up the slick, steep banks of the canal. The taller Americans jumped the canal and assaulted the VC positions with weapons blazing, enabling the little 'Yards to help each other crawl up the canal bank and join the assault. As a result, the enemy position was overrun. The final tally from 2nd Battalion's operations in the swamps and marshes of IV Corps during their early 1970 foray included eleven enemy soldiers captured, along with sixteen bodies of the scores of communists killed by their operations, and the capture of more than one hundred mines and rockets, as well as the destruction of seventy-four sampans.

It was during Chuck's operations in IV Corps that Black and his new Operations Officer, Captain Timothy Boone, went down to observe 2nd Battalion in action. Not long after their arrival there, we got a message directing us to submit their names for the award of the Combat Infantryman's Badge. As there had been no report of significant contact by Randall, I called down there on the KWM-2 radio we used for long-range voice communications, to see what the story was. I learned that Black and Boone had been along with a patrol that had encountered a couple of VC at some considerable distance, and that the 'Yards had fired a few shots at them. I had some question about the validity of the award of the CIB under those circumstances, so I went to the 5th Group Deputy Commander, Lieutenant Colonel Charlie Norton, about it. Norton, one of the original officers of U.S. Special Forces, fired off a message to Black indicating that there was some question about the validity of awarding a Military Intelligence Corps officer the Combat Infantryman's Badge. He recommended that Black resubmit a request for the award of a "CSB"—a "Combat Spook Badge."

I found Lieutenant Colonel Black to be a difficult man to work for—a stickler for paperwork and an officer whose style of leadership struck me as brusque, sarcastic, and out of place in what had been a closely knit team whose main concern was killing communists. I saw little sense, for example, in the need to change the monthly report on the number and condition of our steel Conex shipping containers from a telephonic report—all that was required by the Group logistics section—to a lengthy written report. Black saw otherwise, and kept kicking the report back for various reasons until he was finally satisfied with the flawlessly typed, thirty-six-page report I produced—complete with Polaroid photographs of every Conex container for which we were accountable. When the report got to Group Headquarters, the warrant officer in charge of such reports called to ask me what the hell he was supposed to do with the thing, and asked that, from then on, I either revert to sending in telephonic reports or reduce the written report to something usable.

I was not alone in my distaste for Colonel Black, so some of us devised what was known as the "500 code," which we secretly distributed to like-minded members of the team. The code was a series of numbers beginning with 500, each of which stood for a particular phrase. For example, "501" announced over the compound's public-address system would mean, "Look busy, staff; Black is back on the compound." "505," muttered by one of us during one of his frequent meetings, meant, "Back me up, guys; I'm about to tell the son of a bitch a lie."

Black had a habit of "beating around the bush," of speaking allegorically instead of coming right to the point he was trying to make. McNutt developed a technique called "dumbing him," which we used with considerable success. When we found the colonel leading up—in his usual roundabout way—to something with which we disagreed, or which we didn't want to accept, we would drop our mouths open, wrinkle our brows, cock our heads to one side, and stare dumbly at him. Usually, seeing that he wasn't getting through to us, he would try to make his point from some other indirect approach. If we "dumbed him" again, he would often just roll his eyes back, drop the subject, and start in on something else.

Probably the most difficult problem we had during Black's tenure as the B Detachment Commander was the result of his efforts to "Vietnamize" the Mike Force. It wasn't his decision, as it was the official policy, by then, to turn the war over to the Vietnamese that year. But it wasn't going to work—not with Montagnard strikers whose loyalties were with the Americans and their underground liberation movement, FULRO. A year or so prior, at the insistence of the Vietnamese, there had been an attempt made to field a couple of Mike Force companies more likely to respond to Vietnamese command. One company was composed of ethnic Vietnamese, and the other of ethnic Chinese from Cholon, the "Chinatown" of Saigon. Neither company had performed well in combat, though, so the team had found it necessary to go back to the sources of reliable fighters—Chams and Montagnards—in order to be able to perform missions such as the recovery of camps which had been overrun by the North Vietnamese, or the wresting away of enemy strongholds at places like Nui Coto. As long as there were Americans out at the isolated little garrisons, they deserved to have a reaction force reliable enough to come to their assistance when they were under attack by large North Vietnamese formations.

The Vietnamese Special Forces—Luc Luong Dac Biet— were largely incapable of getting the Mike Force troops to perform well for two basic reasons. First, they were generally of poor quality; many of their officers received commissions only because of family or political ties to the hierarchy, and I suspect that many of the LLDB noncommissioned officers were there only to take advantage of all the additional benefits associated with working with the well-supplied American Special Forces. There were exceptions, of course; Tran Hu Hung, who had been O'Neil's and Clark's counterpart, was a brave and dedicated Northerner whose family had fled from their Hanoi home when the country was partitioned after the defeat of the French. He desperately wanted his homeland to be free from the communists, and he eventually died in battle as a result of his aggressiveness and dedication. But he was an exception.

The second reason for their inability to successfully lead the 'Yards was the fact that, after generations of mistreatment at the hands of the Vietnamese, who still referred to them as *moi*—"savages"—the highlanders hated them. Even the Chams had joined FULRO—the French acronym for "United Front for the Struggle of the Oppressed Races" —which was the secret underground organization dedicated to Montagnard independence.

Khoe, the courageous Cham who was by then the leader of the two Cham Mike Force companies, invited me to his hootch for dinner one night. There, he explained to me that after several centuries of feuding between his people and the Montagnards—the legend being that the feuding had resulted from a Cham marrying a Rhade princess, then murdering her—he had gained FULRO's confidence and was being allowed to lead his people into their underground organization. He wanted to know whether I could supply him with a few thousand blasting caps to put into the FULRO coffers.

"What are they to be used for, Khoe?" I asked him through his interpreter.

"To kill Vietnamese," he replied.

"North Vietnamese or South Vietnamese?" I asked.

"Both," he answered. "They're all the same."

I explained to him that, once we defeated the communists, we would see what could be done to assist in their struggle for equality. But first we had to work together to defeat the communists. I wish now that I had given him the blasting caps.

At any rate, the first real attempt at an LLDB-run operation came shortly before Easter 1970. We were ordered to deploy 1st Battalion down to the B Team camp at Chi Lang, in IV Corps, where we were to conduct combined operations with the IV Corps Mike Force in the vicinity of the nearby Nha Bang Woods—the "Bang Bang Woods," as the local Americans called it.

The LLDB ("Look Long, Duck Back" or "Little Lousy Dirty Bastards," as they were at times referred to by some of the Americans) made their plan, issued their operations order, and the troops moved out to commence the operation.

Shortly afterward, many of the Rhade strikers in Ron Franklin's 1st Company refused to go any farther under LLDB planning and leadership. Arguing that they had joined the Mike Force to fight for the Americans, not the Vietnamese, they simply quit.

Black went out and gave them a heated scolding, telling the rebellious 'Yards that they were South Vietnamese citizens just like the LLDB, and ordering them, in no uncertain terms, to carry on with the operation. That was the wrong argument to use with the independence-minded hill tribesmen, but Franklin was nevertheless able to persuade most of his company to continue the mission, reminding them that the LLDB would probably disappear when the first round was fired, anyway. Ron had a lot of credibility with the Montagnards. He already had about four years' experience working with them, and was even an honorary member of FULRO.

Around thirty of the 1st Company troops still refused to go, however, so we took them back to Chi Lang and put them in an isolated corner of the camp, where I had set up my supply point.

Out in the Nha Bang Woods, the rest of 1st Battalion, commanded by Captain Jim Ficken, was operating in conjunction with an ARVN cavalry troop, and soon had a series of sharp firefights going. The 1st Company "quitters" helped me hump ammunition out to the choppers that were ferrying it to Nick Nicholas's forward mortar positions, from which he was firing hundreds of 81mm mortar rounds in support of Ficken's troops. The surgeon from Chi Lang wanted to watch the mortars in action, so we took one of the resupply helicopters out there. Two things you could always count on from Nicholas and his Nung mortar crews were the most accurate and responsive fire support in Vietnam, and a cup of freshly brewed coffee. It was always a pleasure to watch Nick and his boys raining mortar rounds exactly where and when they were requested, and the wiry old Maine Indian won many a fight for the Mike Force.

Back at the B Team camp in Chi Lang, the communists were delivering mortar and rocket attacks themselves, regularly hitting the camp, the airfield, and a nearby South Vietnamese Army training center. One round had hit a C-7 Caribou aircraft dead in the nose as it taxied down the runway, destroying the plane and blocking the runway for the time being. It was going to be a noisy Easter—although we didn't discover just *how* noisy until early on Easter morning.

Long before dawn on that holy day, a platoon or so of Viet Cong sappers—demolitionists who possessed an uncanny knack for being able to crawl through defensive wire entanglements undetected—approached the camp at the point at which their earlier reconnaissance had evidently indicated the camp was least-well-defended. A number of them were most of the way through the defenses and near the berm of the camp's perimeter before they were detected. Unfortunately for them, the point they had chosen to penetrate the camp was near the corner in which we had placed the 1st Company quitters. When the sappers were detected and taken under fire, the VC support element opened up with machine guns and rocket-propelled grenades, and a heavy battle was soon under way. While the members of the B Team scrambled from their bunks to their battle positions on the inner perimeter, the Mike Force troops began to pour fire into the sappers in the wire, and their supporting weapons' positions outside the camp. Two of our NCOs from the Mike Force were wounded early in the fight. One, a medic, dashed into a machine-gun bunker on the outer perimeter and began blazing away at the VC, when a rocket-propelled grenade hit the bunker. He ran out of the position with his hands over his ears, circled around behind it a couple of times, then ran back in and commenced firing again. Our other casualty occurred when one of our NCOs ran to a 60mm mortar pit between the inner and outer perimeters of the camp and began putting up illumination rounds to assist the defenders in spotting the enemy. Apparently someone on the inner perimeter thought he was a Viet Cong and threw a hand grenade into the mortar pit with him, wounding him severely.

Meanwhile, Master Sergeant Bill Llewellyn, the team sergeant of A-503, 1st Battalion's American Special Forces team, was up on the berm in the midst of the heavy firefight. He was running back and forth along the berm, killing sappers in the wire. As he would empty the magazine of his weapon, someone—he never did learn who—would pass another loaded M-16 up to him, and he would empty it into the enemy soldiers who were continuing to attempt to penetrate into the camp. Llewellyn said later that it re-minded him of the old cowboy-and-Indian movies, when the wagon train was under attack and the men would defend their circled wagons while their wives reloaded the rifles and passed them back up to their men.

At one point, though, Bill ran out of rifle ammo just as he encountered a stunned sapper outside the machine-gun bunker where the medic was located. As Llewellyn reached for the .45 pistol on his hip, the communist recovered and reached for his AK-47. Bill won the draw, emptying his pistol into the enemy soldier just a few feet away.

One of the VC who reached the interior of the camp ran to the nearby dispensary, grabbed a litter leaning against it, and ran back to the wire in an apparent attempt to recover one of his wounded comrades. It was a courageous act, but we still can't figure out whom he expected to carry the other end of the litter for him.

At daylight, there were twenty-two dead communists in the wire. Our troops had suffered only two wounded.

But a couple of days later, out on Nui Khet, a rocky mountain that rose about seven hundred feet out of the Nha Bang Woods five or six miles from Chi Lang, it was a much different story.

—— 14 ——

Atop the rocky mountain known as Nui Khet was a small Regional Forces outpost which the Viet Cong had overrun while the RF troops had gone to town, leaving only a couple of men to defend it. The VC had captured a large quantity of ammunition on the outpost, including a couple of 55-gallon drums of hand grenades which the Regional Forces had put there to throw down onto attackers. The communists were now putting the munitions to good use, and managed to drive off a unit of the IV Corps Mike Force which had made an attempt to recapture the hilltop outpost.

The Vietnamese plan was to recapture the mountain with our 1st Battalion and a battalion of the IV Corps Mobile Strike Force, after firing a 155mm artillery preparation on the peak. The battalion attack positions, it turned out, were on the far side of Nui Khet from the artillery positions, but along the gun-target line. The first round of the artillery prep was a white phosphorous marking round, which landed in the IV Corps Mike Force attack position. Some of the IV Corps troops couldn't figure out what was going on, but those who did quickly realized that it was a long round from the 155's, and that it might be followed by others, and they got the hell out of the area—fast! Those who didn't realize what might happen next were subjected to a devastating barrage of "friendly" 155mm high-explosive fire. Many of the unsuspecting troops were killed, and many others were wounded. It was a foolish, negligent act, and a subsequent investigation revealed that the senior LLDB officer in our counterpart detachment had allowed the fire-for-effect to be fired without confirming the point of impact of the initial marking round. The IV Corps Mike Force battalion was knocked out of the fight before it even began, but our 1st Battalion, untouched by the artillery fire, began its attack up the rocky hill along two separate routes. They got near the top around nightfall, when they began taking casualties—many of them from enemy 82mm mortars firing from the Nha Bang Woods north of the mountain.

Llewellyn and Master Sergeant Chuck Hiner, with a few strikers, had secured a small landing zone in the saddle south of the hill, and one of the medics and I went there with a Huey helicopter we had been using to resupply Nicholas's mortars, and picked up the first load of wounded. A short time later, the LZ came under fire from a small force of the enemy to the south. Llewellyn and Hiner countered with machine-gun fire from the LZ. Colonel Black, who was in the general area in a Huey slick, decided to make a "gun run" at the enemy, so Llewellyn had to hold his machine-gun fire while Black came buzzing by and unleashed a magazine of rounds from his submachine gun—a pitiful dribble of bullets compared to the fire from Lew's machine guns. Black, apparently having a good time, asked the crusty team sergeant how his last "gun run" looked. Using Black's abbreviated call sign, he answered sarcastically, "Go get 'em, Trench." Black, failing to pick up Lew's sarcasm, promptly made another fabulous gun run with his peashooter. "Go get 'em, Trench" became one of our favorite expressions after that, whenever our detachment commander made some decision we felt was unusual.

The situation on Nui Khet remained fairly stable that night, although the 82mm mortars in the Nha Bang Woods caused several more casualties. I went up with a Huey and two Cobra gunships to look for the mortar positions. We

172

couldn't find them after buzzing the area for a while, so the slick pilot sent the snakes to a higher altitude, turned on his lights, and flew slowly around the area in an attempt to draw fire from the enemy positions. We didn't get a bite, though, and ended up flying along the Cambodian border to report on a big battle across the border at Nui O—one of the first big battles the Vietnamese had with the communists in their invasion of enemy sanctuaries in that country.

Around 0300 hours the next morning, Llewellyn and his little force at the LZ were probed by the enemy, but managed to force the attackers away. After daylight the next day, Ficken's battalion continued their attack, and were soon in heavy contact with the enemy on the hilltop. The mortars in the woods began to take their toll again, although the Vietnamese cavalry troop had been ordered to go after them. They made only a halfhearted attempt to get to them, though, so once more the 'Yards and their American Special Forces leaders were made to suffer the result of Vietnamese Army inefficiency.

We went into the LZ several times to pick up the mounting number of casualties, and had gone to Chau Duc to refuel, when I heard Llewellyn call for a truck to come from Chi Lang to pick up more wounded. The helicopter couldn't keep up with the number of casualties the battalion was sustaining. Captain Mel Blow, the B Team Executive Officer, took a couple of trucks with some of the 1st Company "quitters" for security and got to Llewellyn and Hiner's position. From the base of the mountain where his mortars were set up, Nick Nicholas called for a 106mm recoilless rifle. Our troops on the hill were too close to the enemy for his mortars to be used to support them, so Nick wanted the 106 to put direct fire into the enemy positions near our troops. We sling-loaded the big weapon and its ammunition under a chopper, and soon had it in action.

The attack got bogged down as the VC and their mortars continued to inflict dozens of casualties on the Mike Force. Attacking uphill against prepared positions is the most difficult of all assaults, particularly when the enemy is supported by effective mortar fire. When indirect fire is exploding in your midst, there's no way to hide from it. Such was the situation in which the attackers found themselves, and while the Vietnamese who ordered the attack remained in their customary positions well to the rear of the fighting, it fell upon the young American NCOs and their Montagnard strikers to scratch and crawl and claw their way into the communist-occupied bunkers.

Young Sergeant Brian Buker, trying to maintain the momentum of the attack, personally cleared several enemy bunkers and was wounded in the process. Trying to clear yet another, he was killed. He became the first member of B-55 to win the Medal of Honor.

Llewellyn and Sergeant First Class Bobby Bolton went up to assist in the assault, but were both soon wounded by enemy hand grenades as they, too, tried to root the VC from their hilltop positions.

Sergeant First Class Otis Parker, who commanded one of Ficken's companies, arrived at Chi Lang that morning from a thirty-day extension leave in the States, and went directly into the fight. He returned to Chi Lang on a medevac helicopter several hours later, having been wounded three separate times while clearing enemy bunkers. His third wound had been a serious shot in his armpit, and was still bleeding profusely when we medevaced him on to the hospital in Can Tho as he declared, "No sweat. I'll be back. No sweat."

Many on the hill felt that Parker's actions were even more heroic than Buker's, and Parker later was awarded a DSC for his intrepidity on Nui Khet—although he didn't live to receive it.

That night, the gunships found the enemy mortars and put a stop to their cruel effectiveness, and the next day the hill was finally taken. It had been a tough battle for the 1st Battalion, 5th Mobile Strike Force. There were some twenty dead strikers, and more than a hundred wounded. Every American in the battalion was wounded at least once, and about half of them, twice. They had won the battle in spite of the harm from Vietnamese on both sides, and they turned the little hilltop fortress back over to the Regional Forces who had lost it, with the prediction that the RF would only lose it again—a prediction which turned out to be accurate.

Bill Llewellyn was put in for a Silver Star for his actions at Chi Lang, but when General Ewell went out to the camp and heard the full story, he wanted it upgraded to a Distinguished Service Cross. In the end, Lew was awarded only a Bronze Star for his heroics—a real travesty of the awards system, but neither the first nor the last.

The flights of medevac choppers into Chi Lang during the battle had been almost incessant—a steady flow of young men far from home, fighting someone else's battle because the ones to whom the land belonged were unable and unwilling to do so for themselves. And it was not just the Americans who were far from home—to the Montagnards who bled and suffered and died there, IV Corps must have seemed as distant from their jungle homes to the north as it did to the Special Forces troops whose home was halfway around the world. When the battle was finally won, I wrote a letter to my widowed mother which expressed my feelings then better than I could now. Dated 9 April 1970, it read:

Dear Mom,

I'm sorry that it's been so long since I've written. It's been terribly busy these last couple of weeks. Our Montagnards and Americans have just won a hell of a four-day fight for a mountaintop which the Vietnamese had lost, and will probably lose again when we leave for Nha Trang. I wish that our whole country could have witnessed those four days on that mountain. They would never again belittle the young Americans who have chosen to put their lives on the line for the vague ideal of "serving their country." They would clasp each man who came off that hill; dirty and bleeding and dazed and aged—they would clasp them to their breasts, and weep for them, and swear to them that they would never again be asked to do so much without the *full* support of their countrymen. They would never again send them off to do for this miserable Oriental cesspool that which its inhabitants are unwilling to do for themselves.

And they would turn this country over to the Montagnards—the children who only want to be left alone in their hills, to follow their superstitious beliefs and fish their streams and hunt their game, and behave like children all their lives.

It's time for us to come home, and for our Montagnards to go back to the highlands, and for the Vietnamese to be left alone to steal from each other and squat in their garbage-filled streets and pick their noses and eat rotten fish sauce.

I wished so much these last few days that I had an American flag to send to the top of the mountain. And a FULRO flag—the Montagnard underground.

Do I sound bitter? If I don't, then I'm not expressing myself very well. . . .

There was a large amount of captured explosives and ammunition which I needed to get rid of before we left Chi Lang, so I went to the camp's Operations Officer (S-3) to ask for permission to blow it up in a rocket crater near the camp. He agreed, so we put it all in the hole, laced it with detonating cord, and ignited the time fuse. It made a hell of a bang. When I got back to the camp, I was ordered to report to the camp commander, Major Zachary. He raised hell with me about the explosion, until I explained that I had gotten permission from his S-3. He laughed then, and explained that he was upset because he had been briefing some VIP when the detonation occurred, and the shock wave had been so strong that it knocked a light fixture from the ceiling, hitting him on the head. The S-3 hadn't warned him about the explosion, so they thought they were under a rocket attack, and everyone ran for the bunkers.

That was not the only casualty suffered at Chi Lang that day, either. A Chinook helicopter had sling-loaded a pallet onto the camp landing zone earlier in the day, and the commies had rocketed the place. To the dismay of all in the camp, one rocket hit the sling load the Chinook had just dropped off—a precious pallet of beer and sodas.

We were picked up by choppers from near the camp and flown to Binh Tuy air base to await the C-130's which would take us back to Nha Trang, Llewellyn and I, along with my S-4 helpers and the 1st Company quitters being the last to leave. We had some time to kill at Binh Tuy while we waited for the aircraft to return from taking the earlier loads to Nha Trang, so Lew, the other Americans, and I all went to the Air Force NCO club for a beer. I was wearing sterile camouflaged fatigues—no name, rank, or unit patch—and one of the airmen came up to the bar and asked if I was an Aussie. It sounded like a fun idea, so I mustered my best Australian accent, and we fed the airman and his companions a long line of war stories. We couldn't *buy* a beer after that, so Lew and I managed to get totally smashed as a result of the Air Force hospitality. On the way back to the flight line, we walked past an armored car with a group of Vietnamese Air Force Security Police sitting atop it. One of them made a snide comment about us, which I understood. After what I had seen at Chi Lang, I was in no mood for any shit from *any* Vietnamese, so I returned the comment in kind. The Viets yelled a few obscenities, and as I had about a four-foot stick in my hand, I assaulted them. I didn't do the armored car or the Viets much damage—in fact, they took the stick away from me. So I ran around the vehicle and assaulted it again, barehanded. They hammered me on the head a few times with my own stick, so I retired from the field, covering my withdrawal with a barrage of verbal abuse. We returned to the area where the 'Yards were waiting for the aircraft, but meanwhile, the Vietnamese in the armored car had called the U.S. Security Police, and a security platoon in armored cars came rolling up. Llewellyn went out to confront them as a huffy young Air Force lieutenant hopped out and declared, "If anyone crosses this road, we'll rake it with machine-gun fire!" This guy was right out of the comic strips. Lew responded with some such comment as, "If you bring your goddamn vehicles any closer, we'll rake the fuckin' road with *rocket* fire!" and he had a couple of the

'Yards prepare their M-72 66mm rockets for firing. It was all a bunch of hooey, of course, and quite comical. I explained to the lieutenant what had happened, and he took his platoon and left. But I was feeling bad—bad because of the casualties we had taken at Chi Lang, bad because I hadn't been up on the hill with them, bad because the Vietnamese were so damned sorry, and bad because of the job I had. It had been a busy time—humping ammo and supplies, carrying litters, driving trucks out to the edge of the battle—but it wasn't fighting. I was supposed to be leading troops in combat, but all I had been doing was driving trucks. I sat on the side of the road with my head in my hands and wept. "I'm just a goddamn truck driver," I lamented, "just a goddamn truck driver."

My tour was nearly half over, and still I was in the S-4 job I had been given "temporarily" some six months earlier.

Finally the C-130 returned, and we boarded it for the flight back to Nha Trang.

In every war, soldiers manage to find pets or mascots which they adopt, and the Vietnam war was no exception. Lieutenant Colonel Anthony Herbert claimed that there was a duck which the Commanding General of the 173rd Airborne Brigade adopted. He had dog tags made for it, and according to Herbert, everyone was supposed to salute the thing. Herbert claimed he finally killed and ate it. And then there was Co Mau, the puppy smuggled out of a North Vietnamese prisoner-of-war camp by one of our released pilots.

We had a number of pets in the Mike Force too, although most of them met untimely ends.

Like the CG of the 173rd Airborne, our Intelligence Sergeant, Paul Soublet, adopted a duck. He used to drive around Katum with it tethered to the hood of his jeep, and he brought it back to Nha Trang with him when we returned from there. Not long after, Sergeant First Class Jim Osborne was tasked to build a monument on our compound to the Mike Force dead and wounded. One day Soublet came around looking for his duck, but it was nowhere to be found,

178

and he finally concluded that the 'Yards or the Nungs had captured the thing and killed it. But then Osborne took me out to see the monument he had just completed, and invited me to put my ear against it. I did, and from within the cinderblock-and-concrete structure heard a muffled, "Quack . . . quack . . ."

The S-3, Captain Boone, had brought an otter back with him from the trip he and Black had made to IV Corps to visit Chuck Randall's 2nd Battalion, and Boone kept the thing in a cage between the team house and the TOC. Boone was not the best-loved officer on the team, and so a number of the troops took their displeasure out on the poor otter, feeding it everything from booze to hot sauce to laxatives— and God only knows what else. Boone finally determined that the thing wasn't doing very well in captivity and took it down to the river and released it.

Then there was the cat which our mess sergeant, "Bellyrobber" King, put into Staff Sergeant Harry Fields's room while Fields was out on an extended operation. Not only did the cat crap all over Harry's bed, but it finally starved to death in the hot room—days or weeks before Fields returned to discover it. I don't think Harry ever did get the smell out of his room.

Once, someone put a dog into my wall locker while I was gone. By the time I discovered him, the dog had gone mad, and when I opened my wall locker, the big mangy cur leapt out at me, snarling and baring his teeth. I beat a hasty retreat to the shower room, but the dog followed, growling all the while. I turned on the shower in an attempt to ward him off, but he kept after me. Finally I delivered a swift kick to his head, and he yelped and ran off. We found him later out in the street, dead.

Not all of the Mike Force animals fared so poorly, though. Jaw Taylor, our Sergeant Major who went to A Company with Lieutenant Colonel Hinds, kept a sugar bear as a pet at his headquarters. After some considerable red tape and alleged bribing of an Air Force air crew, Taylor managed to get Barney, as he named the bear, shipped to the Atlanta zoo.

But the most bizarre incident concerning a Mike Force pet I ever knew of occurred when Randall's battalion was kicking the VC around down on the Ca Mau Peninsula. They had detained a group of civilians whom they suspected of being communist sympathizers, and took them to the Navy's resettlement location, where they were turned over to South Vietnamese officials. Chuck had formed up his troops to move out, when he discovered one of his teenage 'Yards with a little Vietnamese boy on a leash! Chuck got his interpreter and asked the 'Yard just what the hell he thought he was doing. The young striker was going to keep the Vietnamese kid, he explained, like a pet monkey. He was most indignant when Randall took the little boy and handed him over to the Vietnamese officials. Perhaps he figured that if Captain Boone could have a pet otter, he should be allowed to keep a pet Vietnamese.

Another thing Randall's 'Yards did during that operation, one night while they waited for the VC to show up in a village whose occupants were believed to be communist sympathizers, involved the villagers' chickens, which were all over the little hamlet. The Americans wouldn't let the Montagnards kill and eat any of the chickens, but the next morning, the communist sympathizers awoke to discover that all of their chickens had been plucked by the strikers. There were naked chickens running around all over the VC-controlled village.

—— 15 ——

Beginning on 1 April 1970, the Special Forces camp at Dak Seang, near the tri-border area of Laos, Cambodia, and Vietnam, came under attack from some two thousand North Vietnamese soldiers. The Americans and Australians of the II Corps Mike Force deployed their Montagnards to the area immediately, and were soon fighting the enemy near the camp. The battle around the little camp raged on, the enemy reinforcing to a strength of about five thousand. As of 12 April, when the enemy also attacked Camp Dak Pek, the SF outpost seventeen miles to the north, the dead included eleven Americans, about one hundred Montagnard strikers, and some fourteen hundred North Vietnamese.

As the situation worsened, we were tasked to join in the battle beside our Mike Force comrades from Pleiku, so Chuck Randall was ordered to deploy his battalion into the battle area. While he prepared for departure, I went up there to coordinate his arrival and the logistical support he would require while deployed. I arrived at Tan Can, the Vietnamese Headquarters near Dak To airfield, to discover that enemy rocket and artillery fire had hit the ammunition dump there. It burned and exploded for hours, littering nearly every square inch of the base with shards of shrapnel.

The II Corps Mike Force was supporting their units from the Special Forces camp at Ben Het, the next camp south of Dak Seang, between Dak To and the border of northern Cambodia. We decided to do the same, combining our support effort with theirs. After coordination with the representatives of the Mike Force from Pleiku, and with the A Team at Ben Het—"Been Hit," as they called their little fortress, with ample reason—I returned to Nha Trang to brief Chuck, then accompanied him and his battalion to Ben Het. The communists were active around there by now, as well as at Dak Pek, the SF camp to the north of besieged Dak Seang, and were delivering rocket and mortar attacks at both places with increasing frequency.

Chuck's 2nd Battalion was sent out toward the border to search for the enemy, who seemed to be building their strength for an attack on Ben Het. That night, his people spotted enemy vehicles, suspected to be tanks, moving near the border. He reported that fact, but our higher headquarters seemed skeptical of the report, and all he got in response was a few rounds of eight-inch artillery fire in the general area of the sighting. Angered at the unconcerned response, Chuck was going to go after the vehicles—if he brought back the data plates from some of them, maybe *then* the headquarters skeptics would believe him. Before he could do so, however, the NVA around Dak Seang launched a massive attack on a South Vietnamese Army regiment occupying the hills above the camp, routing them from their positions and forcing them to withdraw in disarray, leaving a large quantity of weapons, ammunition—even radios— behind. The solution? Send in a single battalion of Mike Force soldiers to retake the area. The battalion was picked up by chopper and, after a preparatory air strike, conducted an assault into the area. They managed to get onto the top of the hill—Hill 882—but an element of one of the companies was separated from the rest of 2nd Battalion, and couldn't reach them because of an enemy force entrenched in bunkers in the saddle between them. Randall, in Dak Seang camp with his two Combat Recon Platoons to coordinate with the A Team there, decided to take his two platoons up the hill and try to get his elements linked up. They were soon in heavy contact with the NVA, and one of Chuck's NCOs, Staff Sergeant Tim Drake, was severely wounded. Chuck went after him. He, too, got hit, but managed to get to Drake and drag him back to his two platoons' little perimeter, where Randall again was hit by enemy shrapnel. It soon became apparent that the NVA force was more than Chuck's small party could handle, and they started back to the camp, with the 'Yards carrying the badly wounded Sergeant Drake. Then the enemy hit them again, and the strikers had to drop Drake. Once more, Randall went after his dying comrade, and once more, he was wounded by enemy fire. He got to Drake, destroying a couple of enemy positions in the process, only to discover that the young staff sergeant was now dead. Hit for a fourth time and losing his strength, the courageous captain had to leave the body where he had found it and return to his small force, many of whom were dead or wounded as well. Their situation was desperate as night fell.

Sergeant First Class Jerry Hetzler of the II Corps Mike Force, learning of Randall and his troops' dire predicament, went after him with his company. All night, Hetzler battled his way through the enemy-infested jungle to reach the battered little group, then fought his way back out to see to their evacuation to safety. Sergeant First Class Hetzler was recommended for the Medal of Honor for his actions at Dak Seang—the second time that he was recommended for the nation's highest award. Both times, however, he ended up with the second-highest medal for bravery, the Distinguished Service Cross.

Chuck Randall, with eighteen holes in his body as a result of his actions that day, should have been awarded a DSC. He got a Silver Star, though, and when Colonel Mike Healy presented it to him sometime later, he remarked that Randall's valor had been badly underrewarded, adding that he hoped his own son would be as much a man as Chuck had proved himself to be there near the beleaguered camp in the highlands of Vietnam.

Chuck was medevaced to Pleiku, then on to Cam Ranh Bay for treatment.

Once again, I spent the battle humping supplies instead of leading troops. One evening, some badly needed equipment and strikers arrived at Dak To from Nha Trang. I went in search of some people to go with me for security so I could pick up the 'Yards and the equipment and get them out to the deployed units, as the Vietnamese mechanized infantry unit responsible for security of the road between Dak To and Ben Het had gone in for the night.

I could find no one willing to go with me, so in anger I jumped into a three-quarter-ton truck and drove out of the camp and into the countryside between there and Dak To airfield, some miles away. It soon got dark, and I discovered to my dismay that the truck's headlights didn't work. But I bumped along in the dark, wondering who would hit me first—the enemy or a friendly ambush element. I made it safely, though, and picked up the troops—who thought I was nuts—and the equipment, and returned to Ben Het by the illumination of the 'Yards' flashlights.

The II Corps Mike Force had a refrigerator of beer for their Americans and Aussies to drink when they were at the forward operations base. It was a drink-now, pay-later system—when one took a beer, he made a mark beside his name. If he was killed, his debt was forgiven. Ron Franklin had left the team by then and was working with our sister unit, and his name was one of those on the list taped to the refrigerator door. As the battle was so intense up at Dak Seang where Ron and his troops were, I figured he might not make it back alive, so I began drinking his share of the beer, marking them up beside his name as I did so. By the time I left—before his return—there were some fifty-one marks beside his name. He's been getting even with me ever since.

I was back in Nha Trang the night that Randall got hit. Sometime before that, Frank McNutt was in a meeting with

Lieutenant Colonel Black, and Black had given him some
guidance in connection with Frank's duties as the Intelligence Officer. Jokingly, Frank had muttered, "How you
spell dat?"—the punch line to some joke going around at
the time. Black responded by saying, "If you can't spell it,
you're not my intelligence officer anymore." I suppose we
were expected to be intimidated or something, but we knew
Black had planned on putting Frank in the S-4 shop with
me, and bringing another captain, Russ Driver, in to be the
S-2.

Now, with Randall out of action, I assumed Black would
put me in command of 2nd Battalion. Chuck's fine battalion
Executive Officer, First Lieutenant Dave Barnett, was due to
leave soon, so I asked McNutt if he would replace Dave as
the battalion XO. He was delighted with the idea of doing so
and getting back with the fighting troops. When I mentioned
it to Black, he thought about it, then decided to put *Frank* in
command of 2nd Battalion and to give me 1st Battalion, as
he had previously planned to do when it came open a short
time later.

So Frank took off for Dak Seang and his new command
immediately, taking Sergeants Maxwell and Huggins with
him as replacements for Drake and the NCO who had taken
his company when Huggins was moved into the S-5 section
to give him a break from combat. The chopper managed to
get them through a hail of fire to an LZ within the perimeter
of the smaller element on Hill 882, which was still cut off
from the remainder of the battalion. For nine days the
North Vietnamese attempted to take the position where
Maxwell and Huggins were isolated with only one platoon
of strikers. Efforts to reach them with the rest of McNutt's
troops were unsuccessful, as were several efforts by the
platoon to reach the main force of the battalion. During one
attempt, an NVA 12.7mm machine gun opened up on
Huggins from a few meters away, missing his head by
inches, but striking a splintered tree. A chunk of wood hit
the aging veteran of the Korean War aside the head,
knocking him unconscious temporarily. He came to, to
discover his loyal Montagnard bodyguard kneeling over

him, fiercely determined to defend the American with his life.

Finally McNutt was able to get them linked up with the main element. While part of the II Corps Mike Force deployed to Dak Pek to deal with the enemy there, Frank and his battalion continued to fight the NVA on Hill 882. In dire need of a resupply of ammunition, 2nd Battalion's situation was made even worse when the Operations Officer, Captain Boone, passed high overhead in a helicopter and kicked a load of ammo out, which, according to Frank's report, landed outside his perimeter. The NVA completed its delivery by sending it to 2nd Battalion—at muzzle velocity—with the weapons they had captured from the ARVN regiments which had fled the hill early in the battle.

One morning, as Frank checked his perimeter after a night of probing by the enemy, he found that one of his few remaining Claymore mines had been taken apart, and the C-4 explosive with which it was filled had been taken out. C-4 explosive burns very hotly, and the 'Yards sometimes took it out of the Claymores and used it to quickly heat water to cook their food. Frank was, of course, mad as hell at finding the empty mine, and he called the Montagnard platoon leader over to look at it. The 'Yard thought a moment, then told Frank that he had an explanation for it: the "Viet Minh"—as the highlanders still often referred to the VC and NVA—must have sneaked up, taken the C-4 out of the Claymore, and thrown the empty mine inside the perimeter, so that the Americans would get angry at the Montagnards and cause them to lose morale. . . .

It was during the battle of Dak Seang that Rob Jones came to the team. He was sent immediately to Hill 882 to replace Dave Barnett as the 2nd Battalion XO, where he was promptly given a baptism by fire. On the first day, he earned his Combat Infantryman's Badge and a Purple Heart. The next day, he earned his second Purple Heart. McNutt got a nasty wound in the finger there, and one of his company commanders took a round in the buttocks.

With American forces now rampaging through their former sanctuaries in Cambodia, the North Vietnamese finally could no longer sustain their efforts to overrun the Special Forces camps in the tri-border area. The siege of Dak Seang lifted, and Frank and his battalion came home to Nha Trang.

Chuck Randall, his wounds now sutured and dressed, called from Cam Ranh hospital to say that he was about to be shipped to Japan for hospitalization there. Could we do anything to prevent it? No problem. I hopped in a jeep, drove down to Cam Rahn Bay, and kidnapped him from the hospital. That night, we gathered in the team bar to celebrate the return of the troops from the battle and Chuck's "liberation" from the hospital. Curious about all of Chuck's wounds, we had him strip and stand on a table so that we could examine all of them. There was a second lieutenant there who had just been assigned to the team as the funds officer, and being a second lieutenant, he must have felt compelled to do something dumb—he reached out and grabbed the stitches of one of Randall's eighteen wounds, and yanked on them. We were appalled. I grabbed the guy, and decided to deal with him by ramming his head against the wall. But as I charged the wall with him, my arm slipped from around his shoulders to his neck, so that my head was farther forward than his. I nearly knocked myself out when I hit the wall. There was an NCO from Group Headquarters in the bar who decided to come to the lieutenant's aid, but John Talley grabbed him from behind and held him back. The guy bit Talley's finger—whereupon John looked at his bleeding digit, said, "Hey, you bit my finger!" then proceeded to whip the visitor around the room. Dave Barnett, meanwhile, pounded the second looey across the room and into the latrine, where he left him crumpled in the corner. Not satisfied that the young officer had been adequately counseled, I made him sit in the corner while I sat on the john explaining to him that he had a lot to learn. Before he was allowed to get up, I made him explain the proper procedure for calling in close air-support air strikes. When he proved unable to do so, I gave him a lengthy lecture on the subject.

I was joined by the new 2nd Battalion XO, Rob Jones.

Rob was an excellent instructor. He held a master's degree in English and in "real life" was a university instructor. He always carried one or more concealed pistols, with which he was a superb shot, and a knife from his excellent collection of quality blades. His mastery of the English vocabulary, which he demonstrated by the frequent use of words most of us had never even heard of, brought him considerable kidding from the other members of the team. It never fazed him, though, and he continued to use his fifty-cent words with exaggerated enunciation, made even more grandiose by his deep, booming voice—a result, no doubt, of the effect on his larynx of the strong Picayune brand cigarettes he chain-smoked. I sometimes countered his practice of using big words by sending him encoded messages over the radio, using, instead of the standard military phonetic alphabet of "alpha, bravo, charlie," more appropriate Jonesian words, such as "antidisestablishmentarianism, bituminous, conglomeration," and so forth. Rob's usual response to calls on the radio was "Mighty fine, mighty fine"—whether the call was one saying that there would be a resupply delivery the next day, or that his position was about to be overrun by a regiment of NVA. "Mighty fine. Mighty fine."

Since the arrival of Colonel Black to the team, it appeared to me that the integrity of the awards and decorations system had begun to be degraded. The guys doing the heroic things were being underrewarded, in my opinion, while others—particularly on the staff—were being given undeserved awards. For example, Boone had been recommended for an award of the Air Medal for valor, for flying over Frank's position on Hill 882 and kicking out a resupply of ammunition, even though much of the ammunition missed Frank's position and ended up in the hands—and weapons —of the enemy. Then there was the matter of his recommendation for a Purple Heart for bumping his head on a beam in the underground TOC at Ben Het when enemy mortar rounds had exploded on the camp's airstrip a hundred meters or so away. When I got word of these things, I went to see the Adjutant, Captain Lafayette Sale, a former Special Forces NCO, and asked him about them. "See for yourself," he said, gesturing disgustedly to a pile of papers in his In box. I shuffled through them, found the tainted recommendations, and burned them to ashes in Sale's trashcan. No doubt they would be resubmitted and approved, but at least it made the Adjutant and me feel better for the time being.

The awards situation had gotten so bad, in fact, that Randall and I decided one night to go see the Group Commander, Colonel Mike Healy, about it. Colonel Healy was away at the time, so we started back across the Headquarters compound, Randall still on crutches as a result of his wounds. As we passed the Playboy Club, the name given the enlisted men's club, a group of "legs" from the helicopter outfit at the air base made some comment to Chuck and me about our green berets. We stopped to chew them out, and one kicked Randall's crutches away as several of them gathered around him. I was furious. I roll-blocked them, springing Chuck, but about six of them jumped on me and began to flail the hell out of me. Randall hobbled quickly to the team bar and told our teammates that I was being beaten up outside the Playboy Club, and about a half-dozen ran to my assistance, beating the "legs" so savagely that I ended up having to pull some of my teammates off the helicopter crewmen before they became too badly injured. As it was, several of them had to be taken to the hospital for treatment.

——— 16 ———

At last, in the late spring of 1970, I was given command of a battalion again—1st Battalion, 5th Mobile Strike Force Command, and the A detachment of Americans who led it, Special Forces Operational Detachment A-503. When I had first commanded that detachment two years before, at the time the Nha Trang Mike Force was expanded to a B detachment, it had been temporarily designated A-551, but since then had reverted to its original designation.

By then, American involvement in the war had begun winding down, including the activities of the 5th Special Forces Group. Many of the border camps were being turned completely over to the Vietnamese Special Forces, and the American A Teams withdrawn from them. In the Mike Force, attempts at "Vietnamization," as it was called, had simply not worked. The 'Yards still refused to respond to Vietnamese leadership, so although it was now officially commanded by the members of our VNSF counterpart team, B-22, their true role was seldom more than one of sending one or two people along to report the units' location and activities to their headquarters.

Detachment B-52—Project Delta—was being disbanded, and their Bomb Damage Assessment Platoon was reassigned to my battalion to serve as an additional Combat Reconnaissance Platoon. The Platoon's American leaders, Staff Sergeants Jay Graves and Dickie Pirtle, were assigned to the team as well. The commanders of the battalion's three rifle companies were Master Sergeant Lyle Drake, Sergeant First Class Otis Parker—who had won a DSC at Nui Khet and had been recommended for a direct commission to Lieutenant of Infantry—and Sergeant First Class Williams. My XO, new to the team, was Captain Duane Ramsey, and my team sergeant was that wild and wonderful character Master Sergeant Bill Llewellyn.

With our combat reconnaissance platoons, three rifle companies, and the small headquarters section, we could field a force of some 550 men. With the attachment of mortars and the 105mm howitzer section from Nicholas's Headquarters Company, the number rose to about 600 men. One thing was somewhat disturbing, though: the last time I commanded the battalion, when there were only twenty-eight Americans in the Nha Trang Mike Force, we managed to have at least three U.S. NCOs assigned to each company. But now, even though the number of Americans assigned to the unit had been increased to more than sixty, we did not have enough "roundeyes" down in the battalion to put three with each company. Of the fourteen officers in Detachment B-55, only four were down in the battalions. Lieutenant Colonel Black sure had a nice big staff, though.

McNutt's battalion, too, was undermanned in comparison to the number of men in the B Team, but on one issue we were in full agreement: the NCOs we had leading the Montagnard and Cham strikers into combat were among the best damned soldiers in Vietnam. There is a premise of leadership taught in Army schools which claims that a leader should not get too close to his troops—that by doing so, he might not be willing to sacrifice them when the time comes. Maybe that's true for some people and in some situations, but for Frank and me—and on Special Forces detachments in general—that premise never seemed to hold true. We loved the men under our command, and they knew it. We drank with them, raised hell with them, discussed

191

their personal problems and our own with them, and were, in most cases, closer friends with our NCOs than with our fellow officers. And when the time came to tell them, "Go up on the Grand Summit and attack that regiment with your company," or "Go to Duc Lap and clear the enemy out of the bunkers," they went without hesitation. None was a closer friend to me than Frank McNutt, though. When we were both in garrison, we would go hand-grenade fishing on the reef down at the Coconut Grove, or take some of our 'Yards to the beach to swim, or take off to town together for a session in the Streamer Bar. He took to calling me "Stretch," I was so skinny from my bout with malaria, and I called him "Hawg."

"Hey, Stretch," he said to me shortly after he returned from extension leave in the U.S., "I brought you a present—a pair of bells. Everybody in the States wears bells, so I got some for you." He handed me the ugliest pair of trousers I've ever seen. The legs of the things, one of which was all white on the front half and all red in back, with the other blue in front and solid white behind, flared widely out below the knee. I wore them, though, thinking how much Larry O'Neil would have enjoyed having me wear them downtown to provoke barroom brawls.

I wore them the time the Australian rock-'n'-roll band came to play for us after a gig at the Group Officers' Club. They had agreed to come over and put on a show for the Mike Force in return for meals and lodging. There were two go-go girls with the band, dressed in bell-bottomed white lace jumpsuits. They were quite a hit, with both the 'Yards and the Americans, as one might expect a couple of gyrating, full-busted "roundeyes" to be. One had long blond hair which flowed to her waist, and Frank and I found her to be particularly attractive.

The girls were staying together in the room of one of the officers who was away at the time, and late that night after everyone had gone to bed, I was awakened by a blood-curdling feminine scream for help from the latrine at the end of the hall. I pulled on some trousers and ran to see what the problem was. The blond Aussie girl was bent over the washing machine we had there, and Frank appeared to be wrestling with her. I quickly discovered, though, that the girl had been washing her long tresses in the machine's tub, and her hair had gotten entangled in the rollers of the wringer, pulling her head down and painfully tearing at her hair. After we got her freed from the machine, I laughed and said, "Hell, Hawg, when I heard her scream and found you in there with her, I thought sure your horns had got the better of you, and you'd attacked her!"

"I thought sure *you* had gone after her, when I heard her screaming," he replied.

I believe it was about this time that the communists conducted one of the most heinous atrocities of the war, although back in the United States the news media were too preoccupied with American troops' misconduct to give it much publicity. Late one night, an enemy swimmer-sapper team swam across Cam Ranh Bay, infiltrated the hospital complex, and attacked the wards full of wounded soldiers, female nurses, and other medical personnel, with explosive satchel charges and automatic weapons. One of the attackers was captured by the U.S. Navy element there, and agreed to lead a force into the mountains above the Dong Bo Valley, to his unit's base camp. I was fortunate enough to get the mission of taking the prisoner and one of our companies in to hit the brutal raiders. Accompanied by a Navy intelligence officer, we flew by helicopter into the foothills just north of the bay. The prisoner led us off into the hills, but it soon became evident that he was leading us on a wild-goose chase, with no intention of bringing us to his comrades' base camp. When we came to a water-filled bomb crater, I took the man into it, had my interpreter tell him that I was fed up with his failure to lead us to the base, then shoved him underwater and held him there until he was out of breath. Either he would lead us to the base, I had the interpreter tell him, or I would hold him underwater until he drowned. The Navy lieutenant protested, reminding me that the man was a prisoner of war and that my actions were illegal. "God *damn!"* I replied. "Last night, this lousy son of a bitch was running through the wards of Cam Ranh hospital, blowing up wounded Americans, and all he's done all day is lead us around in circles, and you want me to treat him with kid gloves?" He was right, though, so I added, "Fine. I'll turn him over to his countryman, then." Turning to the LLDB lieutenant with me, I said, "Here, *Thieu Uy,* you take charge of him."

The Vietnamese officer stepped into the crater with the cringing sapper, drew his pistol, and struck the man in the side of the head with it. Then he cocked the .45 automatic, held it to the frightened enemy's head, and spoke briefly to him in Vietnamese. The communist soldier stepped out of the crater and led us directly to his base camp. The remaining sappers had fled the area, although there were signs that they had been there earlier in the day. We were unable to follow their trail very far before we lost it, so we called the choppers for extraction. While we waited, I sat on the edge of the pickup zone with the prisoner and my interpreter. As I shared my ration with him, I had a long and interesting conversation with the North Vietnamese. He was a dedicated soldier, who had only recently made the long walk down the Ho Chi Minh Trail, through Laos and Cambodia and across the highlands to the hill mass where we now sat. The Cam Ranh Bay hospital attack was his first mission, he claimed. He said that he was afraid of the water, but was ordered to become a swimmer-sapper anyway, learning to swim in the northern end of the bay near the base camp. It was his duty to kill Americans, he said, because his countrymen in the south—all of them—were enslaved by us and wanted to be free from American occupation. When I told him to look around, and asked him how he could say that when there were Vietnamese with us who far outnumbered us, he replied that it was only because they were afraid of us. The North Vietnamese would fight to the death until there were none of them left, in their efforts to rid Vietnam of us, he told me with calm assurance. It was a sobering experience, and I wish we could have continued our conver-

sation, but the helicopters arrived and I turned the young
NVA prisoner back over to the Navy lieutenant.

In early June, the 1 Corps Mike Force, racked by battle
casualties and an epidemic of malaria, went on a thirty-day
stand-down to recover and rebuild. We were called upon to
take up the slack for them by going after the enemy in the
jungle west of Camp Thuong Duc.

The night before we left, I was in the shower room with
Llewellyn and Otis Parker, who was now fully recovered
from the wounds he had suffered in the battle to retake Nui
Khet, and back in command of his company. As we lingered
in the luxury of the last hot shower we would have for at
least a month, Parker looked over at Llewellyn and me and
said, "You know, one of us isn't going to make it back from
this operation." Such a prediction was totally out of character for the hard-fighting little sergeant first class, whose
attitude was always so positive.

"Screw *you!*" my team sergeant and I responded. "If
someone isn't coming back, it's going to be *you,* you crazy
son of a bitch!" But his premonition turned out to be an
accurate one.

Such premonitions were frightening to me, because I had
heard them before, and all too often they came true. I had
once had one myself, just before we conducted an airmobile
assault from Nha Trang air base to the Dong Bo area one day
during my previous tour. We were standing beside the
airfield waiting for the choppers to arrive—Bud McBroom,
Sam Coutts, Arnie Estrada, and I—when I turned to the
others and said, "You know, I must have dreamed it last
night or something, but we were standing here like this,
looking across the airfield, and a C-130 crashed right in
front of us." The others gave me a weird look and changed
to some more meaningful conversation. Not five minutes
later, a four-engine Air Vietnam aircraft landed in front of
us, but continued past the end of the airstrip, through the
perimeter fence, and across the road. It crashed through the
Victory Bar and into an orphanage, burning and killing a
large number of civilians, many of them orphan children.

Stunned, the others looked at me in fearful awe. "For God's sake," one of them said, "if you ever have a dream about me getting killed, please don't tell me!"

The Chams had the most astounding record of such psychic incidents, though. Khoe, Coutts's courageous Cham platoon leader, seemed always to know when he could stand in a hail of enemy fire and not be hit, and when he needed to avoid doing so. His company commander had predicted the hot LZ when they were attached to Project Delta for the Samurai IV operation. Many were the times the Chams had stopped, sensing imminent contact, to put on their religious amulets or prayer vests, only to make contact with the unseen enemy moments later. But there was one episode which, beyond all others, defies explanation.

The Chams had been in a battle at one of the camps in II Corps, and their wounded were evacuated to the CIDG hospital in Pleiku. Shortly after the operation ended, the old Cham high priest from Phan Rang showed up at our headquarters, saying that he was there to pick up the body of one of the men who had been wounded in the battle. We checked with the Americans in the company; the wounded man's platoon leader, Sergeant Roberson, said that the young Cham had been evacuated with a minor wound in the arm, and had been in no danger of dying from it. The priest would not be deterred, though; he had had a vision of the soldier's death, and was convinced that the man lay dead in Pleiku. To keep the Cham's religious leader from being alienated, we dispatched him to Pleiku—where he had never been before in his life—and sent Sergeant Roberson to accompany him. At the CIDG hospital, Roberson learned that there was a record of his admission, but no record of the man's release. The medics there and Roberson assumed that, as was often the case, the striker had been treated, and had simply left when he felt well enough to do so, and made his way home to his village to recuperate, without bothering to be properly discharged from the hospital. The old priest was adamant, now claiming that he could visualize the soldier's grave somewhere within the unfamiliar city. To humor him, Roberson borrowed a jeep, and with the Cham priest giving him directions, traveled around Pleiku until the old man stopped him and pointed to a fresh mass grave in one of the city's cemeteries. That was the grave he had seen in his vision. After some difficulty, the skeptical Roberson got permission to have the grave opened. There, to the shocked surprise of the American NCO, was the body of the dead Cham striker. Roberson, and many of the rest of us, never treated Cham premonitions with skepticism after that. The experience had such an effect on him that Roberson even gave up drinking and eating pork, at least for a while.

The day after Parker's dire prediction, we moved up to I Corps and out to the 5th Marines' combat base at An Hoa. We would conduct an airmobile assault in Marine CH-46 helicopters from there out into an area between the SF camp at Thuong Duc and the Laotian border, known to the Marines as Happy Valley.

That night, while we prepared for the next day's assault, there was a firefight in the village nearby, which we assumed to be a battle between the Marines and a communist unit. The next morning, however, we learned that the NVA had raided the orphanage at An Hoa, senselessly slaughtering the orphans and their defenseless guardians. The incident drew little comment from the American press, however; they were too preoccupied with reports of the My Lai massacre investigation.

For many of us fighting the war in 1970, it was a time of severe estrangement from many of our American institutions. The news media reports seemed slanted and all too often disparaging in their reports and editorials, not just about America's policies in Vietnam, but about her soldiers. Except for Bob Hope, John Wayne, Maggie Raye, and a few others, even our country's entertainers had joined the cacophony of antiwar and antisoldier protests. Our former schoolmates were being allowed by Congress to avoid the draft, by going on to graduate school—if their families were wealthy enough to afford it. And the colleges and universities themselves were hotbeds of the antiwar movement, where we were all depicted as baby-killers, and the troops returning to Vietnam brought back tales of alienation and disgraceful comments being made to them, with increasing frequency, by fellow Americans.

Some professional soldiers, themselves fed up with the war, were volunteering to return to Vietnam only because they found the camaraderie there, in spite of the attendant hardships, more palatable than life in a society which mocked and alienated them.

I later tried to recapture their feelings in verse:

This has become our home, this lush
Green jungle where, without a blush,
Pulling us hard into the folds
Between her loins, the whore called Death—
The stink of murder on her breath—
Laughing, raped our virgin souls.

God, had we only seen it then.
But we had come, young, eager men
In search of some mischievous thrill
To take back—just some naughty tale
To tell, to prove how truly male
We were—as young men sometimes will.

Then, fearing what we might become,
We fled—debased, ashamed—for home,
To seek renewal, rid the pain
From in our souls. We found instead
Rejection. Hate. Forgiveness dead;
Ex-prodigals, received as Cain.

Thus turned away from home, we flee
To this, our jungle Purgat'ry,
The choice but one; to die or kill.
Men now, our innocence no more,
We seek to kill the Deadly Whore
In hopes that you'll forgive us still.

MIKE FORCE

Why did you let us, you who knew
The truth? Why did you let us do
This to ourselves? We were but boys
In search of manhood; 'stead, we found
Our lives too quickly over, bound
For hell amid the fire and noise.

We've learned the awful lesson well
And sworn that never to this hell
Will we allow our sons to roam,
Till, victims of this murd'rous toil,
Their young blood soaked up by the soil,
This jungle's their last earthly home.

— 17 —

The Marine Corps ran airmobile assaults a bit differently from the Army—the commander of the helicopter force made all the decisions until the force was on the ground—so I had no commo with my troops en route to our landing zone on the western side of Happy Valley. I was in the second chopper, and as we approached the LZ, I saw what I took to be a canister of napalm from the preparatory air strike still burning on the hill. As we landed nearby, though, I could see that it was the lead chopper, lying on its side and afire. Thinking that the landing was being opposed, I deployed the troops from my ship and attempted to reach the people from the burning CH-46 on the radio. I couldn't raise them, and wondered if they had all become casualties in the crash, or had been finished off by the enemy on the ground.

There was no shooting going on, though, so I moved to the area of the crash site and found, to my relief, that the aircraft had not been shot down, but had struck the hillside with one of its rotors during landing, rolled over, and caught fire. Everyone had escaped from the crash, and the only injury was to one of the LLDB, and it wasn't a serious one.

The others suffered no more than minor cuts and contusions.

We got the rest of the battalion in, and initiated combat patrols around the area to try to contact the enemy. A short time later, a member of Jay Graves's platoon, which was securing the hill where we had established the battalion patrol base, was standing around with his buddies, twirling a hand grenade around by the pin. It came out, and the grenade detonated, killing the man and wounding several of his Nung friends. The operation wasn't off to a very auspicious beginning.

We were to work our way back toward Thuong Duc in search of the enemy, who had withdrawn from the immediate area of the camp, so I put the three rifle companies on parallel axes pointing in that direction. Initially, because we had no feel for what size enemy force we might encounter in the area, I had the three companies converge on the same position each night and form a battalion night defensive perimeter.

The day after we left the LZ patrol base, we began to see signs of the enemy—well-used trails, human feces, paper which had been used to burn leeches off them, still wet from the uncoagulated blood. On the second day, we made several light contacts, capturing two weapons, although the dead and wounded were recovered by their comrades before we could get to them. The next day, we found a recently occupied defensive position, but no one in it. Just beyond there, though, Sergeant First Class Parker, patrolling with one of his squads, made contact with a small enemy force and charged off after them with his squad. He came upon a series of bamboo-and-thatch shelters, put his squad on line, and assaulted into them. His attack yielded two dead NVA, a Montagnard woman, a half-dozen rifles, and some documents of good intelligence value. Some of the documents indicated the presence of large enemy units in the area the same ones that had recently attacked Thuong Duc. Another of the documents, when sent back to the rear for analysis, turned out to be written in Katu Montagnard dialect. The

Katu were not believed to have a written language at the time, although it was reported that a missionary had been in the area several years earlier, putting Katu into a written language. I never learned the contents of the notebook, but it was either the missionary's, or he had succeeded in teaching some of the Katu to write their language.

At that point, we couldn't tell whether the Katu were cooperating with the enemy willingly or not, but it was obvious that, in either case, the North Vietnamese had control over at least some of them.

We began to find location after location where the enemy had recently been in large numbers—command-post areas, abandoned bivouac sites, and several small hospitals, each with several bamboo-and-thatch hootches, bunkers, an occasional fresh grave, and sometimes a document or two. The documents, taken together, began to give a pretty clear picture of NVA activities in the area.

The whole region we were patrolling had been used as a staging area where a large number of enemy units had equipped themselves, conducted planning and training, and supported their offensive operations against the populated outposts and villages between Danang and the mountains, particularly during the recent attack and siege of Camp Thuong Duc. They had been using the sites we were now finding to treat their wounded, reequip, and redistribute troops and matériel. Apparently the battalion-size airmobile assault in Marine helicopters which we had made into their staging area at a time when they were still licking their wounds from the battles around Thuong Duc had caused them to withdraw into their sanctuaries in nearby Laos. They had apparently left only a few small forces behind to maintain surveillance of the area, to manage the Katu 'Yards, and to tend the corn and tobacco crops we occasionally encountered.

For the next couple of weeks we continued to make about one light contact a day, getting an occasional kill, capturing several weapons each week, finding a document or two now and then, and finding a store of corn or a small cache of equipment. It was, if not a particularly action-packed operation for a Mike Force battalion, at least a very educational one. I learned more about how the NVA lived, staged, and organized their areas of operation during that trip to I Corps than I did during the rest of my time in Vietnam.

We were pleased when we began finding the caches of corn, because our only logistical support consisted of a resupply by helicopter of food and ammunition every four or five days. The Oriental patrol rations we ate—mostly rice—were inadequate to keep us going after weeks of constant patrolling through the mountains in the intense heat—especially since the little tins of mackerel in tomato sauce which we were supposed to receive as a daily supplement to our rice packets were in short supply.

We were wearing down, beginning to lose considerable amounts of weight, and the captured corn was our favorite find. We would roast and eat all we could, and destroy the rest by throwing it into a nearby river or contaminating it with persistent powdered tear gas.

A few weeks after we got to the jungle west of Thuong Duc, we got word that McNutt's battalion was coming up to join us. I didn't see much sense in it, as we weren't getting into any fights that even required the company making the occasional contacts to be reinforced by another. Someone speculated that because Black was nearing the end of his tour and hadn't had both battalions out on the same operation together, he needed to do so to assure himself an award of the Legion of Merit.

In any case, one afternoon while we were cutting an LZ to receive a resupply, Frank called on the radio to say that he was in the area in a chopper conducting a visual reconnaissance. As we guided the helicopter to our location, I got a captured NVA pith helmet, made a long bamboo cigarette holder, and borrowed someone's eyeglasses. When Frank's chopper arrived, hovering low above us, I put on my best imitation of Artie Johnson's "verrry interesting" Nazi soldier from the popular *Laugh In* television show. I could see Frank sitting in the chopper, pointing at me and roaring with laughter. I liked to see my good friend laugh. As he flew off to conduct his reconnaissance, he waved a hearty good-bye.

It was the last time I ever saw Frank.

When 2nd Battalion arrived at An Hoa combat base, the Marine commander was, as most Americans were, suspicious of our little dark-skinned Montagnards. He wanted them off his base and into the field as soon as possible. Black agreed that they should get out to the field, so plans were made to move them across the river which runs west-to-east just north of An Hoa. I was told later that the Marine intelligence officer, on hearing of the plan to move them there, remarked that it would be "murder," that there was "nothing over there but booby traps."

"We're Mike Force. We can take it," Black was alleged to have said.

"It is easy to be brave from a safe distance," Aesop once wrote.

Sampans were commandeered, tanks were positioned to support the crossing, if necessary, and Frank and his battalion began crossing the river. Once a sufficient number to secure the far bank were across, the point element moved out away from the river. They had moved only a short distance when they hit a booby trap. Several of the 'Yards were badly wounded, and Frank—not knowing whether there were enemy soldiers present, not knowing how many more mines or booby traps were there, knowing only that some of his beloved troops were hurt—rushed forward. Another mine, probably command-detonated, exploded. Shrapnel tore his belly open.

We were out of radio range of An Hoa much of the time, but we could hear occasional snatches of conversation between the forward operations base there and the people across the river. Someone was calling for a medevac. Several 'Yards, and apparently one American, were badly wounded. We were moving to a higher elevation, and I began to pick up more of the conversation. The people across the river were becoming more and more concerned about the condition of the wounded. No one could seem to ascertain where the medevac chopper was, or when it was coming. That didn't seem right, because there were always helicopters sitting right there at the combat base. It had been nearly an hour since the explosions. I began to sense that Frank was the American who was hurt—badly hurt—and I began asking the people at An Hoa about the status of "Hawg." I kept getting evasive answers. Finally Colonel Black came on the radio and informed me that the "Five-Four"— that month's suffix meaning "Commanding Officer"— of my sister battalion was "Kilo." KIA. Killed in action. Dead.

I had known a lot of good men who had been killed—far too many. But none of them had been as close to me as Frank was. Nor was that the only reason his death struck me so hard. It just wasn't right. There was something about Frank McNutt which made it seem so wrong for him to die in combat—something of naiveté, of innocence about him. He loved people too much to be involved in their intentional killing of each other. He especially loved the Montagnards; I never met anyone who cared more for his troops. He seemed out of place, being at war. He was a good man, a good soldier—but there was something about him which made his death utterly wrong.

Nevertheless, he *was* dead, though I really couldn't bring myself to believe it at first—I expected to awake the next day and see him there picking at his thumbnails or fiddling with a matchbook as he usually did.

He had a classmate in OCS—a guy named William Calley, who would soon be tried for the massacre of civilians at My Lai. What madness is it that leaves a man like that alive, while robbing someone like Frank McNutt of life? He had so much left to do, so much happiness left to find.

He spent much of his short life playing second-string ball at Kansas and at Texas Western. But he died on the varsity team. An All-American. A United States Army Special Forces officer in command of a battalion in combat—an awesome task for a man so young.

MIKE FORCE

I will remember you, my friend; ah, yes,
I will remember you,
Not as this stiff'ning heap of bones and flesh
You've suddenly become;

I will remember you a year ago
When, cradled in your arms
As I now hold you, cradled in my own,
I wept, alive, at death.

A year ago, when I'd first killed a man,
You said to me, "Yes, weep.
Weep for us all, who kill as if we have
The rights of God.

"But when your tears are spent, remember this;
We do what must be done,
And, wretched as this deadly duty is,
For freedom's sake, it's ours.

"For, being honor-bred, could we do less?
Our heritage is this:
America will risk what must be risked;
Her finest sons, her best.

"So rest your injured soul. For now
You understand, my friend,
That killing is the one great risk we face—
To *die* is not a sin."

And now you've paid the price, for freedom's sake—
". . . to die is not a sin."
I hope you're right. God knows, I hope you're right.
I'll see you soon, my friend.

——— 18 ———

The night of Frank's death, I was with Otis Parker, with whom he had also been close, and with other members of the team, and we talked about what we might do in McNutt's memory. We wanted to do something, and discussed the possibility of establishing a scholarship at Plant City High School, near Tampa, Florida, where Frank had played football. It would be for kids like Frank—guys who needed financial assistance, perhaps, but most important, guys who gave 100 percent to the game. Youngsters without enough size, or not quite enough ability to play first-string ball.

We figured we could sell the several dozen weapons we had captured on the operation, to rear-echelon types, and we would each donate a sum of money as well.

At about that time, Captain Boone—who, like Black, was nearing the end of his tour—called on the radio to say that he had been polishing up one of the weapons Parker had captured, and that he wanted to take it home as a trophy. Parker didn't particularly care for Boone—a sentiment shared by many of us—and he certainly didn't like people taking the weapons we planned to sell to establish the scholarship, so he told Boone, "Not only no, but hell, no!"

Black got word that we were refusing to give away the weapons we had captured, and called to say that the weapons were the property of the LLDB team, and not ours to keep or to give away. Bullshit. Maybe that was technically correct by some obscure regulation, but it was contrary to a long-standing tradition in the Mike Force and to the idea that, "to the victor go the spoils." The LLDB seldom saw contact, rarely took part in firefights, and never, that I knew of, captured any weapons themselves.

I told Black my feelings about it, but it was to no avail. We later learned that both Boone and Black, who left for the States before we got out of the field, took some of the weapons home with them as war trophies. I was incensed when I learned that. How despicable! To me, it amounted to stealing from men who were out risking their lives, and that, in my opinion, is criminal. I also learned later from Sergeant Major Richardson that Black had him go downtown and have a big black flag made for Black to take home with him. It had a skull and crossbones on it, above which was written in large letters, "Black's Death Brigade." Richardson also told me that it was paid for with S-5 funds, which were intended to be expended for psychological warfare and civil affairs.

Two days after Frank's death, we received a resupply of food, ammunition, and uniforms, and learned more about what had happened when Frank got hit. The medic got an IV into him, and called the B Team for a medevac. For some reason, an Army medevac was called, from all the way back at Danang. Why weren't the helicopters right across the river at An Hoa used? Why did it take nearly an hour to get him out? He continued to lose blood, and was given another IV of blood expander. When he was finally evacuated the fifteen hundred meters to the Marine aid station, the doctor there found that he was dead, from what should have been a nonfatal wound. The doctor kept saying aloud, "Why did he die?"

But he was dead, and nobody could undo that.

We were operating along both sides of a river at the time, finding plenty of corn, tobacco, and political documents. We took our resupply, and got in a replacement—Specialist Ed Nicely, who had been the detachment clerk.

Several days earlier, at about the time 2nd Battalion arrived from Nha Trang, Black had flown over our area, and I had commented on what a good operation it was to break new people in on—to let them see how the enemy operated and to get them into a little contact. Russ Driver, the intelligence officer, was out with us, and was learning a lot, as well as earning his CIB.

Parker and I had been trying for some time to get Nicely assigned to the team, because although he was trained as a clerk, we could see in him the natural talents of a combat leader. He was the sort of guy who succeeded at anything he tried, and Parker wanted him to fill a vacant platoon leader's slot in his company.

As Black flew over, I asked him about it, but he wasn't very receptive to the idea. That evening, after we had closed into our night defensive positions, Russ Driver called me on the radio and asked me what my earlier conversation with Black had been about. I told him, then added that Black had been unreceptive to my suggestion, ending with, "If he doesn't want to do it, then fuck him."

As luck would have it, the colonel was up in a chopper and monitoring my frequency. "That's right, Five-Four: 'Fuck him!'" I was careful about the conversations I had on the battalion internal net after that.

But, for whatever reason, when our next resupply came in, Ed Nicely was on the helicopter and ready to go to war as a Mike Force platoon leader. Parker welcomed him to the company on the resupply LZ as easily as if he were an experienced Mike Force NCO, introduced him to the 'Yard indigenous platoon leader, and gave the young but capable ex-clerk the direction and distance to the next patrol objective. Then he gave the order of movement; Nicely's platoon was to take the point. As the company moved out, Parker looked back at me and smiled, then fell in a short distance behind Nicely. "The young ex-clerk may be inexperienced," I mused, "but he's going to learn quickly, working for Ranger Parker."

We finished breaking down and distributing the rest of the chow and ammunition to the other two companies, then moved out for the other company objectives, when we suddenly heard firing and explosions from up the river, where Parker's company had moved. We used unofficial call signs on the battalion internal radio net—Parker's was "Groover," mine was "Buckshot," and, on his arrival at the LZ, we had given Nicely the call sign of "Good Guy." When we heard the firefight, I called Groover. Good Guy answered my call and calmly reported that they had come upon a couple of enemy-occupied hootches just north of the river, and Parker was assaulting. A few moments later, he called me again. He needed a medevac; Parker was down, wounded.

I asked him for the priority required of his request for a medical evacuation, and heard that ugliest of possible responses: "Urgent."

When they had come upon the enemy position not long after leaving our resupply LZ, they saw several enemy near the hootches. Parker assaulted immediately, almost single-handedly, firing his rifle and throwing hand grenades at the surprised enemy. He killed two of them immediately, but two more grabbed their weapons and ran. Parker charged after them at a run, while the few 'Yards with him fired at the fleeing enemy. A striker armed with a 40mm grenade launcher fired his weapon at the communists, but hit a tree just in front of the charging Parker. Otis halted, slumped slightly, and turned toward the grenadier.

"God damn you," he said to the Montagnard whose round had wounded him. Then he sank to his knees. Frenchie Bordeaux, the medic with Parker's company, got to his company commander immediately and tore open his shirt, finding a small wound in his chest. It didn't look bad, but Otis' aorta had been severed. As Frenchie did the best he could to treat the deep wound, I called the B Team and made certain that they understood that the medevac request was an urgent one. I wanted a chopper *now,* and if there was one at An Hoa, I wanted *that* one, rather than wait for one to come from Danang.

Parker's company was about fifteen hundred meters from us when they made contact, and John Talley and I, on learning of Otis' wound, ran the whole way there. The medevac ship from An Hoa arrived at about the same time we did. Parker told Frenchie, "I'm going fast," as the young medic tried to keep him from going into shock. It was to no avail, though. With a severed aorta, Parker was doomed. Only if he had gotten to an operating-room table within a few minutes of being wounded could he have been saved. Bordeaux's efforts to keep his company commander alive until they arrived back at An Hoa were futile. Another good, dedicated Special Forces NCO was dead.

When we arrived at the location of Parker's company, I found that Ed Nicely, who had been on the ground as an infantry platoon leader for all of one hour, had taken charge of the situation and had the company deployed in a defensive perimeter. He had done a good job of communicating with me and securing a pickup zone for Otis' evacuation while Bordeaux, the only other American with the company, tried to keep Parker alive. I was proud of him, but as Larry O'Neil had done with me, I made it seem as if that was only what was expected of him. I had him show me around the perimeter of his company. Satisfied with his dispositions, I got on the radio to An Hoa to check on Parker's status.

The tough little sergeant was dead. He had predicted that one of us—me, Bill Llewellyn, or Parker himself—would not return from the operation alive. He had proved his premonition correct.

I was terribly angry at the enemy. Just two days ago, they had killed my best friend, and now my best NCO—one of the most professional and courageous in the Army—was dead. And both deaths had been so needless.

One of the 'Yards near me was carrying an M-79 grenade launcher, and in frustration I snatched it from him, firing round after round in the direction toward which the enemy had long since fled. I called for more and more ammunition, until I had fired about thirty rounds and my shoulder ached so badly from the recoil of the weapon that I could fire no more. Then I called for an immediate air strike, and when two F-100 fighters arrived, I had them pound the area toward which the enemy had run.

Parker's death struck me differently than McNutt's had. Otis was the type of hard-charging career soldier for whom it was only fitting to die in battle, and he knew it. As Patton had once said, he wanted to die by "the last bullet in the last battle of the last war."

Parker once claimed that he fought for medals, for decorations. It was deeper than that, of course, but that was the image he wanted and the image he displayed in such acts as chasing after the enemy by himself and performing heroics at Nui Khet. It was fitting, somehow, for him to die in battle—but what a loss for those of us he left. There was so much left for him to do, so far for him to go professionally. But he was gone to Valhalla.

We were just preparing to pull in the perimeter and move out of the area when there was a burst of fire nearby. I rushed over to see what it was, and found an NVA soldier, his AK-47 still slung over his shoulder, lying on his back in the trail with his face blown away. One of the 'Yards on the perimeter had heard the man coming, raised his 40mm M-79, and hit the communist in the face with a canister round. We searched up the trail for others, but apparently the man was moving alone. We searched the body and the rucksack he was wearing. He had on a Russian watch, and his bag contained a large quantity of medicines made in China, Rumania, and the United States. There were medical instruments and a diary, from which we learned that he was the NVA physician for the region. It was a severe blow to the enemy in the area, and I was glad that the assault-rifle-carrying doctor was dead. I wanted to take the empty M-79 shell back with us and have it mounted on a plaque with the inscription "With this round, the death of SFC Otis Parker was avenged. 'And thine eye shall not pity; but life shall go for life, eye for eye, tooth for tooth, hand for hand, foot for foot.'"

An animal impulse took hold of me then, and I told Talley and a couple of the others to drag the three enemy bodies out into the clearing near a tree. Then I told them to find me a rope.

"For what?" Talley asked.

"I'm going to string these communist bastards up by their heels and skin them, that's what," I replied.

Talley approached me, his face close to mine, and looked me in the eye. "Over my dead body, you are. Have you lost your damned mind, *Dai Uy?*"

I stared at him for a long moment, then at the bodies of the dead. Talley was right. They were the enemy, but they were soldiers, just as Otis and Frank and we were—far from home and doing what they felt was their duty. I thought of the conversation with the NVA sapper who had attacked Cam Ranh hospital. I thought of what Frank and Otis would do if they were standing where John Talley and I now were.

"Take charge of this company, Sergeant Talley, and let's move out. You're the company commander now."

He stepped into the task easily, and got the unit up and ready and on its way. That was no surprise. John had come to the Mike Force before I had left the first time, nearly two years before. He had led platoons in the tough battles at Camp Duc Lap, and up the VC-infested slopes of Nui Coto, and on a score of other operations. After a brief stint as intelligence sergeant of the B detachment, he was back where he was at his best—leading a rifle company into combat.

That night, after we had set up our night defensive position and got our ambush parties out, the Vietnamese officer from the artillery forward observer team we had attached to us came to me to complain indignantly that one of the American NCOs had been disrespectful to him, and he had "lost face"—been embarrassed in front of his subordinate. I checked out his complaint and learned that he and his radio operator had built a cooking fire in the middle of the perimeter. One of the Americans had walked up and kicked it out.

The forward observer party had proved useless to us anyway; the one time we had used them, I had called for fire to our front, and the rounds had impacted behind us, so we hadn't used them anymore. We were beyond the range of their guns most of the time anyway, and I had frequently had to correct them for violations of noise and light discipline myself.

"Very well, *Thieu Uy,*" I said. "From now on, any corrections will be made by me or my XO. But if you build another unauthorized fire, I'll not only kick your fire, I'll kick your ass as well. I'd rather have *you* lose *face* than one of these troops lose his life because of your sorry light-and-noise discipline."

We continued to search the jungled mountains and valleys west of Thuong Duc, and though contacts with the communists remained light, we were doing the enemy considerable harm. We continued to reap valuable intelligence, and we were finding caches of food—tons of it—which the enemy had placed in the area to support their next offensive against Thuong Duc, the villages between there and Danang, and apparently Danang itself, for we had found copies of leaflets depicting NVA flags flying over the city, with bodies of dead Marines lying around, and the victorious communists being greeted by the civilians with flowers.

Other caches yielded 107mm rockets, a new weapon in the war—much easier for the small Vietnamese to carry, and nearly as destructive as the larger 122mm Katusha rockets—and a large quantity of communications equipment.

Physically, we were wearing down badly, though. The corn we found helped some, and the 'Yards were getting some additional nutrition from an occasional banana-tree heart or bamboo shoot, as well as such delicacies as lizard and red ants. It was terrible to be around them after they had eaten a lizard. Their body odor, bad enough from being out for more than a month without a chance to bathe, was made *terrible* as a result of some reaction to the lizard flesh.

The leeches were the worst I have ever seen. Most were of a tiny species, small enough to get through the eyelets of our boots. Sometimes we found the leeches so thick on the jungle floor that they looked like a field of grass waving in the breeze as we approached. We sometimes got low on leech repellent, so that we were unable to put it around our boot tops. On one occasion we were humping along, and one of my boots was "squishing" each time it hit the ground, when I thought to myself: Hey, we haven't crossed a stream lately, so why's my foot wet? I looked down to discover that it was from a leech which, having gorged itself on my blood, had fallen into my boot. Blood from the eating-hole he had bored into my ankle was running into the boot also, as leeches exude an anticoagulant which prevents the blood from clotting at the wound. Leeches don't usually cause pain, but one 'Yard had a leech which crawled into his penis and attached itself. We had to medevac the poor guy to get it taken care of.

The steep mountains were taking their toll too. As we each had five days of rations and a large quantity of ammunition and radio batteries, since our scheduled resupply was only once every five days, our rucksacks were a back-bending burden, their straps cutting into our shoulders and their weight causing our frequent and steep uphill climbs to become thigh-searing, knee-wrenching agony. The hills weren't as bad as the bamboo thickets, though. Sometimes we would hit bamboo that we couldn't get around, and we'd have to go through it. The only way to get through bamboo is to crawl through it on hands and knees, and although a number of 'Yards would precede us larger Americans through, it was impossible for us to get through without removing our rucksacks and either pushing them through ahead of us or dragging them behind. Fifty or a hundred meters of that was totally exhausting.

My 'Yard radio bearer, Y Sam—just "Sam" to me—was a tough little Rhade tribesman who was always beside or just behind me. With the radio in his pack, and the new KY-38 speech-security device in mine, as well as spare batteries for each, our loads were heavier than most.

Once, the two of us were moving together up a steep mountainside from the company at the base of the hill, to another company at the top, with two more 'Yards for security. It was a tough climb for Sam and me, and he began to fall behind. I called a halt, and found that Sam was coughing and spitting up blood. I was checking on him when one of the two 'Yards Talley had insisted on sending with Sam and me for security saw two men with M-16 rifles and wearing the "tiger suit" camouflage fatigues we all wore, walking down the trail toward us, about twenty meters away. They were ethnic Vietnamese, and the 'Yard, thinking they must be LLDB from the company atop the hill, called out to them. One of the two startled men cut loose at us with his M-16, and we hit the dirt. They disappeared before we could bring them under fire. They were apparently NVA reconnaissance troops, employing a technique our own reconnaissance units sometimes used—dressing and arming themselves like the enemy forces in the area being reconnoitered. Their ruse saved their lives, and had we not had the two men along for security, they would have come upon me kneeling over Sam, checking on him. No doubt we would have been killed or captured, and the radio, with its classified speech security device, as well as my keylist and signal operating instructions, also classified, would have fallen into the hands of the enemy. It was a close one.

I called the company on the summit and told them to lay an ambush for the two men; then the four of us started up the hill. I didn't want my own men to ambush us by mistaking us for the two NVA, so I took the point, figuring that it would be easier to recognize me by my size and lighter hair color.

"Dai Uy," Sam said as we moved out, "you only battalion commander ever point man." We linked up with the company a short time later. Nothing was seen of the two NVA soldiers with their M-16's and tiger suits again.

Sam was suffering from tuberculosis, and I had, reluctantly, to evacuate him. He had been a good friend and a loyal radio bearer. Each time we had made contact with the enemy, Sam had always handed me first the radio handset, followed immediately by a lighted cigarette. When we reached our RON—remain overnight—position each evening, I would invariably return from checking the dispositon of the troops, crew-served weapons and Claymore mines on the perimeter, to find that Sam had erected my poncho hootch and had brewed us a canteen cup of hot, sweet coffee. I never saw the young Montagnard soldier again after the day he had to be evacuated for treatment of his tuberculosis.

—— 19 ——

My new 'Yard radio bearer was a youngster named K'ba. K'ba spoke only a few words of English, but we got along well nevertheless. He had apparently conferred with Sam about my likes and dislikes, because he, too, always handed me first the radio handset, then a lighted cigarette, when a firefight started. He had also learned that I liked coffee, and every time we halted, K'ba began heating a pot of water with a heat tablet. Even when everyone else was out of coffee and heat tablets, K'ba always had some. I had a little aluminum cook set—a Girl Scout item that was one of the best investments I ever made—and K'ba could have the little covered pot from it boiling in about a minute, to make coffee and to heat water to reconstitute the dried rice of our indigenous rations. The rations each had rice, plus a small amount of sausage, dried minnows, chunks of jerked beef, dehydrated shrimp and mushrooms, or mutton. Unfortunately, K'ba had been advised that the shrimp-and-mushroom ration was my favorite, and when we got resupplied, that's all he ever got for me. Week after week, that's what he fixed for me at every meal. I didn't have the heart to tell the little guy that I was sick to death of it, and that's what I ate for the rest of the long operation.

He also knew that I liked hot pepper on my ration, and he put two packets of it into the pot each time. It was hot as hell, but I'm convinced that it was the reason that, unlike many of the other "roundeyes" from the battalion, I didn't suffer from parasites—internal parasites, at least.

About two weeks before we were ordered to a hilltop to build a fire base for Nicholas and Alex Visena's mortars and an ARVN artillery battery, I was out on patrol with a platoon of strikers when a freak accident occurred. We were walking beneath a tall dead tree, and a limb broke off it, striking one of the 'Yards in the back of the neck. He went into immediate respiratory arrest and unconsciousness, and I had to give him mouth-to-mouth resuscitation. I got him breathing again, sporadically, and called for a medevac, going along with it to An Hoa to continue the mouth-to-mouth resuscitation.

We got there, dropped him off at the dispensary, and while I waited for the chopper to refuel and take me back out to the field, got the urge to defecate. I went to the nearby shithouse of K Company, 5th Marines, and gave birth to a couple of North Vietnamese, then returned to the LZ. As the chopper approached to pick me up, I noticed a big column of black smoke from the K Company area, and asked one of the Marines what it was.

"Oh, that's the K Company shithouse they're burning down," he replied. "Everybody who's taken a crap there lately has caught the crabs."

I jumped on the chopper, went back to the field, and didn't give it another thought until a couple of weeks later when we reached the hilltop where we were to build Fire Base McNutt.

After we secured the hilltop, the 'Yards found a large spring, and I went there to bathe for the first time in about two months. After washing in the cold water, I noticed that there was what appeared to be coagulated body oil and dirt still at the roots of my pubic hair, so I heated a helmetful of water and washed again. It was still there, so I picked at it with my fingernails, and was examining a speck of the stuff—when it began walking away. Crabs. I was mortified. I got on the B Team radio net and called the medic at An Hoa to get him to send me something to get rid of them. That was a mistake. Every clown in I Corps must have been monitoring the call, because I immediately began receiving unsolicited advice from everyone on the net about how to rid myself of the malady.

Rob Jones led off, using his best enunciation, with, "Try boiling them for several minutes, then serving them with lemon and butter."

"Get some lighter fluid, an ice pick, a razor, and a match," someone else recommended. "Shave one side, soak the other with lighter fluid, and light it. When they run out into the open, stab them with the ice pick."

Another suggestion was to take them to a movie and buy each of them a box of popcorn. Then, when they all got up to get a drink of water, just leave. And on and on it went.

There was no supply bird coming out soon, and I couldn't stand the thought of the things crawling around my private parts, so I doused myself with GI insect repellent. It did the trick, but I had to spend the next hour or so dangling my burning scrotum in the cool spring water.

We carved a fire base and a landing zone out of the hilltop with the help of a small Marine Corps bulldozer, and soon had Fire Base McNutt in operation. When we began receiving supplies at the fire base, K'ba got three small wooden pallets, on which he spread my poncho. He called me over and proudly showed me my new bed. There was about a three-quarter-inch gap between each of the boards of the pallets, and they were hard as hell. I thought I'd never be able to get any sleep on the thing, but K'ba had put so much effort into leveling out a place for it, and was so proud of it, that I gave it a try anyway. After two or three nights I got used to it, and spent the next couple of weeks sleeping comfortably there.

Second Battalion was airlifted in to the southwest of us, and we in 1st Battalion used Fire Base McNutt for a patrol base.

The supply section sent us the little tins of mackerel in

tomato sauce which had been in short supply, but which we sorely needed to improve the protein deficiency from which we were all suffering after two straight months of humping through the jungle-covered mountains. They also sent us new tiger suits, which we also needed badly. After a few weeks of constant wear, they would begin to rot. The stitching would break, the buttons would fall off, and they would tear at the knees. By the time we got new ones, many of the troops were running around with their buttonless flies open—not a good situation for those of us who wore no underwear, especially in the leech-infested area where we were.

Major Louie Lopez, who had been the B Team executive officer, assumed command of the team from the departing Lieutenant Colonel Black, and came out to visit us. He wanted us to fire a "mad minute" from the fire base, during which all weapons are fired from the fire-base perimeter at once, for a period of sixty seconds. I had heard of American units doing it to discourage the enemy from considering an attack on the position, but we had never done so. I had all of the crew-served weapons in the battalion moved to different positions from the ones in which we had emplaced them, as I didn't want any NVA recon patrols nearby to be able to locate their real locations, and at dark we opened up. Almost immediately, one of the strikers some distance away hit a tree about five meters in front of me with a grenade from his M-79, and one fragment from the exploding round tore into my elbow. One of the Montagnard leaders, seeing it happen and no doubt recalling what had happened to Parker, rushed over and flailed the hell out of the errant grenadier.

While out with a small recon patrol one day, I was in contact with a Marine FAC, and when he learned of our location, he said that we weren't far from the site at which an armed Huey had been shot down two months earlier. The Air Force rescue chopper that went in after the crew came under heavy fire, and was able to pick up only two of the three crewmen. The third, though he had probably been killed in the crash, was still carried as missing in action. The

FAC wanted to know if we could try to find the crash site and check it out to see if the crewman's remains could be found.

We agreed to do so, of course, and climbed to the crash site. We found the destroyed chopper, which the rapidly growing jungle vegetation was already beginning to overgrow. We poked around in the wreckage, found a confidential document in it—which, strangely, the enemy hadn't recovered—and finally found a few human vertebrae, ribs, and other bones. I was afraid that jungle animals might have taken the rest of the man's remains off into the jungle, and that the bones we had were inadequate to positively identify the man. Finally, though, we found the man's skull some distance away from the wreckage. There was a large hole in the side of it, and Frenchie Bordeaux, the medic with us, remarked that at least it looked as if the poor Marine airman hadn't suffered before dying. Bordeaux, whose speech was stuttered, was really angry at the Marine Corps for leaving the man's body out there for so long, remarking that his widow or parents must have been terribly distraught these months that the man had been listed as MIA and they didn't know whether he was dead or alive. We had no body bag with us, but Frenchie placed the dead American's bones in his rucksack. There wasn't enough room for the skull, so he attached it to one of the straps on the outside, and we headed back to Fire Base McNutt. We were pleased that we had been able to find the man's remains and relieve his family from further uncertainty about his fate.

On the way back, we discovered an unexploded five-hundred-pound bomb. As the enemy used such unexploded munitions to make mines and booby traps, we needed to destroy it. We had two Claymore mines with us, so I took the explosive and blasting cap from one of them and placed the charge on the bomb. As we had only two fifty-foot lengths of firing wire, I had to find a place to take cover within one hundred feet of the bomb so that I could blow it with the Claymore's electrical firing device. I found a small shelf of rock nearby and hid behind it while Talley, Bordeaux, and the others took cover some distance away. I cranked the charge off, and the shock nearly knocked me over, but it worked. We were preparing to move out when somebody noticed a small cave beneath the rock outcropping. In it we found two elephant tusks, several earthen jars, and a number of beautiful blue-and-white Chinese porcelain rice-wine jars and ginger jars, as well as several brass gongs. Not realizing what Black and Boone had done with all of the weapons we had captured, we felt that the sale of some of the items would give us a valuable addition to the Frank McNutt Scholarship Fund.

We loaded up our booty and moved out, and arrived back at the fire base to find a number of people—including the detachment of Marines—waiting at the edge of the perimeter to morbidly view the dead man's remains. Bordeaux, still upset at the Marine Corps for leaving the body there at the known crash site for so long, pointed at the skull on his rucksack and stammered, "S-s-see what's l-l-left after you knock the sh-sh-*shit* out of a M-M-*Marine?*"

A Marine Corps helicopter arrived a short time later to pick up the body, and as it touched down, I ran to the gunner's window and set the bones, inside the rucksack, into the chopper. Not realizing what I had placed aboard, the crewman threw out a body bag and gestured for me to put the body in it. I shook my head and pointed inside to the rucksack. He opened it, looked in, and his eyes widened. Then he said something into his microphone, and as the chopper lifted off, he saluted—not the traditional salute, but the V peace sign, modified with the thumb sticking up between the fingers—the GI version of the sign, the literal meaning of which is "Fuck peace."

The recovery of the Marine airman's remains was, somehow, particularly significant to me. If the killing of the NVA medical officer was revenge for the death of Otis Parker, then the recovery of an MIA American's body was appropriate "revenge" for the loss of Frank McNutt. That's the kind of man he was—one whose death would only be avenged by an act of compassion.

We shipped the beautiful jars out on the next chopper

from the B Team, a Marine CH-53. They were offloaded at An Hoa, but the big helicopter lifted while they were still on the ground behind it, and the powerful rotor wash blew them over onto the steel planking of the LZ, destroying most of them and dashing our plans to establish a scholarship in Frank's name.

The 'Yards kept the gongs at the fire base, made flutes from bamboo, and played their haunting traditional music on days that they were not on patrol.

We were allocated preplanned air strikes every now and then, and I was selecting locations from the map which looked like the sorts of places the NVA might use for bivouacs near areas where we had made contact. Several days after one such strike, we received an intel report that indicated the location of a possible POW camp. I checked the coordinates on my map and discovered, to my dismay, that it was the exact location I had chosen for one of the air strikes. As all too often occurred, the information from intelligence channels was slow in getting out to us. I was sick, until I finally got a patrol there and discovered that there had, indeed, been an enemy facility at that location, but that the air strike had missed it. It looked as if it had been abandoned for some time, and there was nothing to really indicate that it was a prisoner-holding facility. If we had gotten the intelligence in a timely manner, though, at least we might have caught the enemy there, and even if they had no prisoners, dealt them another blow.

Back at the fire base, John Talley discovered that the telescope he had ordered for his son from the PX catalog had arrived, and the B Team had sent the package out to the base with the rest of our mail. There was a manned mission on the moon at the time, so we set the telescope up one night and let the 'Yards have a look at it with the powerful scope. They were amazed by the detailed view of the moon, and by the fact that there were Americans there. They peered through the telescope, jabbering away, so we asked one of the interpreters what they were saying. "This one say he no understand why Americans want to go to moon," he explained, "'cause there nothing up there but water." Another wanted to know what kind of airplane they had taken up there, a fighter or a C-130, and we explained that it wasn't an airplane, but a giant rocket—"Same same beaucoup big VC rocket."

The hill on which we had built Fire Base McNutt yielded some "beaucoup big" fauna, as well, which made the superstitious 'Yards think the place was charmed. We had found giant earthworms, some more than two feet long, and insects of the walking-stick variety of about ten inches in length. I had never heard of insects or worms so large, and wanted to send samples to the Smithsonian, but figured they would never make it through customs. It was another of those places I was going to revisit after the war, like the Coconut Grove beach and reef at the end of the Dong Bo Valley, where I used to consider the possibility of building a scuba-diving and wild-game-hunting camp.

——— 20 ———

By this time we had been on the operation some two months, and the number of contacts we were making with the enemy had dropped off considerably. Second Battalion wasn't getting much action either, although I recall Jim Osborne calling on the radio to Rob Jones, in command of the battalion since Frank's death, reporting that he was in heavy contact, and Jones replying with his customary, "Mighty fine, mighty fine."

My XO, Duane Ramsey, patrolling with Lyle Drake's company, called one day to say that they had detained a Katu Montagnard. He was an emaciated old man, and he told us that the NVA had forced him and the other Katu to grow food for them, leaving them very little for themselves. He said that there had been large numbers of North Vietnamese soldiers in the area but that they had all left, moving west, several weeks earlier, taking the healthier 'Yards with them as slave laborers.

Our strikers had already missed one payday and were about to miss another. With the news from the old Katu of the enemy's departure, they saw no reason to stay in I Corps beating the bushes; they wanted to go to Nha Trang, get paid, and take money to their dependents. Besides, the I

Corps Mike Force, now under Vietnamese command, had come to the field, run a short operation, and returned to Danang.

They were all good points, but General Lam, the Vietnamese Commanding General of the ARVN in I Corps, or Military Region 1, as it had been redesignated, insisted that we remain in the field. The general—who was later relieved of command for performing poorly during the invasion of NVA sanctuaries in Laos—said that we could take a five-day stand-down on Fire Base McNutt before going back to the field. All that would consist of, though, was a five-day break on the hill, which still had to be defended with perimeter security and local security patrols; and the shipment to the base of some fresh food. The 'Yards declared the hilltop stand-down unacceptable. Unless they got a five-day stand-down in Nha Trang, one beer and a pack of cigarettes per man each day for the rest of the operation, and the immediate departure of representatives from each company to go home and pay the dependents, they were going to quit. Actually, except for the beer and that many cigarettes, their demands were quite reasonable. But General Lam refused to yield. In an attempt to appease them, he sent out a few live hogs, some rotting vegetables, and a big bag of dried tea. We were all hurting for fresh food after months of subsisting on almost nothing except dehydrated rice, and the long climb back up to the fire base after each patrol had become an agonizing, thigh-muscle-straining ordeal. But the 'Yards wouldn't touch the "fresh" food, although they cooked and ate the monkey we had captured sometime earlier and given the name "General Lam." Finally, though, their hunger got the better of them, and they ate the vegetables and hogs, except for one the medics declared inedible, as it was riddled with trichina-worm cysts.

The ARVN artillery battery on the fire base was packing up to leave, and this, too, made the strikers angry, since they had been in the field for much less time than we. Also, the artillerymen had been living on B rations—canned vegetables and tuna and such things—which we had none of. In their haste to get off the hill, they left much of their chow and equipment in cargo nets for us to sling out under their helicopters. Talley and I, noticing that the nets contained large amounts of the canned food, promptly removed all that we figured the 'Yards and we could eat before hooking them up to the choppers. We had a real feast that night, while Major Lopez and Chuck Randall, now serving as Louie's XO, negotiated between our Montagnard leaders and the general.

Finally it was decided that we would be allowed five days to get to An Hoa, then on to Nha Trang, pay the troops, and get back up to the area of the operation. We would go for the first five days, then 2nd Battalion would get five days. The only thing I regretted about going on stand-down was the fact that the beautiful red two-month-old beard I had cultivated would have to come off.

It didn't seem right to be back in Nha Trang without Frank there. Just before the operation, we had moved into what had previously been the Detachment B-57 supply room, a spacious little building away from our rooms near Black. Except for the fact that we could no longer routinely piss under his door when he was gone, we could sit in our new hootch and raise hell with our NCOs instead of having to be in the team bar with Black and his cronies from Group Headquarters.

When we learned that Black and Boone had taken some of our captured weapons home with them, and given the rest to the LLDB, I wrote each of them a nasty letter demanding that they send a check for the weapons, payable to the Frank E. McNutt Scholarship Fund, but I never got a reply from either of them. Also, I never found the Browning 9mm that my good friend from the IV Corps Mike Force, Bruce Lombard, had given to me, and which I'd loaned to Boone.

The newsmagazines from the States we finally had a chance to peruse were full of stories about our countrymen taking to the streets to protest the war, draft-dodgers flocking to Canada and Sweden, the upcoming trials of Calley and some of his men for the My Lai massacre, and members of Congress threatening to cut off funds for all U.S. military activities in Southeast Asia. The invasion of enemy sanctuaries in Cambodia was over, and all American troops had been withdrawn to Vietnam after killing thousands of communists, but suffering the loss of more than 350 young American men and the wounding of nearly 1,700 more.

There was so much disheartening news that I thought about taking the leave I had coming and going to Australia to look for a new homeland.

We had one hellacious stand-down party, then headed back to I Corps to complete what turned out to be the longest combat operation in U.S. Special Forces history. Contacts with the enemy remained light and infrequent, although after we finally left there, the North Vietnamese moved back around Thuong Duc, where, in a two-day battle, they lost 163 dead and 20 captured in action. The captives confirmed that our operation had badly damaged their ability to sustain the battle for a greater length of time.

We returned to Nha Trang, refitted, and sent home as many of the strikers as we could to see their families. A number of us Americans were due for R&R or leaves as well. Staff Sergeant Bobby Bolton, who was into his fifth year of Vietnam duty, was one of them. Bobby had missed the last thirty-day leave he was authorized each time he voluntarily extended his tour for six months, and he was nearing the time he would lose the leave he was authorized for his current extension. In addition, his mother had contacted the Red Cross to get them to find out when he was coming home. I got hold of Bobby and told him to go home on leave. He agreed, but added that he would like to go to Bangkok for a while after he went home and saw his mother.

Just a few days after he left, we got a message from the embassy in Bangkok—Staff Sergeant Bolton had been admitted to the hospital there in serious condition. His liver, deprived of rich food and strong drink the previous couple of months, was about to quit as a result of the sudden overload of those things

Ed Nicely and I had been contemplating a leave in Bangkok or one of the other Asian R&R centers, so when we learned of Bolton's illness, we decided to go there. We packed up and caught a hop to Saigon the next day, where we checked into the 5th Group's Command Liaison Detachment. There, we learned that, as we were on leave and not normal R&R, we would be required to have passports to go to Bangkok. No sweat. We bummed a ride to the embassy and went to the reception desk, where I informed the Vietnamese woman there that we needed to get passports for a leave in Thailand.

"Too late today," the woman declared as she concentrated on painting her fingernails a bright red. "You come back Tuesday."

It was only Friday, and midafternoon at that.

"Tuesday?" I asked. "What do you mean, 'come back Tuesday'? We're only on leave until Thursday. We need passports *today!*"

"Monday holiday—Labor Day. Too late to get passport today, we closed till Tuesday. You come back then."

"Oh, yeah? Well, listen, lady, if I'm going to be told we can't get passports until Tuesday, I'm at least going to be told that by an American. Now, I want to talk to an *American.*"

She shot me a look of disgust, then got up and walked to a nearby office, where she informed the occupant, "These two GI want passport. I already tell them too late today, come back Tuesday."

Nicely and I had followed the woman to the office, and peering in, we saw a small, pale, bespectacled man of about my age sitting behind a typewriter, chewing vigorously on a wad of gum. Without looking up from his typewriter, he said to the woman, "Well, tell them again."

I pushed by the Vietnamese woman and leaned over the bureaucrat's desk. "Listen," I said, "it's only three o'clock Friday afternoon. We can't wait until Tuesday to get passports—we need them today."

The man glanced up from his typewriter for a second, then continued typing as he said, "It's too late to get them processed today. We're closed on the weekend, and Monday's Labor Day. You'll have to come back on Tuesday."

"Why, you little . . ." Nicely said as he made a move

toward him. I blocked Ed's move toward the man with my arm, then leaned forward and lifted the typewriter about a foot off the man's desk and dropped it. That got his attention, and he looked up at me with a mixture of fear and disgust.

"Let me tell you something, you little bureaucrat son of a bitch," I said as my voice raised in anger. "We have one week—*one week* off from this stinking war! Nicely here has just come back from a long, tough operation in I Corps, and, by God, he's going to get the break he's earned! Now, I may not get a passport issued today, but if *he's* not going to get one, it'll be because the goddamned *ambassador* refuses to issue him one! So why don't you just get your little gum-chewing, bureaucrat ass up from behind that desk and go find someone with some *authority?*"

"What's the problem here?" asked a deep voice from behind me. I turned to see a large man with Polynesian features standing there looking curiously at me. The gum-chewing bureaucrat stood, giving me the impression that this was a man with some authority.

"Sir," I said, "I'm Captain Burruss. And this is Specialist Nicely, one of my troops. We've got a week's leave, and we want to go to Bangkok, but we're being told that we can't get passports until Tuesday. Hell, sir, we've got to be back to our team on Thursday . . ."

The big man smiled. "Oh, I don't see any problem, Captain. You can get your passports. In fact, Smith"—or whatever his name was—"here, will type them up for you. . . . Do you have photos?"

"No, sir. We don't."

"Well, you can get them made right down the street in about an hour. Go ahead and fill out the applications, and Smith can type them up while you go get the photos made."

"Thank you, sir," I said, turning to the man behind the typewriter and giving him a look of undisguised triumph, then grinning at Nicely as we turned to leave.

"Oh, and, Captain," the big Hawaiian called, "try to be back before eight o'clock. I have an appointment to keep."

We went to the passport photo shop down the street, got

our pictures taken, then went to a bar for a couple of beers while they were being developed and printed. We took our time, returning to the embassy a couple of hours later to find the bureaucrat typist impatiently waiting with our passports. He affixed the photographs, then took them in to have them signed by the big Polynesian, "Anthony O'Boyle, Vice Consul."

We spent the evening checking out some of Saigon's more famous bars, and the next morning we caught the first flight from Tan Son Nhut airport to Bangkok.

It was a Royal Thai Airlines flight, with the best in-flight service I've ever experienced. There were cold towels offered before takeoff, steaming-hot towels before landing in Phnom Penh, and cigars and brandy in between, served by gorgeous Thai stewardesses in silk dresses. It was such an incongruous hour, that flight from Saigon to Phnom Penh to Bangkok. One moment we were amid the now-familiar squalor of Vietnam; the next, we were on an elegant international luxury flight, the war seeming far away and far behind.

With civilian clothes and passports, we managed to avoid the delay of having to wait for the military R&R briefing, with its long list of "don't do this" and "don't do that." We hired a taxi from one of the throng of taxi drivers at the airport and headed immediately for the hospital in search of Bolton. I approached the attractive lady at the reception desk and said, "Ma'am, I'm here to check on Staff Sergeant Robert L. Bolton."

An American nurse who happened to be passing by overheard me, and said, "Oh, Bobby left this morning. We sure hated to see him go."

Apparently the gregarious Bolton had made a favorable impression on the nurses.

"Did he say where he was going?" I inquired.

"No, he didn't."

I went back to the taxi driver and asked him which hotel most of the Special Forces soldiers on leave or R&R in Bangkok stayed in. Without hesitating, he replied, "Opera Hotel. Special Force and Peace Corps all go to Opera."

The driver took us to a small hotel while I wondered if his information could possibly be correct—Special Forces soldiers and Peace Corps volunteers seemed a strange combination of clientele. Or maybe it wasn't so strange; after all, President Kennedy had been the champion of both, and although their political views tended to be at opposite ends of the spectrum, at least they were both groups of zealous young people who translated their beliefs into action. I recalled that Dick Chamberlain, who had performed so bravely when we attacked an NVA regiment with a company of Chams up on the Grand Summit, had been a Peace Corps volunteer before he joined the Army.

We pulled up to the hotel and I went to see if Bolton was registered there. From the bar I heard a blood-curdling scream, and the mock warning, "Anybody who doesn't want to fight, stand by to carry out the wounded!"

Yep, I thought, this must be the place. I found Bobby there in the bar. In deference to his recovering liver, Bobby was drinking his Scotch mixed with milk. He was surprised to see us, and after briefly scolding him for coming straight to Bangkok instead of going to the States to see his mother first, I checked into the hotel and joined him in the bar.

Bolton knew Bangkok well, and served as our guide. We made the obligatory trips to jewelers, tailors, a kick-boxing match, and a gondola trip on the canals of "the Venice of Asia," as well as the other attractions for which Bangkok is well-known. *Patton* was playing at one of the movie houses, and Bobby and I went to see it. We stayed to see it three straight times—we would have followed George C. Scott anywhere after that.

In Thai theaters, the audience stands during the playing of the national anthem, while the king's picture is displayed on the screen. Bolton and I complied with that tradition, of course. And we also stood when George C. Scott made the opening speech of the film, which was Patton's gung-ho speech to his staff before he took the Third Army into France. The rest of the audience, unsure of protocol, stood with us. We congratulated ourselves heartily for that.

By the time we left Thailand to return to Vietnam, I had

somewhat overspent my budget, and was unable to pay for the formal uniforms I had ordered, so I left them at the tailor's, intending to pick them up when I returned to Bangkok for R&R during my next tour to Vietnam. I guess they're still there. . . .

The long operation in I Corps in the summer of 1970 turned out to be the last significant Mike Force operation of the war. The other Mobile Strike Forces had converted to ARVN Ranger units under Vietnamese command by then, as ours eventually did.

I doubt that there will ever be another unit quite like the Mobile Strike Force. I had grown up there—had become a man, done manly things. I had known the best men in the world—American Special Forces noncommissioned officers. I had fought beside them, drunk and sung with them, sometimes even wept with them.

When the skies cloud up, and thunder rumbles across them, I still look up and think: It's the Big Rangers again, McNutt and Parker, up there in Valhalla, reminding us that they're still there—up there with all those 'Yards, and my Old Man, and Buker, and Hall, and Davan, and all the others.

I only wish our countrymen had loved them as they loved our country. They died believing that they were fighting for the United States, regardless of whether or not they were correct in that belief.

On the tenth and eleventh of November 1970, the United States reported that, for the first time in five years, there were no U.S. combat fatalities in Indochina. But I was gone by then.

One day in late October, I threw my duffel bag into a jeep and exchanged hugs and handshakes with my teammates. "You sweet motherfuckers, don't you never die."

K'ba, good ol' K'ba, came running up with a Montagnard bracelet for me. I accepted it humbly, tousled his hair, and as we both wept, I left the Mike Force and headed home. Home to the United States of America, to the country and the people whose freedom was worth it all. Oh, they didn't care much for us at the time, most of them. Our uniforms had become the symbol of a divisive war they didn't understand. But no matter. We knew what we had done, and why we had done it.

In the last war my martial ancestors had lost, their Commanding General sent his soldiers home with these words, which are good enough for me:

> You will take with you the satisfaction that proceeds from the consciousness of duty faithfully performed, and I earnestly pray that a Merciful God will extend to you his blessing and protection.
> —Robert E. Lee, General, Confederate States Army

III
1971–1987

Victories have a thousand fathers, but defeat is a bastard.

—John F. Kennedy

—— 21 ——

For me, the war was over. I went to Fort Benning for the Infantry Officers' Advanced Course, where the emphasis in training had already shifted to the potential battlefields of Europe. Chuck Randall went back to Vietnam, working for Mike Healy, the former 5th Special Forces Group Commander who was now a general officer, trying to figure out a way to prevent the Domino Theory from becoming a reality. We exchanged letters about the possibility of forming Mike Force–type units again—this time under purely American leadership. We still couldn't accept the fact that the U.S. government was prepared just to abandon the effort to prevent a communist takeover of Southeast Asia. But it was, and our hopes of at least assisting the Montagnards in establishing a highland nation of their own faded. So when the Infantry Branch representatives came down to discuss our next assignments, I asked to be assigned to the Joint Casualty Resolution Center—the Thailand-based unit tasked with trying to resolve the fate of the MIAs by going into crash sites to recover the remains of our missing comrades, and by trying to determine if any were still being held prisoner in Laos and Cambodia. "No way!" was the branch rep's reply to my request. There was to be a drastic reduction in the numbers of officers in the Army, and as I was still a reserve officer with no conventional-unit time, I was a prime candidate for the RIF—Reduction in Force. My only hope of retaining a commission, I was told, was to go to a conventional unit and command an infantry rifle company. So I volunteered for an assignment to the regular infantry in Europe.

The "RIF gun" began a heavy volume of fire almost immediately, and there were many casualties. Special Forces officers and aviators seemed to be the primary targets, especially those without college degrees. As many of those officers were former enlisted men who had gone to OCS to receive their commissions, many of the Army's best combat soldiers were lost, and their invaluable experience with them. Incredibly, Bud McBroom, now an aviator qualified in both fixed-wing and rotary-wing aircraft, as well as one of the most experienced Special Forces soldiers around, was among them, because he had spent his college-age years instructing scuba and developing military free-fall-parachuting and "skyhook" techniques, and leading hill tribesmen into combat, instead of sitting in the classroom learning Einstein's Theory of Relativity and Milton's *Paradise Lost*. And there were many others, swallowed up by the "Green Machine" to lead young troops into combat, who now found themselves being spat out at the other end, their services as officers no longer needed. It was a sad time; the "riffed" officers got the same kind of parade they got when they returned to the States from the war—none at all. There was one officer in the Advanced Course who picked up his pay voucher to find it included the notation "last pay before estimated time of separation." When he went to the finance section to advise them that the notation was a mistake, the clerk made a quick check, then informed him that there had, indeed, been a mistake—someone had failed to inform him that he was no longer in the Army.

Somehow, the RIF gun missed me, and I ended up commanding a rifle company in the 509th Airborne/ Mechanized Infantry in Germany. The Great Rot had taken root deeply there—drugs and racial incidents and poor discipline were rampant in the United States Army, Europe. Bill Edge, whom I had gotten to know and respect during my first tour in Vietnam, was the Command Sergeant Major of the battalion. I was stunned and confused by what I saw going on in the ranks of what had been dubbed the "Modern Volunteer Army," and expressed my dismay to Edge. He had it pretty well figured out, and he sat me down and explained it. I had, it seemed, missed a revolution.

"When a country looks at its fighting forces," British General Sir John Hackett said, "it is looking in a mirror: if the mirror is a true one, the face that it sees there will be its own." I had not been looking in a true mirror. I had been looking at the Talleys and Parkers and Couttses and O'Neils, and what I had seen was a reflection of tough, dedicated, professional soldiers who believed in what they were doing, believed that soldiering was the noblest of professions. For the past five years I had been isolated in a society peopled by Special Forces soldiers and, more recently, young Infantry officers fresh from combat—men whose values, unlike those of their civilian peers, had been tempered in the caldron of firefights and dying friends and steaming-hot jungles with seemingly endless humps up enemy-infested hillsides. We had drifted out of the mainstream of American society of the sixties—of sexual abandon and mind-altering drugs; of protest against everything except the right to practice the credo "If it feels good, do it."

Perhaps without realizing it, we had, by mutual consent, isolated ourselves from the realities of the new America of our civilian peers. And the civilians were, as we were sworn to ensure, in charge.

As I am, Bill Edge is prone to quote others when trying to get a point across, and he reminded me of Kipling's words about soldiers of an earlier time:

> Oh, it's "Tommy this," and "Tommy that,"
> And, "Throw 'im out, the brute!"
> But it's "Savior of his Country"
> When the guns begin to shoot.

"We're the bastard sons, for the time being, *Dai Uy,*" the wise old Sergeant Major went on, "and it's up to us to hold it together, to make the best of what they give us, until 'the guns begin to shoot' again."

He went on to remind me that, with the draft ended by demand of the American electorate, they no longer had the same stake in their Army that they had when their sons were apt to be called in. In order to fill the ranks with volunteers, 100,000 soldiers whose mental deficiencies would previously have made them unacceptable for military service were allowed—*encouraged,* actually—to enlist; "McNamara's Hundred Thousand," they were appropriately dubbed.

Nor did the new wave of permissiveness end when recruits entered the Army. Military justice was liberalized to the point that it seemed nearly impossible to punish drug pushers and thieves and malingerers. "Rehabilitate them" was the predominant word from above—so we ended up spending the vast majority of our time with the minority who were troublemakers.

Furthermore, many—not most, but many—of the officers now in the grade of lieutenant colonel and up were of a new breed. Education had become more important to an officer's career than experience, management more critical than leadership. Bill Edge, who had been in the trenches most of his long career, had a theory about how that had come about. He blamed it on the helicopter. The officers who were now finding themselves in command of battalions, brigades, and divisions had missed World War II and the Korean War. In Vietnam, with the ever-increasing number of staff positions versus field leadership positions which were created (there were funds officers and psychological-operations officers and liaison officers and civil-affairs officers and air-operations officers and race-relations officers), the norm was for a captain to spend six months in command of a company—at best, barely enough time to learn the job. And while he was spending that brief stint on the ground with the "grunts" under his command, he was learning a new technique from his battalion commander, which Edge liked to call "leadership from three thousand feet." "The C&C bird" was the villain—a heli-copter crammed with radios from which the commanders at every level from battalion up were able to fly over their subordinate units and "command" them from a vantage point high above. From that lofty position it was very easy for a battalion commander to direct not only the companies under his command but also the platoons and even squads. "Get that left-flank squad up and moving" was an effortless thing to demand over the radio. That was easy to say from a position high above, where the air was cool, the fatigue of having humped a rucksack all day was nonexistent, and the deadly stream of steel from a hidden enemy machine gun was well out of range. But it was all the vogue of the recent Vietnam War, and it was carried over into the Army afterward. It created role models that must have made George Patton want to return from his grave. This distanc-ing of the commander from his troops may even have been the villain responsible for the attitude that I found in the lieutenants under my command—many from West Point, as the 509th was a plum assignment for recent graduates of the U.S. Military Academy in those days. As doctors were taught about their patients, they had somehow gotten the idea that they shouldn't get too close to their soldiers—that emotional involvement with their men might cause them to hesitate to risk their men's lives when it was necessary. Bullshit. That's a weakling's excuse for so distancing oneself from his troops that he won't have to bear the sacred responsibility for their lives; so that the officer's own sense of kindredness which he should have with his soldiers could be avoided, thereby making them mere pawns instead of fellow human beings, and enabling him to sacrifice them with emotionless, electronically delivered commands from high above or far to the rear, instead of with the traditional order of the Infantry officer—an order shouted above the din of battle from the combat leader's rightful place—at the front and center of his soldiers, looking at them eye-to-eye, his arm motioning them forward to do what they might not be able to hear him shout above the rattle of machine guns and the cacophony of exploding artillery: "Follow me!"

"Don't get too close to your troops." Bullshit. Once they got that heartless idea out of their minds, the lieutenants I was fortunate enough to have in the 509th were as good as any I have ever seen.

Don't get me wrong—there still has to be that line between the leader and his men. God knows, I've stepped across it many times in my desire to be their brother instead of their leader, their father figure—too many times, some would say. But I have no regrets about becoming close to the men it was my honor to command. I had the sort of kindred feeling for them that the magnificent ancient warrior Sun Tzu must have felt when he said, "Regard your soldiers as your children, and they will follow you into the deepest valleys; look on them as your own beloved sons, and they will stand by you even unto death."

When he had finished bringing me back to the realities of the Modern Volunteer Army—"VOLAR" was the acronym used—I looked Bill Edge in the eye and asked him, "So, how should I handle it, Sergeant Major? What should I do?"

"The same thing good American officers have done for the last two hundred years, sir," he counseled. "The same damned thing you did in the Mike Force when you were given a mission; *attack* it, sir. Attack!"

It was a different kind of battle, fought with the Manual for Courts-Martial and mass urinalyses, and middle-of-the-night "health-and-welfare" inspections. And it was fought with fatherly counseling sessions, and meaningful training, and the pride of coming out on top in field training exercises and tactical evaluations. Now and then, it meant turning away from the accidental discovery of a platoon sergeant or squad leader off in a corner of the motor pool, motivating a malcontent private with his fists.

But, thanks to the hard work of a handful of good NCOs and a crop of promising platoon leaders, our attack on the Great Rot was slowly but surely succeeding.

It was a shock, therefore, to be called before the third of the five battalion commanders I served under, shortly after what I felt was one of the better attacks we made against the Rot. The authority to conduct unannounced mass urinalyses in the battle against drug abuse had just been issued, so at three in the morning on the Monday after the next payday weekend, I assembled the platoon leaders and platoon sergeants, woke the troops, and had every man present for duty in the company submit—under close supervision—a urine sample for analysis. Some held out until two that afternoon, but at last we had "pissed" the whole company. The results were alarming, if not unexpected. Twenty-one men were found to have traces of illicit drugs in their urine.

But, instead of being told that my actions in trying to determine the extent of the problem were commendable, I was told that my company was a disgrace to the battalion. "You have a severe drug problem in your company, Captain!"

No shit, Colonel. Every company in the battalion did; every company in U.S. Army, Europe, for that matter—and most, I daresay, worse than mine. But at least I had got it out in the open, and now had it where I could attack it better. Wrong answer. It would look bad in the quarterly statistics. And that would make the battalion commander look bad. And that might hurt his Officer Efficiency Report, which could hurt his chances for promotion.

I wasn't as surprised at my battalion commander's reaction as I was at that of one of my fellow company commanders, though. "You're a damn fool, Burruss," he said. "As long as I can get a few of them to pass the Expert Infantryman's Badge test, and pass the Division Maintenance Team's inspection, I don't give a shit *what* these sons of bitches do after duty hours." Then, with the battalion commander's concurrence, he proved it: he took his company out to the Taunus Mountains for tactical training with *sticks* instead of rifles. The Great Rot wasn't confined to the bottom of the apple.

I missed the Mike Force. It had been much simpler there, and I am a simple man who likes simple things. In Vietnam—I suppose in any war—the tasks were relatively few and straightforward: Train your soldiers to shoot, move, and communicate. Teach them how to fire and maneuver. Ensure that they are equipped, fed, rested when possible,

245

and paid what they have earned. Promote those who deserve promotion, decorate those who display valor, tend to those who are wounded, and see to the dignified burial of those who have been killed. Know how to call for and adjust air and artillery. Enforce light, noise, and fire discipline. Always maintain flank security and never walk on trails—unless you do so in a conscious trade-off of security for speed. Ensure that you have the right mix of weapons, that the men know how to use them, and that they are kept clean and at the ready. Know where you are at all times, and where your troops are in relation to you.

When you find the bastards, attack. Find 'em, fix 'em, fight 'em. Keep the pressure on, hit them with everything available, and remember George Patton's sage advice, that "the only tactical principle which is not subject to change is 'to inflict the maximum amount of death, wounds, and destruction on the enemy in the minimum time.'"

The U.S. Army, Europe, in the early '70's, had different, less simple rules:

Always know how many of your soldiers are classified as black, Hispanic, Native American, Oriental American, and "other." Foster ethnic pride by having "rap sessions," at which everyone, regardless of rank, calls everyone else by his first name, or, if you can't remember his first name, "honky," "nigger," or just plain "motherfucker" will do.

Ensure that your troops all wear their fatigue uniforms with the shirttails out and the sleeves rolled up today, the shirttails in and the sleeves rolled down tomorrow, and that they have white T-shirts on—no, make that OD T-shirts today, and white T-shirts next week.

If you're looking for a missing pistol, and you open a soap dish and find that it's full of heroin, don't prefer charges against the owner, because a pistol won't fit in a soap dish; therefore, your search was illegal.

Be certain that you have your prescribed load list of repair parts on hand—so that they can be taken from you and shipped to the Israelis on a moment's notice, while your own vehicles rot in the motor pool.

"Make sure your soldiers all have haircuts exactly like one

of the six models on the poster you are required to have posted next to the ones of General Davidson, in which his hair is curling down over his collar."

"Oh—and if you have a chance, train your troops to defend West Germany against the Soviet bloc forces—but for *God's* sake, don't get off the roads; that will cause maneuver damage, and the Germans will charge us *millions* of marks for the honor of defending the land you damage. . . ."

It was a time of strange priorities and weird values, brought about, I believe, by the Army's being forced to adapt to the cultural revolution in American society which had occurred while we were focused on the task at hand in Vietnam. And those who had distanced themselves from the young men now filling the ranks of the Army, as my battalion commander had apparently done, were having the toughest time of all: on the one hand, they were passing down edicts of permissiveness from a hierarchy which was bent on making the Army—at a time when soldiering was probably the least socially acceptable profession around— an all-volunteer force, by catering to the troops' every whim. But on the other hand, they wanted the Army to be as it *had* been, a disciplined, well-trained, and battle-ready force. So they ended up demanding both, leaving the company-grade officers to figure out how they could allow the troops to do damned near anything they wanted to do one minute, and respond to orders to go risk their lives the next.

Worse than distancing themselves from the troops, though, many of the officers above company level had distanced themselves from their NCOs. I suppose that was partly as a result of the "don't-get-too-close-to-your-men" syndrome—those who had been their "men" when they were lieutenants and captains were now their NCOs. And it was also partly the result of having spent too little time with troops, I think. Schools and staff assignments—the longer the school and the higher the staff, the better—had taken precedence over the experience of dealing with soldiers; many of those who had stuck with troops had been victims

247

of the RIF—or of combat. So when there were problems, they were the officers' problems; the NCO's were ignored. No Army can function long in that manner.

For me, it was a difficult time. I loved my troops—most of them, anyway. I couldn't ignore the good NCOs I had, and I couldn't refuse my second lieutenants the right to make mistakes from time to time. My First Sergeant, Sergeant First Class Perpetuo Delagarza, was a superb soldier—but he couldn't make Master Sergeant because he had never been to an NCO academy. So I ordered him to go. When my battalion commander learned of this, he called me in and chewed my ass. "How can you send your First Sergeant to school when such-and-such is coming up?" I sent him anyway.

One of my NCOs—a veteran of the 173rd Airborne in Vietnam, where he had won two Silver Stars—had been a "payday drunk." I reduced him to E-4 after one such episode and enrolled him in the Drug and Alcohol Abuse Program. One day his counselor came to me and requested that the man be allowed to extend for sixty days in order to complete his rehabilitation. "He's got orders back to Fort Bragg, but if he goes back right now, he'll run into some of his old buddies and fall off the wagon immediately," the counselor said. "Give me another sixty days with him, and I think he'll make it." I approved the extension, and was again called before the battalion commander. "Supported marginal NCOs" was the comment he later included in my efficiency report. Maybe he was right, but for my money, you don't shitcan a soldier with that kind of combat record without doing your best to help him get his act together first. The extension stood. So did the efficiency report, including the comment "Captain Burruss' previous assignments did not properly prepare him for command of a rifle company." That was strange, I thought, since I had twice commanded rifle battalions in combat, which he had never done—and never would. Maybe that was the problem, maybe it wasn't. At any rate, I found that I couldn't run my company the way I thought it should be run without suffering a bad efficiency report. So I did what any good Mike Force soldier would do in that situation: I ran my company the way my First Sergeant and I thought it should be run. I've never regretted it.

It was a relief, though, when I left that battalion for the battalion down the street (albeit with an efficiency report which ensured that I would never be considered for Staff College), to discover a different set of values. Instead of concerning themselves with how the battalion looked on paper, they concerned themselves with how it looked in the eyes of its members. Instead of ignoring our NCOs, we (as the battalion commander expressed it) "turned the NCOs loose." As a result, we ended up with troops who were proud, happy, and who kicked the asses of their counterparts in our sister battalion in virtually everything, with the possible exception of the Division Quarterly Statistical Review, which, I daresay, the Soviets feared far less than a battalion of battle-ready American soldiers.

As my tour in Germany drew to a close, the Infantry Branch flesh-peddlers showed up to counsel us on our careers and future assignments. One look at the Officer Efficiency Report I had received from down the street, and the officer reviewing my file said, "Well, you might as well go to an assignment you'll enjoy."

The RIF gun was about to fire again, and my chances of surviving it looked pretty grim. A bad command OER was the kiss of death. Nor did the command of a Mike Force battalion in combat carry any weight in the Military Personnel Center, where the barons of paperwork ruled; as far as they were concerned, the Mike Force battalion was only an A Team command. "The same as squad-leader time," as the branch representative put it.

"So, where do you want to go?" my counselor asked.

"Back to Special Forces," I replied. I was going back home.

—— 22 ——

Bill Edge was now the Command Sergeant Major of the John F. Kennedy Center for Special Warfare—the senior enlisted man in all of Special Forces. I went to see him to find out what Special Forces company-commander jobs might be available. Special Forces companies are commanded by majors, but I had heard that some were being commanded by captains, and that's what I wanted to do. There was an Engineer Corps major in his office, so I waited until Edge had finished with him, smiling at the heated discussion emanating from the Sergeant Major's office. Actually, it was a mostly one-sided discussion, with Edge doing the talking. It seems that he had found some of the NCOs in his charge trimming the grass around JFK Center with scissors, so Bill had put in a request for some "weedeaters," to make the job easier and quicker, and so that his troops could "get the goddamn job done, and get back to training, where they belong," as he was now telling the engineer.

"But, Sergeant Major," the engineer officer sniveled, "those things cost a lot of money, and the troops will only tear them up."

Edge's voice raised several decibels. "Goddammit, sir,

how dare you? We give privates in the Tank Corps million-dollar tanks and tell them to go out on the battlefield and kill communists with them. You expect these sons of bitches to go to war with nothing but a five-dollar bayonet? You just order the goddamn weedeaters, and I'll worry about whether or not they get torn up . . . *sir!"*

It was good to see that my old friend was still attacking. I found out from him that there were no companies available for captains, but he checked around and found the next best thing—a company whose commander was on extended temporary duty and who had no executive officer to act as commander in his absence. I went to 5th Group Headquarters, and got the job—Acting Commander of B Company, 2nd Battalion, 5th Special Forces Group. When the 5th had returned from Vietnam, the old 6th Group was deactivated, and its detachments were redesignated with 5th Group designations. B Company, 2nd Battalion, had previously been Detachment B-64, Company B, 6th Special Forces—the same unit I had commanded between tours to Vietnam, some six years earlier. As the Company Sergeant Major, Pete Morakon, took me around to meet the troops, I found a number of them were those with whom I'd served earlier. But the big surprise came when I met one of the medics; it was Larry O'Neil, the son of my old team leader, whom I had not seen since he was medevaced with a shattered femur seven years earlier. There were none of my old teammates from the Mike Force in the company, but there were many in other assignments at Fort Bragg, and I ran into them often. We would have a few beers together, and spoke often about having a team reunion. But we never seemed to get around to getting it organized.

That spring, Vietnam fell to the communists. As we all expected they would, the North Vietnamese ignored the "peace-with-honor" pact Kissinger had negotiated in Paris. And they did so without fear of interference from the United States. The will of our people to sacrifice more American blood for the corrupt government of that distant land was gone. The war was lost—finally and fully.

I learned from the Vietnamese wife of one of my Mike

Force teammates that Miss Ling, the Vietnamese girl who had been our secretary in Nha Trang, had managed to escape, and was living near Washington, D.C. I wrote her a letter to ask if she had news of any of the others who had worked there. She replied with a poignant letter from which I learned that the 'Yards had been converted to border Rangers and used as cannon fodder in an effort to stem the tide of North Vietnamese sweeping south toward Saigon. *Dai Uy* Hung, the bravest LLDB fighter I had known, had been promoted to Major and sent to a beleaguered camp in I Corps. The camp had been overrun, with no survivors. The one bit of good news Miss Ling had was that K'Phe Cil, the Montagnard nurse, had escaped Vietnam and was studying in California.

Sometime later, Bill Edge invited me to his office to look at some intelligence reports from the highlands. The Vietnamese were having a hard go of it, trying to "liberate" the highlands. The 'Yards were still fighting—fighting for their highland home and their freedom.

As the years crept by, memories of the Mike Force slipped ever deeper into the recesses of my mind. There were new challenges: military free-fall-parachute training, and an assignment with the Free-fall Committee. A tour as an instructor with the Special Forces Operations and Intelligence Course, and as a faculty adviser for the Special Forces Officers' Course.

Then, one day, my boss in the SF School, Colonel Charlie Beckwith, called me in and told me that there was a move afoot to form a new elite unit in Special Forces, modeled after the highly regarded British Special Air Service, which had successfully countered communist insurgencies in Malaya and Oman, and was now engaged in counterterrorist operations against the Irish Republican Army. He needed someone to go to Britain and give their arduous selection course a try, so that we could devise a similar course for the new unit. Was I interested?

Hell, yes, I was interested! I went, managed to hang with it, and as a reward, was allowed to be one of the two officers

Beckwith brought in to help him form the unit—which came to be known as the Delta Force. When we went in search of volunteers, I sought out my aging comrades from the Mike Force. Some of them were still up to it, as were a number of NCOs from the other Mike Forces, one of whom is presently serving as Delta's Command Sergeant Major.

There was a spirit in the Delta Force much like that of the Mike Force—the sort of spirit which develops among men whose duty it is to react on short notice to conduct dangerous missions. And there was a new spirit emerging in the nation. Military service was recognized as a noble occupation again. Vietnam was no longer a dirty word, and the veterans of that now distant war finally got their parade and their monument—all except the nurses, that is.

But even though, from time to time, I got to hear the rattle and crack of AK-47 rounds passing nearby again, the true spirit of those days two decades ago, when we were so young and the battles so frequent, could never be recaptured—not by one whose innocence and idealism had since fallen victim to the realities of middle age and a peacetime Army.

We finally had a Mike Force reunion, in the summer of '85. Bob Gilstrap and his wife came all the way to Fort Bragg from California. Sam Coutts, now a hunting guide in Wyoming, was there. And Larry O'Neil, recently recovered from heart surgery, came—and although the leg he had had shattered by an NVA bullet is now a couple of inches shorter than the other one, he managed to win the impromptu disco contest we held at the Green Beret Sport Parachute Club.

Jack Tobin, a reserve Special Forces captain, showed up, as did Tommy Batchelor, J. C. Cooper, Rob Jones from Florida, and Russ Driver from Oklahoma. Sam Carter, Dick Bishop, Sam Huggins, and "No Thumb" Wright made it, as did several others. Walt Hetzler couldn't come—but he sent his son. And Bud McBroom, whose job as a Boeing 737 pilot in Saudia Arabia wouldn't allow him to be there, had us a bunch of Mike Force pins made for the occasion. Dick Chamberlain sent his regrets from Germany, and a couple of old Mike Force patches.

We sang the old songs: "Mary Ann Barnes," and "Rat-a-tat-tat," and "The Friendly FAC and the Green Beret." We made fun of each other's paunches and receding hairlines, and told war stories now barely recognizable as the truth after twenty years of exaggeration.

Tommy Batchelor's wife made us a beautiful Mike Force wreath which we solemnly placed at the foot of the Special Forces statue, as we recalled the names of our fallen comrades and pictured them in our minds—their faces, unlike ours, forever young and smiling. Hall. Busby. Zamiara. Davan, McNutt, and Parker, and Buker. Greene, Grottke, Tim Drake, and all the other Mike Force leaders whose young lives had ended on the mountains and in the jungles and swamps and rice paddies and streets of the Republic of Vietnam. From the A Shau Valley in the north, to the mud of the Mekong Delta, their blood had drained into the soil, mixed with that of their troops—Montagnards and Chams and Nungs with names like Ksor, Eban, Mang, Y Dok, Y Sam, K'tien, Chau, and Kut Nie.

Larry O'Neil treated us all to brunch at the Officers' Club, where we drank up all the free champagne, then moved to the golf course and drank up all the Killian's red ale. There, a couple of newly commissioned officers seated nearby asked Larry, "Say, what's this 'Mike Force' you guys keep talking about, anyway?"

O'Neil explained it to the young men, and then we took them with us to the main post parade field, where we held a Retreat formation, and saluted, with tears in our eyes, as "To the Colors" was played. The young officers said they didn't want to be helicopter pilots any longer—now, they said, they wanted to be Special Forces officers. So we took them back to the golf club and bought them a couple more pitchers of beer.

And then we said our goodbyes, and drifted away after vowing to get together again—soon. "You sweet mother-fuckers, don't you never die!"

I retired the following year, not long after we learned that some two hundred Montagnards, now known by their rightful name—the Dega—had managed to slug their way across Laos and Cambodia and into Thailand, where they were being readied for resettlement in North Carolina. In hopes of seeing some familiar faces, I went to the airport when they arrived. Most were, as I should have expected, too young to have fought in the Mike Force—these were the sons of those brave Rhade and Jarai and Koho troops of yesteryear. Yes, it was time for me to do as these young warriors' fathers had done—to turn the duties of soldiering over to younger, harder men, whose idealism and vigor are better suited to the rigors of battle.

But I couldn't let it go completely. Among my treasures were two notebooks I had written fifteen years ago, when the memories of the Mike Force were still fresh, and the sounds of crackling rifle fire and exploding hand grenades—of Frank McNutt's laughter and Otis Parker's "No sweat. I'll be back . . ."—were still ringing in my ears. So I pulled the notebooks out, determined to make a lie of that sign someone found tacked on a tree deep in the jungle so long ago and far away. And I began to write.

> The strikers are the only
> ones who die in the jungle
> and nobody cares. . . .